Christianity and Homosexuality Reconciled

New Thinking for a New Millennium!

by
Rev. Joseph Adam Pearson, Ph.D.

Paper Book Identifiers:

ISBN-10: 0985772883

ISBN-13: 9780985772888

Electronic Book Identifiers:

ISBN-10: 0985772891

ISBN-13: 9780985772895

Library of Congress Control Number: 2014908419

Christ Evangelical Bible Institute, Dayton, TN

Dedication

This work is dedicated to the untold number of gay, lesbian, bisexual, and transgender people worldwide who have been rejected, abused, tormented, and murdered in the name of the Lord God Almighty and to those who have injured themselves or taken their own lives because of the pain they experienced from victimization, oppression, and abuse. The message of this work is simple for those who are still alive and struggle with the unjust condemnation of others: Take back your lives and be victorious. Today, in Christ Jesus, you can have new hope!

This work is also dedicated to those in the future who will live in more sensible times — when Christ Jesus rules on earth for 1,000 years.

Table of Contents

Foreword

Dear Reader,

The book version of *Christianity and Homosexuality Reconciled*, first copyrighted in 1999, has been available for free on the internet in various digitized formats from 1999 up through the publication of this edition in 2017. During that period of time, this book had more than 200,000 downloads. This book will remain free in its current digitized pdf format because: 1) it is a free-will offering from the author to the Lord God Almighty; and 2) the information contained within it needs to be widely disseminated and easily accessed globally.

This book was written through the prompting and guidance of God's Holy Spirit. Therefore, the God of the Holy Bible deserves all praise for this book because it is He who has blessed the author with: salvation, spiritual gifts, wisdom, understanding, longevity, and success as well as all opportunities for education, personal growth, and Christian ministry. Indeed, this author is grateful that the Lord has used him in spite of his considerable weaknesses, frailties, and vulnerabilities.

Because this book also needs to be available in pulp print (i.e., in paper media) to satisfy instructional requirements as well as to satisfy requests for gift copies and paper copies for highlighting and handwritten notes during personal study, it is also available for purchase through *print-on-demand* at www.amazon.com and https://www.createspace.com/4775617

If you have not paid for this book because you have accessed it for free in its pdf format via the internet, and if you would like to make a financial contribution to Christ Evangelical Bible Institute (CEBI), then please purchase paper copies of this book to distribute for free to others, especially those who may not have access to it on the internet. All net proceeds from the sale of paper copies of this book go to support branch campuses of Christ Evangelical Bible Institute outside of the United States. If you like, you can also make financial contributions directly to Christ Evangelical Bible Institute to help promote Bible education internationally. Feel free to contact the author via drjpearson@aol.com for additional details.

This book is meant to be read, reread, and studied. I pray that you take to heart the truths contained within it, that the truths help you to grow spiritually, and that you are inspired and better prepared to discuss and share these truths with others.

Finally, this book is intended to serve God by serving others and to serve others by serving God. Although it is the author's hope that this book is pleasing to its readers who have struggled with the topic, this book can have no value unless it first pleases the Lord God Almighty. Consequently, I submit this book to the God of the Holy Bible for His approval, and I ask that He bless this book in the name of our Lord and Savior, Christ Jesus.

Much love in Christ Jesus,

Joseph Adam Pearson

Rev. Joseph Adam Pearson, Ph.D.

P.S.

Digital copies of this work in its original pdf format may be made with the following provisions and stipulations: (1) This pdf publication may be reproduced, stored in a retrieval system, and transmitted in any form and by any means (electronic, mechanical, photocopying, audio recording, or otherwise) — but only as a complete work, without any changes from its title page to its last page: (a) provided that it is NOT sold, bartered, exchanged, and/or used to proselytize any particular Christian denomination; and (b) provided that commercial advertising is NOT superimposed on, in between, or around (i.e., in the margins of) any of its pages. (2) This work may be translated into other languages only if this original English version is appended to all digitized translations. (3) Published paper copies of all translations must include facsimile copies of the original English title page (page i), the original English copyright information page (page ii), and the original English Foreword (pages vii through ix).

I encourage you to send digitized pdf copies as well as paper copies of this book to family, friends, colleagues, and others who might benefit from it. You also have my permission to post the entire book in its original pdf format (i.e., exactly as you see it now) on your own web site or in other media formats that do not currently exist in 2017. However, you must never post your own comments as "balloons" (i.e., captions) on any of its pdf pages and you must not highlight any area other than on your own personal copy. Finally, no one has the right to sell copies of this book except the author, his publishing company, and retail book stores that have purchased the book at its wholesale value.

For the duration of my life, I intend to maintain the original English version of this book in pdf format at:

http://www.dr-joseph-adam-pearson.com/CHR.pdf
and
http://www.christevangelicalbibleinstitute.com/CHR.pdf

Notes

As used in this book, *KJV* is an abbreviation for the public domain King James Version of the Holy Bible. Other abbreviations used in this book include: *JNT* = Jewish New Testament, *JPS* = Jewish Publication Society, *LB* = The Living Bible, *ML* = The Modern Language Version, *NAS* = The New American Standard Bible, *NKJV* = The New King James Version, *NLT* = The New Living Translation, and *RSV* = The Revised Standard Version.

To ensure their accuracy throughout this book, all paraphrases of the public domain King James Version of the Holy Bible were finalized only after first checking: 1) the Masoretic Hebrew text of the Tanakh (the Jewish Bible) for accuracy of passages from the *KJV Old Testament* and 2) the earliest Greek text extant for accuracy of passages from the *KJV New Testament*.

Each transliterated Hebrew and Greek word referenced within the text of this book is noted by its corresponding number [in brackets with a preceding "H" or "G"] from the *Dictionary of the Hebrew Bible* and the *Dictionary of the Greek Testament* found in *Strong's Exhaustive Concordance of the Bible* by James Strong (Copyright 1890), Crusade Bible Publishers, Inc., Nashville. The most important Hebrew and Greek words are presented in a table immediately after each Biblical citation — or each group of related citations — in which they are used.

Although God the Father (i.e., the *Lord God Almighty*) and God the Son (i.e., the *Lord Jesus Christ*) are consubstantially united in the Godhead along with God the Holy Spirit, in order to distinguish *God the Father* from *God the Son*, an upper case "H" is used for personal pronouns specifically referring to *God the Father* (*He*, *His*, and *Him*) and a lower case "h" is used for personal pronouns specifically referring to *God the Son* (*he*, *his*, and *him*).

CHAPTER ONE

Reconciliation and Coming Out

I consider it a privilege to have the opportunity to write, revise, and edit this book version of "Christianity and Homosexuality Reconciled: New Thinking for a New Millennium!" In the early 1990s, I began teaching a seminar and workshop by the same name through Christ Evangelical Bible Institute (CEBI) in Phoenix, Arizona. The seminar and workshop eventually became so popular that I responded to invitations from churches in North America, South America, and Africa to present it to their congregations in order that they might better understand the scriptural basis for the affirmation that God loves and accepts both heterosexual people and homosexual people alike (that is, without viewing one as better than the other).

In order to help meet the demand for this information, I ended up professionally video-taping the seminar and workshop and offered the resulting three-and-one-half hour video series through CEBI as both part of its "Christianity and Homosexuality" correspondence course as well as on a stand-alone basis for those who were not interested in pursuing course completion certificates or program certificates. Overall, the video tape series did quite well, not only having sold throughout most of the United States, but also in such diverse places as Vancouver (British Colombia), London (England), and Harare (Zimbabwe).

Although the video tapes were designed so that they could be used without ancillary materials, I also developed an accompanying workbook and manual as a precursor to this book that provided pre-viewing activities, Biblical citations, and post-viewing questions for each video segment as well as transcripts of the video tapes, edited to enhance comprehension, so that students might more effectively study and better reflect on the lessons contained therein. To date, the complete package — consisting of video tapes, workbook and manual, and transcripts — has been used by many students of the Bible in individual, small group, and large group study.

Recognizing that it was time for new thinking and new ideas on the issue of Christianity and homosexuality to be presented to a significantly greater number of people for this new millennium, in the late 1990s I took all of my previous writings and additional notes and committed them to book form in order to meet the ever-increasing demand for information on this topic. It is important for more people to be exposed to this information in order to better facilitate discussion, Christian dialogue and debate, and eventual understanding and acceptance that Christianity and homosexuality are, indeed, reconcilable to one another.

In 2010, I recorded an mp3 audio series based on this work to facilitate easy listening and convenient learning. My seven one-hour broadcasts can still be found on the internet. You may download the mp3 files and send or broadcast them to anyone provided that each one hour broadcast is not partitioned or segmented in any way. (In other words, each audio file must be sent and/or broadcasted in its entirety.)

There are three reasons that my materials on this topic are free:

1. I have taken to heart Proverbs 23:23, which states that we should be willing to buy the truth but not to sell it.

2. I have also taken to heart Matthew 10:8 (KJV Paraphrase), which states, "Because you have received freely, then give freely."

3. I desire that this information be accessed easily and quickly, especially by people who live in economically-emerging nations and cannot afford to purchase paper copies.

I have written this book: 1) to help resolve conflict within people's minds concerning the reconcilability of Christianity and homosexuality; 2) to better equip heterosexual people and homosexual people to combat tyranny from those who would try to rob homosexual people of what is rightfully theirs through Christ Jesus (i.e., salvation, spiritual power, peace, joy, faith, hope, and love); and 3) to bring more honor, glory, and praise to our Creator, Savior, and Sovereign King, Christ Jesus, by drawing more people closer to his cross and, thereby, closer to each other.

There are many homosexual people whose guilt has been etched deeply by the official positions of various Christian denominations. And there are many homosexual people throughout the world whose pain has been exacerbated by the unkindness shown to them through the actions and reactions of church-goers. These include family-of-origin members, co-workers, and longtime friends. It is my hope and prayer that the seeming dilemma between homosexuality and Christianity be resolved, and that a higher spiritual understanding of gender and sexuality be settled within their minds, once and for all, both now and throughout the rest of their earthly days.

This book also attempts to provide a rationale for traditional churches to become *open*, *affirming*, and *reconciling* — which is to say, *welcoming* to gay, lesbian, bisexual, and transgender[1] (GLBT) people.

There are at least seven reasons for Christian denominations and local churches to become *open*, *affirming*, and *reconciling*:

1. First, churches need to become open, affirming, and reconciling to more effectively reach homosexual Christians as well as their loved ones who may have erroneously concluded that God does not desire to have a relationship with them.

    Many homosexual people and their loved ones have been driven out of local churches by hateful sermon messages, and some have even been asked to leave by church leaders and congregational members. Christ Jesus does not approve of such rejection!

2. Second, churches need to become open, affirming, and reconciling to more effectively reach non-Christians who may believe that

---

1   *Transgender* is a word whose meaning is still in flux and currently used as an umbrella term applied to a variety of individuals, behaviors, and groups involving tendencies to vary from traditional and customary gender roles or cultural norms.

accepting Christ Jesus as their personal Savior is not an option for them.

After concluding one of my workshops in San Francisco (California), one of the attendees came up to me and expressed gratitude for the information he received. Although he was not a Christian, he attended the seminar to find out if Christianity could be an option for him. He was grateful because he learned through the seminar that Christianity is, indeed, an option for non-Christian homosexual people.

3. Third, churches need to become open, affirming, and reconciling to better minister to homosexual people already in their congregations.

When presenting my seminar and workshop at a non-affirming church in Lake Forest (California), I was told by a church leader there, "We know what to do with homosexuals who no longer wish to be homosexual, but we do not know what to do with those who do not desire to change." This view, of course, is borne of ignorance by those who think that, in order to not be homosexual, all that is required is to not have sexual intimacy with someone of the same sex. (Such people equate homosexuality with a sexual act and not with a psychosocial orientation.)

It was very telling when the same leader told me that their church had "ex-gays." To this leader, however, "ex-gay" meant to refrain from romantic expression with someone of the same sex. The leader acknowledged that the so-called "ex-gays" still had desires for people of the same sex; they just did not act on those desires. In the final analysis, there is no such thing as "ex-gay" for truly homosexual people. Perhaps there is such a thing only for bisexual people or for others on a broad gay-straight (i.e., homosexual-heterosexual) sexual orientation continuum, who choose someone of the opposite sex as their lifelong, covenant-based spousal partner.

4. Fourth, churches need to become open, affirming, and reconciling to more effectively demonstrate Christian love and inculcate morality throughout the entire population.

It is no wonder that many homosexual people have decided that, if they are going to hell because they are homosexual (an erroneous assumption, of course), then they might as well do whatever they like. Churches unwelcoming to homosexual people actually promote promiscuity within the homosexual community and within society as a whole.

5. Fifth, churches need to become open, affirming, and reconciling to help activate and better utilize the spiritual gifts God has given to homosexual people.

    Homosexual people have substantial God-given gifts and talents that need to be used for the greater good of the Body of Christ — which is, indeed, *the Church Universal.*

6. Sixth, churches need to become open, affirming, and reconciling to continue to meet the needs of the changing landscape of the local church.

    For example, there are more divorced people than ever attending local churches. If local church leadership continued to harp on the sinfulness of divorce, divorced people would be driven out of the church in droves in the same way that homosexual people have been driven out. Let it be known that God requires mercy from local church congregations and their leadership and not arrogance or condemnation!

7. Seventh, churches need to be open, affirming, and reconciling to help heal and unite the Body of Christ.

    From beginning to end, this book is meant to present a body of evidence to Christian *jurors,* so to speak, who have mostly, or only, heard the prosecution's side of the story. I present this work as a body of evidence in defense of reconciliation, — not "reconciliation" between sinner and God (because the shed blood of Christ Jesus does that) but "reconciliation" between the seeming incongruity of Christianity and homosexuality that still exists due to unchallenged traditional thinking. This book is meant to challenge such thinking.

Coming out means "revealing your sexual orientation or gender identity to others." To be sure, *coming out* about one's sexual orientation or gender identity definitely includes *reconciliation* with one's Christian faith. Reconciliation also means being reconciled to oneself and others as the gay, lesbian, bisexual, or transgender person that one is.

Before you can *come out* to your loved ones and friends, you really must first reconcile who you are for yourself. Such reconciliation includes these four things: 1) acknowledging who you are as a GLBT person; 2) understanding who God made you to be as a GLBT person; 3) accepting who you are as a GLBT person; and 4) loving and celebrating who and what you are as a GLBT person.

Education is really the key here. You must learn about yourself. You must learn about others who are like yourself. You must learn about the history of those who have had a Christian faith walk as well as those who have had an active prayer life at the same time that they were coming to acknowledge, understand, accept, and celebrate who God made them to be as GLBT people. Also, you must learn that the Holy Bible does not condemn who and what you are.

Coming out requires that you not only grow in acceptance of who you are but also grow in understanding that God accepts you and loves you just as you are. According to Scripture, God knew you before you were born. (For the sake of clarity, the Holy Bible is the only true Scripture.) It says in verses 13 and 14 of Psalm 139 that God knew everything about you even when you were still developing in your mother's womb and that you are "fearfully and wonderfully made." It says in verse 16 of the same Psalm that all of the days that God has ordained for you were written in God's *Book of Life* before one of them ever came to be. It also says in verse 4 of that Psalm that God knows what we are going to say even before we say it (and, therefore, what we are going to write even before we write it).

You do not need to *come out* to God. God already knows everything about you. However, you do need to *come out* to yourself so you can be a whole person — at the same time that you seek God to lead, guide, and direct you; and you need to *come out* to your loved ones and friends so they can begin to see you as a whole person.

Just as your Christian faith walk is a personal journey, so is *coming out* to yourself and others a personal journey. If you are a loved one and/or friend to a GLBT person, your personal acceptance and understanding of what you cannot control is also a personal journey. We human beings understand incrementally. Understanding takes time. Be patient with yourself, be patient with others, and be patient with society as a whole.

Readers of this book might include: 1) a GLBT senior adult who is married to someone of the opposite sex as well as 2) a GLBT secondary school student. If, by chance, you have already *come out*, what I have written may be useful to you as you counsel and advise others who are new to *coming out*.

Concerning *coming out*, God does not want GLBT people to put themselves in an unsafe place. God does not want you to be reckless with your life or someone else's life. And, as stated in Matthew 7:6 (KJV Paraphrase), God does not want you to "cast your pearls before swine." The word *swine* here does not represent your loved ones or friends; *swine* include those who are pig-headed (i.e., stubborn) or have their minds in mental swill. God does not want you to put yourself in jeopardy when someone is going to physically, emotionally, mentally, or spiritually abuse or victimize you. And God does not want you in a church where the leadership and congregation butcher GLBT lambs and, more likely than not, other innocent people.

Concerning disclosure, Christ Jesus himself purposely did not disclose his identity as Messiah on certain occasions for three different reasons: 1) because the timing was not right; 2) because the people with whom he was surrounded were not in the right frame of mind; or 3) because people were not sufficiently prepared to receive that information. Similarly, God wants you to be circumspect and judicious in *coming out*. Being circumspect and judicious includes being aware of the right time, the right set of circumstances, and preparing both yourself as well as others so that they can best receive the information.

God does not want you to be reckless in *coming out*. That is why you should first *come out* to your loved ones and friends. To be sure, you need to be aware of possible ramifications. If you are in a secondary school and your parents are going to throw you out of your home, then the timing might not be right and their frame of mind might not be right for you to *come out* to them *without substantial and significant practical preparation* on your part. If there is a strong possibility that your friends are going to betray your confidence: 1) at work to your employer or other co-workers, 2) at school to a teacher or other students, or 3) at church to a church leader or other congregational members, then the timing might not be right and your friends might not be in the right frame of mind for you to disclose to them who and what you are *without significant and substantial practical preparation* on your part.

You will note that I have emphasized the phrase *significant and substantial practical preparation*. You were made in the image and likeness of God. Because God's intelligence is part of that image and likeness, God wants you to act intelligently. God is smart. Therefore, God wants you to be smart. God does not want you to deny who you are. However, God wants you to proceed methodically, with due diligence, one step at a time.

God does not want you to put yourself in an unsafe place. God does not want you to place yourself in, or remain in, an abusive or dangerous situation. God does not want you to put your well-being in jeopardy. If you are being bullied, or if your GLBT child is being bullied, then you must act swiftly to protect yourself or to protect your child. If authorities at school are not *immediately* responsive, and you are being harassed and threatened on a daily basis, or if your child is being harassed and threatened on a daily basis, then you must remove yourself or your child *immediately* from that abusive and potentially dangerous situation.

As recorded in Matthew 5:39, Christ Jesus teaches us to turn the other cheek. However, he did not teach us to run up and get our faces slapped (or even worse). Fortunately, today, there are alternatives to dangerous school environments through: 1) home schooling; 2) education in parochial, private, and charter school settings; or 3) education at the local community college through early entrance or customized dual enrollment/concurrent enrollment opportunities — all of which might better meet the specific needs of GLBT young people today.

It would be irresponsible if anyone encourages you to put yourself in harm's way. That is not what is meant here about *coming out*. You need to protect yourself as well as protect your loved ones and friends if they are *not* emotionally or mentally stable enough to receive the information without putting you in harm's way or themselves in harm's way. If you are married to someone of the opposite sex, and your husband or wife is emotionally or mentally unstable, then you must not disclose who you are until you have made *significant and substantial practical preparation* for them to understand without blaming themselves.

Why does God want you to disclose who you are by *coming out* to loved ones and friends? Our Creator is a God of truth and not a god of lies. God does not want you to be less than whole. Being less than whole includes: 1) pretending that you are someone you are not, 2) denying who you are, and 3) not standing up for others who are less able to protect themselves. As recorded in John 8:44, Christ Jesus teaches us that it is Satan who is the father of lies and that lying is Satan's native language. We need to speak the truth about ourselves without shame or embarrassment. It is unhealthy for us to live our lives in secret or for us to lie to those who are our loved ones and friends.

In our Christian faith walk, we each should have a prayer life. In our prayer life, we should ask the Lord God Almighty for direction and guidance relative to preparation, timing, and educating others concerning who we are. Of course, educating others requires that we first educate ourselves before we *come out*.

I remember the first time that I jumped off the high platform at our neighborhood's newly-built Olympic swimming pool when I was twelve years old. I had to walk up each flight of stairs. I had to walk to the end of the platform. I had to listen to the lifeguard tell me to point my toes. And, after surveying the swimming pool and whether or not someone was in my diving and landing path, I then closed my eyes and jumped. Yes, my heart raced before that jump. And it raced in subsequent jumps, but each time my heart raced a little less until the jumping became natural and matter-of-fact. To be sure, I never learned how to dive gracefully or elegantly like the Olympic champion Greg Louganis. But it felt good to me that I met my fears and was able to jump. So, too, is *coming out* like jumping into a swimming pool from a high platform. With each disclosure, it gets a little easier until you are able to say with confidence and trust in God: "I am gay," "I am lesbian," or "I am transgender;" or "my son is gay," "my daughter is lesbian," or "my child is transgender."

The first few times I jumped from that high tower, I forgot the advice of the lifeguard to point my toes and I paid the price for not being sufficiently prepared to enter the water. So, too, must you listen to the good advice from others before you take the plunge of *coming out*. My prayer for you, in Christ Jesus' Name, is that you learn to trust in the Lord to lead, guide, and direct you as well as to sufficiently strengthen you. When the Prophet Daniel entered the lions' den,[2] his courage was not his own. Daniel had courage because he trusted in the Lord. The point intended here is that our strength and courage really come from God. Like Daniel, you need to turn to the Lord God Almighty concerning *coming out*. You will find that, in response, He will turn to you and grant you sufficient courage and wisdom to *come out* as the GLBT person you were created to be.

Reconciliation is a part of *coming out*, and *coming out* is a part of *reconciliation*. For a Christian GLBT person, reconciliation requires understanding that the Holy Bible does not condemn homosexual people nor transgender people. That is what the rest of this book is about.

---

2   Read more about Daniel in the lions' den in Chapter Six of the Book of Daniel in the Old Testament of the Holy Bible.

CHAPTER TWO

Controversial Human Rights Issues in the Christian Church

Throughout the history of the Christian Church, there have been at least five major controversial human rights issues that have developed, including:

1. Judaization and the rights of Gentiles

2. Anti-Semitism and the rights of Jews

3. Slavery and the rights of racial and ethnic minorities

4. Female clergy and the rights of women

5. Homosexuality and the rights of gay and lesbian people.

Unfortunately, at different times in history, what many people have done relative to these issues is to select out particular verses and passages from the Bible to support less than whole and less than circumspect views on Gentiles, Jews, slavery, women, and homosexual people. Have all such people been malicious and stupid? Unfortunately, no. Many were well-intentioned and earnest in trying to apply what they thought the Lord God Almighty wanted them to believe and how He wanted them to practice their faith. I used *unfortunately* because it would be much easier to attribute all xenophobic, misogynistic, and anti-homosexual attitudes and biases to malice and stupidity.

To be sure, some readings of Scripture can result in two different conclusions even among intelligent people of good will. However, it is important to also remember that, although Christians of good will can disagree on an interpretation of Scripture relative to a serious issue, they should still remain in fellowship as they await a more perfect and complete understanding from God.

Judaization and the Rights of Gentiles

Because the earliest converts to Christianity were Jews, many of them struggled with the role of Gentiles in the Church and the degree to which they would be permitted to retain their non-Jewish cultures, mores, and customs. When the twelve Apostles were sent out to preach, Christ Jesus himself gave them these instructions: "Do not go among the Gentiles or enter any town of the Samaritans. Instead, go to the lost sheep of Israel" (Matthew 10:5-6 KJV Paraphrase).

Because Christ Jesus also taught that "salvation is of the Jews" (John 4:22 KJV), many early Jewish converts to Christianity believed that in order for Gentiles to be received into the body of Christ (i.e., *the Christian Church*), they would have to first convert to Judaism.

The Apostles had also heard Christ Jesus refer to Gentiles as "dogs" (that is, lawless pagans, barbarians, and idolaters). Consider what Christ Jesus said when the Gentile woman of Canaan had sought a healing from him for her daughter. At first, Christ Jesus ignored her. However, after his disciples asked him to make her stop bothering them by sending her away (Matthew 15:23), Christ Jesus told her that he had been sent to the house of Israel (Matthew 15:24) and not to the *dogs*. He said to her, "It is not fair to take the children's bread and throw it to the *dogs*" (Matthew 15:26 RS [italics mine]).

Students of the Bible know that the Canaanite woman's response to *the Christ* (i.e., *the Messiah*) was not only respectful but worshipful as well: "Yes, Lord," she said, "but even the dogs eat the crumbs that fall from their master's table" (Matthew 15:27 KJV). Christ Jesus marveled at the faith behind her answer and, in response, he healed her daughter based on her mother's faith. Similarly, today, Christians who happen to be gay, lesbian, bisexual, or transgender are being healed by Christ Jesus, not of their sexual orientation or gender identification, but of the pain of rejection from their fellow Christians who think of them as modern day *dogs* — which is to say, rejected by God, incapable of receiving salvation, and unable to take a place among God's elect. Such thinking, of course, is erroneous and incompatible with the entirety of God's Scripture.

Early in Church history, the Apostle Peter also believed that Gentiles were unclean and impure. However, the Apostle Peter was then taught directly by God not to demean the people God chooses to save. The Apostle Peter was told, "What God has cleansed, do not call common, or unclean (Acts 10:15b KJV Paraphrase). Later, that Apostle recounted his revelation to Cornelius, a Gentile at whose house Peter was staying:

"You are well aware that it is against the law of Moses for a Jew to associate with Gentiles or visit them. But God has shown me that I should not call any person impure or unclean."

Acts 10:28 KJV Paraphrase

Even though our Lord Jesus had ministered to the Apostle Peter personally and directly when Peter "fell into a trance" (Acts 10:10 KJV), Peter eventually succumbed to his old way of thinking as well as to the peer pressure from the Jewish legalists of his day. To be sure, without guidance from God's Holy Spirit, the human mind cannot escape defaulting to legalism. It is impossible. For many people, legalism is the brain's natural default in order for it (i.e., the brain) to more easily interpret right from wrong. Religious legalism is worse than civil legalism because the people who use it to guide their thinking erroneously believe that God is on their side.

The Apostle Peter himself could not resist thinking that Christian Gentiles needed to be fixed. To be sure, many other early Christians tried to impose Jewish traditions and customary laws on Gentile converts to Christianity — even going so far as to convince them of the necessity for all believers to follow Jewish practices, including circumcision:

> And certain men that came down from Judaea taught the brothers, "If you are not circumcised after the manner of Moses, you cannot be saved."

Acts 15:1 KJV Paraphrase

This narrow thinking is just like the narrow thinking of those who currently admonish homosexual people, "Unless you are heterosexual, according to the custom taught by Moses, you cannot be saved."

In Acts 15:5 (KJV Paraphrase), it is recorded:

> But there rose up certain people of the sect of the Pharisees who believed in Christ Jesus, saying that it was necessary to circumcise Gentiles, and to command them to keep the law of Moses.

The religious legalism of the early Christians who were Pharisees is just like the legalism of Christian leaders who currently teach that "homosexual people must be made heterosexual and required to obey the laws of Moses. Homosexual people must change."

The Apostle Peter's entrenchment in legalism, nationalism, ethnocentrism, and elitism eventually became so detrimental to the early Christian movement that the Apostle Paul "opposed the Apostle Peter to his face because he was clearly in the wrong" (Galatians 2:11 KJV Paraphrase).

Today, Christians who happen to be gay, lesbian, bisexual, or transgender need to oppose those who are clearly in the wrong about who they are and what they can do or cannot do in the body of Christ.

Just as the Apostle Paul had to admonish the Apostle Peter almost 2,000 years ago for his unwillingness to fellowship with Gentile Christians by telling Peter that "he was clearly in the wrong," so should enlightened Christians rebuke the preachers, pastors, teachers, evangelists, and so-called prophets of today for their unwillingness to allow full participation and involvement by Christian GLBT people in the modern Church.

When the Apostle Paul described his evangelistic team as co-laborers alongside mainstream leadership in the Lord's harvest field, he acknowledged that the hardships they endured included being regarded by those mainstream leaders as "deceivers" even though they were "true" (2 Corinthians 6:8 KJV).

Although Paul was personally called by our Lord Jesus to be an Apostle, he was regarded by others as suspect because he had not been discipled by Christ Jesus when he was in the flesh. He was also regarded as suspect because he was called to minister to Gentiles — who were the *dogs* of his day. The Apostle Paul was part of God's chosen leadership and, yet, he was viewed by many of the earliest church leaders as a second class citizen in the Kingdom of God or as no citizen at all. The same erroneous thinking is true of modern church leaders who view Christian GLBT people as unsaved or reprobate.

Today, Christians who happen to be gay, lesbian, bisexual, or transgender can relate to how the Apostle Paul and members of his evangelistic team were viewed two thousand years ago. Today, they are: 1) rejected outright as imposters, even though they are genuine; or 2) they are assigned to second class citizenship within the local church — permitted to sit in pews and donate their financial resources but not permitted to minister to others with their unique, God-given talents and spiritual gifts.

Can you see how the issue of Judaization and the rights of Gentiles in the early church is applicable to the plight of modern day Christian homosexual people? This issue is relevant to Christianity and homosexuality because Scripture was once used against Christian people who happened to be Gentile, just as it is now used against Christian people who happen to be homosexual. Christians must learn not to run to verses in the Holy Bible that are used against homosexual people without first running to the rest of the Bible. In order to be good students of the Holy Bible, all Christians must hold the whole Bible while they simultaneously attend to its various parts.

Anti-Semitism and the Rights of Jews

Gradually, as Hellenist Christians (i.e., Gentile Christians) outnumbered Hebraist Christians (i.e., Jewish Christians), there was a shift from the Judaization of Christianity to de-Judaization. In *Our Father Abraham: Jewish Roots of the Christian Faith*, author Marvin R. Wilson notes:

> Although a few Jewish Christians apparently still attended synagogue in {St.} Jerome's day (ca. A.D. 400), the parting of the way seems to have been largely finalized by around the middle of the second century. By the time of Justin Martyr (ca. A.D. 160) a new attitude prevailed in the Church, evidenced by its appropriating the title "Israel" for itself. Until this time, the Church had defined itself more in terms of continuity with the Jewish people; that is, it was an extension of Israel.[3]

Wilson traces how de-Judaization gradually gave way to anti-Judaism and even anti-Semitism:

> In the fourth century, when Constantine made Christianity the official religion of the Roman empire, Jews experienced a further wave of discrimination and persecution. They lost many of their legal rights; they were not permitted to dwell in Jerusalem or to seek converts. In 339 {A.D.} it was considered a criminal offense to convert to Judaism. Several decades later the Synod of Laodicea ruled against Christians feasting with Jews, classifying those that did so as heretics. Around 380 {A.D.},

---

3   Wilson, Marvin R. *Our Father Abraham: Jewish Roots of the Christian Faith*. William B. Eerdmans Publishing Company, Grand Rapids, 1989, page 83. {brackets mine}

Ambrose, bishop of Milan, praised the burning of a synagogue as an act pleasing to God.[4]

Ironically, even Christ Jesus addressed the Jews of his day as illegitimate heirs to the promise given to Abraham:

"If you were Abraham's children," Jesus said, "then you would do the works of Abraham. But now you seek to kill me, a man who has told you the truth that I have heard from God: Abraham did not even do this. You do the things of your own father."

John 8:39b-41a KJV Paraphrase

"You belong to your father, the Devil."

John 8:44 KJV Paraphrase

"You do not understand because you do not belong to God."

John 8:47 KJV Paraphrase

Yes, there is a rather sharp and bitter polemic against nonbelieving Jews in the Bible, but, when found, it is spoken or written by other Jews (that is, those who believed in the Lord Jesus as the Messiah). As such, it was a family fight. Consequently, Gentiles should not take those passages and others like them out of their historic context and use them to justify their own anti-Semitism. They need to remember that, in Chapter Eleven of the Epistle to the Romans, the Apostle Paul teaches that God has not rejected the Jews (verse 1) and that all Israel eventually will be saved (verses 25-26).

It is recorded in Scripture that the chief priests and Jewish elders persuaded the crowd in Pontius Pilate's presence to ask for the prisoner Barabbas to be released instead of Christ Jesus and to demand Christ Jesus' execution (Matthew 27:20). Finally, when Pilate washed his hands concerning the fate of Christ Jesus, it is recorded in Matthew 27:25 that

---

4   *Ibid.*, page 95. {brackets mine}

the Jewish crowd who condemned him then responded, "'Let his blood be on us and on our children!'" [or, in other words, *on us and on our descendants*] (KJV Paraphrase).

Unfortunately, some nominal Christians have distilled from the Holy Bible the idea that Jews are *Jesus-killers* and use it as their foundation for anti-Semitism. However, true Christians should be strongly opposed to anti-Semitism because the family of Jehovah (Yahweh) includes our brothers and sisters who happen to be Jews. (By extension — so, too, must seemingly anti-gay passages be interpreted in their historic context and never used by straight people to bash gay people.) Be reminded that the Holy Bible states that "there is neither Jew nor Greek [i.e., Gentile]… for you are all one in Christ Jesus" (Galatians 3:28 KJV Paraphrase).

God is not done with the Jewish people or the nation of Israel. The Jews are still among God's chosen people, just as Christian homosexual people number among God's chosen.

Can you see how anti-Semitism and the rights of Jews are applicable to the plight of modern day Christian homosexual people? The issue of anti-Semitism is every bit as relevant to Christianity and homosexuality as the Bible passages that are used against homosexual people. Christians must learn not to run to verses in the Holy Bible that are used against homosexual people without first running to the rest of the Bible. In order to be good students of the Holy Bible, Christians must hold the whole Bible while they simultaneously attend to its various parts.

Slavery and the Rights of Racial and Ethnic Minorities

Concerning slavery and human rights, students of the Holy Bible can find different passages, especially within the first five books of the Bible (*Torah* or *the Pentateuch*[5]), to find verses that support slavery. *For example*:

> Your male slaves and female slaves shall be from the pagan Gentile nations around you; from them you may buy male and female slaves. Moreover, of the children of the aliens that live

---

5   The first five books of the Bible are called "Torah" by Jews and "the Pentateuch" by Christians.

among you, of them shall you buy slaves, and of their families that are with you, which are born in your land: and they shall be your purchased property. And you shall take them as an inheritance for your children after you, to inherit them for a possession; they shall be your slaves forever: but over your brothers and sisters from the nation of Israel, you shall not rule as slaves.

Leviticus 25:44-46 KJV Paraphrase

And if a man hits his male or female slave with a rod, and he or she dies as a result; he shall be surely punished. However, if he or she continues to live a day or two, he shall not be punished because the slave is his property.

Exodus 21:20-21 KJV Paraphrase

And if a man hits the eye of his male or female slave and the slave's eye becomes blind, he shall let the slave go free for the eye's sake. And if he knocks out his male or female slave's tooth, he shall let the slave go free for the tooth's sake.

Exodus 21:26-27 KJV Paraphrase

It is absolutely phenomenal that — on the floor of the United States Congress in the 1830s, 1840s and 1850s — many congressmen supported slavery. For example, on February 1, 1836, United States Senator James Henry Hammond said the following on the House floor concerning Black Americans:

The doom of Ham has been branded on the form and features of his African descendants. The hand of fate has united his color and destiny. Man cannot separate what God hath joined.[6]

---

6   Miller, William Lee. *Arguing About Slavery: The Great Battle in the United States Congress.* Alfred A. Knopf, New York, 1996, page 139.

In order to bolster their case that slavery should be the law of the land, many elected representatives in the United States Congress held up passages like those previously quoted from Leviticus and Exodus as well as those written by the Apostle Paul that express his tacit approval (or seeming endorsement) of slavery. *For example*, the Apostle Paul stated:

Slaves, obey in all things your masters who rule over you in the flesh; not only when they are watching you but continually, fearing God.

Colossians 3:22 KJV Paraphrase

The burden of my argument is not to point out how horrible, unethical, and immoral slavery is; civilized, educated, and cultured people already know that. Rather, it is to point out that, for the majority of time that Christianity has been on the earth, there also has been slavery and that many Christians either owned slaves themselves or condoned slavery (or even been a part of slave trading), and that nowhere in Scripture are Christians specifically forbidden from owning slaves.

This illustrates that a majority of Christians can be wrong a majority of the time, just as they have been wrong about GLBT people. Nonetheless, as the children of God mature in Christ Jesus, each and every Christian can come to a more enlightened and moral understanding relative to specific human rights issues involving racial and ethnic minorities as well as GLBT people. (For the sake of accuracy, it should be noted that, throughout history, some enslaved people in certain countries have actually constituted a numerical majority.)

Why should slavery not be the law of this land or any other land? *Because it is inconsistent with the entirety of God's written Word.* God has no preferred socioeconomic status and God makes no social distinctions among people:

There is neither… slave nor free… for all are one in Christ Jesus.

Galatians 3:28 KJV

Similarly, why should anti-homosexual feelings not prevail within the Christian Church? Because they are inconsistent with the entirety of God's written Word.

Can you see how slavery and the rights of racial and ethnic minorities in the Christian Church are applicable to the plight of modern day Christian people who happen to be homosexual? The issue of slavery is every bit as relevant to Christianity and homosexuality as the very Bible passages that are used against homosexual people. Christians must learn not to run to verses in the Holy Bible that are used against homosexual or transgender people without first running to the rest of the Bible. In order to be good students of the Holy Bible, Christians must hold the whole Bible while they simultaneously attend to its various parts.

Female Clergy and the Rights of Women

Even in this day and age, there are some people who will not enter a church where a woman is pastoring or preaching because they feel that it is against God's written Word and codified Will. Often, to justify their misogynistic position, they quote these Bible passages:

> Let your women keep silent in the churches: because it is not permitted for them to speak; but they are commanded to be under obedience as the Law of Moses states. And, if they will learn anything, let them ask their husbands at home: because it is shameful for women to speak in the church.
>
> 1 Corinthians 14:34-35 KJV Paraphrase

> Let a woman learn in silence in submissiveness. Regardless of what she learns, I do not permit a woman to teach, nor to usurp authority over a man, but to be silent.
>
> 1 Timothy 2:11-12 KJV Paraphrase

Those who would quote such passages to support an anti-feminist viewpoint fail to realize that the distinct separation of the sexes in the Apostle Paul's day, not only determined where women sat within the synagogue, but also curtailed their opportunities for education and leadership as well. All society was distinctly different then. It was still a mostly patriarchal, male-dominated, and male-dependent society that had been borne out of hunter-warrior days when brute strength alone provided the survival advantage and edge. However, things are much different now — at least in some parts of the world.

In 2001, when I was in Salvador, Brazil to do my seminar and workshop, a newspaper reporter asked me what I thought the future held for homosexual people in Brazil.[7] I answered that not until women had equal rights and parity within the country could we hope for much progress to be made in the arena of human rights for homosexual people. During my first mission trips to Uganda and Tanzania in East Africa and to India, I was somewhat surprised to find that males and females still sit in separate groups during church services. To be sure, different cultures and societies throughout the world are at different stages in their development concerning the issue of equality for women.

Perhaps the unique cultural situation regarding women that the Apostle Paul was addressing in the previously-quoted Bible passages is no longer fully understandable to us. (Many Biblical references to ancient situations and cultural practices are no longer fully understandable.) However, because Scripture cannot contradict Scripture, these difficult passages must be interpreted in the light of other Bible passages that indicate parity of the sexes in God's eyes (such parity is discussed in Chapter Three of this book). In summary, the previously-quoted passages must be properly contextualized in order to interpret them correctly and relate them to practices in the modern world.

To be sure, the Apostle Paul's actual practice, which included an extensive use of female co-workers in the gospel, as well as the whole

---

7   *Tribuna da Bahia*, Ano XXXI - N° 10205 Pagina 8 Salvador, Terça-Feira, 19 de Junio de 2001, "Palestra prega aproximção entre Igrejas e homossexuais," Andréa Cristiana (Reporter).

Bible's understanding of *human* as both male and female made in God's image, must be factored in:

> So God created humanity in His image, in the image of God humanity was created male and female.

> Genesis 1:27 KJV Paraphrase

An enlightened view of gender includes an understanding of the following Bible verse:

> Christ Jesus said, "When people shall rise from the dead, they neither marry, nor are given in marriage, but are as the angels that are in heaven."

> Mark 12:25 KJV Paraphrase

During the 1950s and 1960s, I regularly attended the healing services of the well-known evangelist, Kathryn Kuhlman. She would come to the McCormick Place Convention Center in Chicago, Illinois (U.S.A.) a few times each year. Each time that I saw her, she was flanked on the stage platform by as many as one hundred seated males from the Full Gospel Businessmen's Association. She would say to the audience, "I know that some of you are wondering why I am standing here instead of one of these men." She knew that there would be those in the audience who would object to having a female in such a prominent Christian leadership role. She would then say, "If God can speak through a donkey, then He certainly can speak through Kathryn Kuhlman." (Rev. Kuhlman was referring to Numbers 22:28-30, where it is recounted that the Angel of the Lord spoke through Balaam's donkey.

Our Creator-God is not a sexist. God has no gender preference. Consider the Old Testament roles of Miriam, Deborah, and Huldah and the New Testament role of Anna as well as other female prophets referred to in the Holy Bible. Indeed, "there is neither... male nor female... for all are one in Christ Jesus" (Galatians 3:28 KJV Paraphrase).

Once, when I reached the point of discussing the role of the Old Testament Judge and Prophetess Deborah during my seminar and

CHRISTIANITY AND HOMOSEXUALITY RECONCILED

workshop in Indianapolis, Indiana (U.S.A.), a male attendee stated, "Well, I tend not to count the passages about Deborah because she is an exception." I responded to him, "As we build our own personal theologies based on Scripture, we must remember to factor in all exceptions in the Holy Bible."

Can you see how female clergy and the rights of women in the church are applicable to the plight of modern day Christian homosexual and transgender people? This issue of the role of women is every bit as relevant to Christianity and homosexuality as the very Bible passages used against Christians who happen to be homosexual or transgender. Don't run to the verses in the Bible that are used against homosexual or transgender people without first running to the rest of the Bible. If Christians are going to be good students of the Holy Bible, they must hold the whole Bible while they simultaneously attend to its various parts.

Homosexuality and the Rights of Gay and Lesbian People

To be sure, individual Bible verses have been used to foster ethnocentrism, racism, and sexism throughout millennia. However, it should be clear that only half-truths are presented when the Bible is not taken in its entirety. That is why, rather than building church doctrine on only a few selected verses, Christians need to hold the whole Bible while they simultaneously attend to its various parts. They must do this as they seek to understand the fundamentals of their faith. They should understand that the Bible is a divinely-inspired book, and that its continuity is unequaled and unparalleled by any other book — especially when one considers the number of individuals who were involved in its writing. They should also understand that the Bible's truths are inerrant — but *only* when its verses are properly contextualized. It is only when Scripture is taken in its entirety and accurately contextualized that one comes to a more perfect and complete understanding of the whole truth on any particular topic, subject, or issue.

One's approach to Bible study, interpretation, and application needs to be hermeneutically-sound if one is to derive and practice the truer, deeper, and higher meaning of Scripture. For the sake of clarification, *hermeneutics* is herewith defined as "the science and methodology of interpretation, especially of the Bible."[8] In other words, students of the Bible must resist using only a few words or verses of Scripture to represent the entirety of God's Word, just as they should resist using only a half-truth to represent the whole truth: "Study to show yourself approved unto God, a worker who need not be ashamed, rightly dividing the word of truth" (2 Timothy 2:15 **KJV** Paraphrase). Quality study involves time, effort, and energy and a consistent interpretation of a topic, subject, or issue based on understanding the entirety of God's written Word.

If we selectively pull out a Bible verse here or there, and build a theology around it, we really are not bringing honor and glory and praise to the Lord God Almighty. What we are doing is furthering a personal, political, and/or social agenda that cannot be pleasing to the Lord. Such has been the case with Bible passages that have been used to support Judaization, anti-Semitism, opposition to female clergy, slavery, and the general idea that one group of human beings is superior to another. Though I believe that the writing of the Holy Bible was under holy guidance (meaning, that it was authored by the Holy Spirit), selective dependence on single verses or passages will lead to error in overall interpretation and general application. Also, while individual Bible verses express absolute truth, sometimes the truth does not have universal application.

For example, the Bible verses that are commonly used against homosexual people to tell them that their sexual orientation is an abomination to God have been interpreted out of their historical, literary, and etymological (i.e., word origin) contexts. Their historical, literary, and etymological contexts are even largely ignored and misunderstood by most clergy. In other words, they have been interpreted without holding the whole Bible while simultaneously attending to its various parts. This, of course, I will attempt to prove through careful analysis and synthesis of those verses against their historical, literary, and etymological backdrops (that is, in their historical, literary, and etymological contexts). A proper understanding of Bible verses includes understanding passages immediately adjacent to them as well as those located in other parts of the Bible that provide insights to their intended meaning as well as potential multiple meanings. Sometimes, when there are no adjacent

---

8   *Webster's II New Riverside Dictionary*, Riverside Publishing Company, 1984, page 577.

verses, or verses elsewhere in the Bible, that will help with the meaning or meanings of a verse, we can only turn to its historical context in order to elucidate its truer, deeper, and higher meaning.

Thus far, you have been introduced to: 1) Judaization and the rights of Gentiles; 2) anti-Semitism and the rights of Jews; 3) slavery and the rights of racial and ethnic minorities (or, in some cases, majorities); and 4) female clergy and the rights of women. Discussing these issues and related passages in the Holy Bible is just as important as explaining the so-called passages that are used abusively against homosexual people, against homosexuality, and against the homosexual orientation. Sometimes, those who use Christian apologetics to defend the doctrine of reconciliation between Christianity and homosexuality are accused of having their own so-called *gay theology*. This is not true. We have theology and our understanding of it. Rather, it is those who accuse us of having a gay theology that are the ones who really have a gay theology because of the importance they place on convincing others that what they believe about homosexuality is true.

If you are a Gentile Christian and a Jewish Christian came up to you and began to focus on passages in the Bible that put Gentiles in second class status, you would know immediately that the person had his or her own personal, political, and/or social agenda.

If you are Jewish and a Gentile Christian came up to you and began to focus on passages in the Bible that put Jews in a bad light — perhaps relative to their disobedience to Yahweh or relative to the murder of Christ Jesus — you would know immediately that the person had his or her own personal, political, and/or social agenda.

If you are a racial and/or ethnic minority and someone from a more privileged class came up to you and began to focus on passages in the Bible that directly or indirectly support a caste system or slavery, you would know immediately that the person had his or her own personal, political, and/or social agenda.

If you are a female and a male came up to you and began to focus on passages in the Bible that directly or indirectly support women as second class citizens or, even worse, as the property of males, you would know immediately that the person had his own personal, political, and/ or social agenda.

Similarly, if you are a gay, lesbian, bisexual, or transgender person and a heterosexual person came up to you and began to focus on passages in the Bible that are interpreted to be against homosexual, bisexual, or transgender people, you would know immediately that the person had his or her own personal, political, and/or social agenda.

Do I have an agenda in writing this book? Yes, of course. This work is dedicated to the untold number of gay, lesbian, bisexual, and transgender people who have been rejected, abused, tormented, and murdered in the name of the Lord and to those who have injured themselves or taken their own lives because of the pain from their rejection and victimization. The message of this work is simple for those who are still alive: Take back your lives and be victorious. Today, in Christ Jesus, you can have new hope! Thus, my agenda is 1) to help GLBT people recognize that they can have hope as well as 2) to help educate all people who struggle with the issue of reconciliation between Christianity and homosexuality.

Sometimes, when I share my seminar and workshop with groups who believe they already know all there is to know about the topics of Christianity and homosexuality, attendees want to get immediately to the half dozen or so passages in the Bible that seem to be anti-homosexual. In their zeal, they often fail to gain insights from other passages in the Bible that are equally important to this issue. *For example*, 1 Corinthians 1:27-29 (KJV Paraphrase) states:

{27} But God chose the foolish things of the world to shame the wise; God chose the weak things of the world to shame the strong. {28} God chose the lowly things of this world and the despised things — and the things that are not — to nullify the things that are, {29} so that no one in the flesh is able to boast before the Lord.

According to the Holy Bible, no earthly flesh should boast — neither *heterosexual flesh* nor *homosexual flesh*. Boasting is an outward manifestation of false pride. And God hates false pride.

What do the Anti-Gentile Church, the Anti-Semitic Church, the Racist Church, the Misogynist Church, and the Homophobic Church all have in common? They have in common the sin of arrogance. Arrogance is a manifestation of false pride. God hates all forms of false pride, and God hates all forms of arrogance — including doctrinal arrogance. We are to love and respect our Roman Catholic brothers and sisters. We are to love and respect our Baptist brothers and sisters. We are to love and respect our Apostolic brothers and sisters. And we are to love and respect people in every other Christian denomination and group — regardless if we agree or disagree with all of their doctrinal positions.

CHAPTER THREE

The Seeming Dilemma

The God of the Bible is No Respecter of Persons

One of the principles that we are taught through God's written Word is that God is "no respecter of persons." To be sure, this is a commonly-used phrase in the King James Version of the Bible. (See Acts 10:34; 2 Samuel 14:14; 2 Chronicles 19:7; Romans 2:11; Ephesians 6:9; and 1 Peter 1:17.) Other translations of the verses just cited use similar phraseology, indicating that God does "not show favoritism" and that God has "no partiality." In other words, our Creator-God is not impressed by our outer human appearance. And God does not respond to us based on our individual human personalities.

As a trained biologist,[9] I can attest that much of the human personality is physiologically-predisposed, neuroendocrinologically-inclined, and

---

9   The author received his Bachelor of Science and Master of Science degrees in Biology from Loyola University (Chicago). Additionally, the author spent one year in a doctoral program in Human Anatomy at the University of Illinois Medical Center and one year in a doctoral program in Biology at the University of Chicago. The author's earned doctorate is a Ph.D. from Arizona State University and is in Education with specializations in Language, Literacy, and Linguistics.

genetically-determined. Indeed, genetically-determined hormone levels impinge on groups of neurons and cause the brain to act and react the way it does. This is one of the reasons that children are so very much like their parents relative to not only appearance but also personality and temperament. Often, adult children display virtually the same animated behavioral profile, or lack thereof, as their parents (*for example*, in having a "flat affect"). Regardless, in the final analysis, there should be no value judgments associated with whether someone has an "effervescent" or a "low key" personality. God really does not care. He understands that much of the human personality is predisposed and not chosen.

Instead, what God cares most about is what is within our individual hearts. We find this as a good object lesson in 1 Samuel 16:1-13. As recorded there, the prophet Samuel evaluated the sons of Jesse relative to whom God was going to choose as the second king of the nation of Israel. As the first son, Eliab, passed by, Samuel looked at him and thought, "My, Eliab is an impressive individual. Surely, this is the one whom the Lord is going to choose" (1 Samuel 16:6 KJV Paraphrase). However, the Lord responded to Samuel by instructing him that He does not evaluate outward expression as human beings evaluate it:

> But the Lord said to Samuel, "Do not look at his appearance, or at his height, because I have rejected him: the Lord does not evaluate as human beings evaluate; for human beings look at the outward appearance, but the Lord looks at the heart.

> 1 Samuel 16:7 KJV Paraphrase

In other words, the Lord looks at the inner core of an individual and the attitude and intent of the person's heart. According to God, the true stature — or measure — of a person is determined by how much sacrificial, selfless, and forgiving love is in his or her heart. It is very important for us to understand that our human persona, including our physical appearance as well as personality, is merely an outer expression that may or may not accurately reflect our inner core or our attitude and intent. That is why God is not a "respecter of persons," and that is why God shows no favoritism or partiality based on our anatomically-determined appearance or physiologically-determined personality.

Indeed, God is not impressed by our physical appearance. God is not impressed by our personality. And God is not impressed by our sexual orientation. He does not really care about any of these things — unless, of course, we do not act in a godly manner in relation to them, or unless we do not act in keeping with what it is that God would have us do relative to them. To be sure, abuses related to our physical nature — such as vanity, self-loathing, sexual addiction, and deception — are repugnant to the Lord. (For the sake of clarity, *deception* here includes presenting ourselves to others as other than who or what we are.)

Human personhood includes outward expression, physical appearance, genetic makeup, personality traits, and sexuality, the latter of which includes gender identity, sexual orientation, and, in the case of bisexuals, sexual preference. Spiritually speaking, *true man* is really the expression, or person, of God because, collectively, we constitute the body of His Christ. What I mean by the last statement is that, although we are not God and can never be God, when we invite God into our lives, and when He lives within us and we do His Will, then He really is our one true and only real Self. In other words, our true being and real identity come from God. As the Apostle Paul clearly stated, it is in God that "we live, and move, and have our being" (Acts 17:28 KJV). And, as John the Baptist declared when he saw Jesus, "he must increase, but I must decrease" (John 3:30 KJV). Paradoxically, it is in losing ourselves to God that we end up finding ourselves in Him.

An Enlightened View of Gender

We need to come to a better understanding and more enlightened view of gender by apprehending the meaning of these two verses from the Holy Bible:

> There is neither... male nor female... for we are all one in Christ Jesus.

> Galatians 3:28 KJV Paraphrase

For when they shall rise from the dead, they will neither marry nor be given in marriage; but are as the angels which are in heaven.[10]

Mark 12:25 KJV Paraphrase

Ultimately, God does not evaluate us in terms of our physicality. To be sure, He is aware of who and what we are, but He does not evaluate us on the basis of features or characteristics that have null value or neutral consequence. He does evaluate us in terms of our earthly circumstances. Most importantly, the Lord God Almighty looks at the righteousness that has been imparted to Christians through the shed blood of His only-begotten Son, our Lord and Savior, Jesus Christ.

As attested to in Mark 12:25 (previously quoted), when we go to heaven, we are not going to be gendered males or females. Rather, we will be "like the angels in heaven." Often, this boggles the mind because, as human beings, we have the tendency to think only in terms of images and allusions that relate to human referents — or, in other words, in terms that relate to what we now see and with which we are currently familiar. Of course, such thinking is understandable, but we really do need to elevate our thinking by focusing on things supernal — that is, on heavenly things:

{1} If you are in Christ, seek those things which are above, where Christ sits on the right hand of God. {2} Set your affection on things above and not on earthly things. {3} For you are dead, and your life is hidden with Christ in God. {4} When Christ, who is our life, shall appear, then shall we also appear with him in glory.

Colossians 3:1-4 KJV Paraphrase

In the reality of God, are we spiritual beings, physical beings, or both? In the Fifteenth Chapter of 1 Corinthians, we read:

And as we have born the image of the earthly, we shall also bear the image of the heavenly. Now, this I say, brothers and sisters,

---

10   See also Matthew 22:30 and Luke 20:35-36

that flesh and blood cannot inherit the Kingdom of God; neither can corruption inherit incorruption.

> 1 Corinthians 15:49-50 KJV Paraphrase

To be sure, human beings are both spiritual and physical. However, what we now *wear* is a corruptible body — a body that perishes. But one day we will have a new body — a body that is incorruptible and that does not perish. And that body will be glorious because we shall be wearing the glory of God. In other words, in heaven we will be enveloped by — as well as reflect — the brightness of God's *Being*.

I believe completely in the triune nature of God (i.e., *God the Father*, *God the Son*, and *God the Holy Spirit*). As I search Scripture, I find everything that points to that particular doctrine being sound as well as providing a solid foundation for understanding the one Godhead. Some people misinterpret the phrases "God the Father," "God the Son," and "God the Holy Spirit" to mean that Christians are polytheistic because they worship three gods. That could not be farther from the truth. All authentic Christians, independent of what they call themselves, believe in one God, regardless of semantics or how they articulate their views.

I also believe that there is a triune nature to God's created (we are God's *created* individually, collectively, and corporately) and that the triune nature for each individual consists of "spirit and soul and body," as stated in 1 Thessalonians 5:23 (KJV).

Thomas L. Constable, Professor of Bible Exposition at Dallas Theological Seminary, defines this threefold nature as follows:

> The *spirit* is the highest and most unique part of {a human being} that enables {the human being} to communicate with God. The *soul* is the part of {the human being} that makes {the human being} conscious of himself {or herself}; it is the seat of {the} personality. The *body*, of course, is the physical part through which the inner person expresses himself {or herself} and by which he {or she} is immediately recognized.[11]

---

11   Constable, Thomas L. "1 Thessalonians." In *The Bible Knowledge Commentary* by John F. Walvoord and Roy B. Zuck (eds.), Victor Books, USA, page 710. {brackets mine}

So, the human body is the form in which the individual literally *takes shape*; it is the individual's physical appearance or somatic identity. We know what shape we are in right now (that is, how we presently appear), but we do not yet know what we will look like in heaven. In response to the uncertainty of our heavenly appearance, the Apostle John wrote:

> Beloved, now are we the heirs of God, and it does not yet appear what we shall look like, but we know that, when the Lord Jesus shall appear, we shall look like him; for we shall see him as he is.

> 1 John 3:2 KJV Paraphrase

In other words, one day we will have a glorious body and heavenly form just as our Lord Jesus now has a glorious body and heavenly form. For this reason, we eagerly await the redemption of our bodies:

> {20} For the human creature was made subject to vanity, not willingly, but by reason of God who has subjected the same in hope, {21} Because the human creature itself also shall be delivered from the bondage of corruption into the glorious liberty of the children of God. {22} For we know that the whole creation groans and travails in pain together until now. {23} And not only the whole creation, but we ourselves also, who have the firstfruits of God's Holy Spirit. Even we groan within ourselves, waiting for our adoption in the redemption of our bodies. {24} For we are saved by hope: but hope that is seen is not hope: for what a person sees does not need to be hoped for. (We look forward to what we do not now see.)

> Romans 8:20-24 KJV Paraphrase

A few verses later, Scripture states that God's servants are "predestined to be conformed to the image of God's Son" (Romans 8:29 KJV Paraphrase). How exciting! Let us praise God that we have this to look forward to.

God reveals Himself to His people in terms they can understand. The invisible God does not have a penis and testes. In all probability, God presented Himself to primitive people in masculine terms so that they (who easily understood the concept of physical strength in hunting and defense) might better relate to His power and might. My point here is that God is neither gender-focused nor genital-enthralled.

Organized Religion

To date, organized religion has really served as a stumbling block, hindering many homosexual and transgender people from coming to terms with the Creator-God as well as coming to understand who the Creator is as our Father through His only-begotten Son, our Lord and Savior, Christ Jesus. This stumbling block exists in contemporary Christianity, in particular, but also in much of contemporary Judaism as well, although it has been less difficult for many Jews to reconcile their religion with variances in sexual orientation and gender identity. For example, in the December, 1993 issue of *Bible Review*, Rabbi Jacob Milgrom provides us with one Judaic perspective of the Levitical prohibition of same-sex activity in his article entitled "Does the Bible Prohibit Homosexuality?"

> From the Bible we can infer the following: Lesbians, presumably half of the world's homosexual population, are not mentioned [in Leviticus 18:22]. More than ninety-nine percent of the gays, namely non-Jews, are not addressed. This leaves the small number of male Jewish gays subject to this prohibition. If they are biologically or psychologically incapable of procreation, adoption provides a solution [to compensate for any loss of their seed].[12]

Many rabbis would tell Gentiles that the God of the Tanakh (i.e., the Old Testament of the Christian Bible) only requires Gentiles to obey the rules, regulations, and commandments written in the Bible up through the time of Noah. Noah is considered a Gentile by Jews

---

12 Milgrom, Jacob. "Does the Bible Prohibit Homosexuality?" In *Bible Review*, December 1993, page 11. [brackets mine]

because the Semitic people technically originated through Noah's son, Shem. Therefore, Noah is a Gentile and not a Jew. "Noachide Laws" specifically refer to laws in the Bible up through the time of Noah.

Rabbi Milgrom added this footnote to his work:

> It is true that some rabbis would include homosexuality under the Noachide Laws, binding on all humanity, but this is a later interpretation, not the plain meaning of the Biblical text.[13]

To be sure, Rabbi Milgrom does not take into consideration the Christian perspective that God's grace fulfills as well as supersedes the Law of Moses, nor does he take into account the role that male temple cult prostitution played in causing the Lord God Almighty to originally institute the Levitical prohibition against idolatrous, same-sex behavior. (Male temple cult prostitution, Levitical Law, and God's grace will be discussed in detail in Chapters Four and Five of this book.) Additionally, please keep in mind that, in Judaism, there are Orthodox and Conservative perspectives as well as Reform perspectives, and that I do not mean to suggest that all three are capsulized by Rabbi Milgrom's comments.

Here, I would like to point out that there is a difference between the phraseology "same-sex behavior" and "homosexual orientation." People who are uneducated, under-educated, or miseducated about the homosexual orientation often conclude that sexual activity itself determines whether someone should be called *homosexual* or *heterosexual*. They fail to realize that same-sex activity does not determine the homosexual orientation. In fact, behavior does not determine who is homosexual or heterosexual. Not all people who have had an opposite-sex experience are heterosexual. Not all people who have had a same-sex experience are homosexual. Not all people who are heterosexual have had an opposite-sex experience. And, certainly, not all people who are homosexual have had a same-sex experience. Behavior does not determine who is homosexual or heterosexual nor, for that matter, who is supposedly *ex-gay* or *ex-straight*.

Concerning Christian perspectives, the Roman Catholic Church has historically taken the hard-line stance that sexuality is for procreation

---

13 *Ibid.*, page 11.

and procreation alone. Thus, the Roman Catholic Church is opposed to masturbation, birth control, and homosexual acts because they do not serve a reproductive purpose. In the 1986 document, "On the Pastoral Care of Homosexual Persons," the Sacred Congregation for the Doctrine of the Faith states that the homosexual "inclination itself must be seen as an objective disorder" — which view, of course, is in contradistinction to prevailing psychiatric and psychologic views. This document was prepared by Joseph Cardinal Ratzinger, who was then Prefect of the Sacred Congregation for the Doctrine of the Faith. (Some readers may recognize the name of Joseph Cardinal Ratzinger as the Cardinal who would become Pope Benedict XVI.)

In a 1975 document entitled "Declaration on Certain Questions Concerning Sexual Ethics," the Sacred Congregation for the Doctrine of the Faith put forth the idea that, for some individuals, homosexuality is an "innate instinct." It is very curious that the two words *innate instinct* are used in the document, and that, despite their use, homosexuality is still condemned. If one takes "innate instinct" to its logical conclusion, one should recognize that God would not condemn people for a condition into which they have been born. Indeed, such a position is not only contradictory, it is illogical as well.

In many ways, Roman Catholicism has distanced itself from homosexual people, and many homosexual people have felt unwelcome in Roman Catholic churches. However, Roman Catholicism really has not been responsible for the extreme activism against homosexuality that has been demonstrated by many Protestant sects, denominations, and local churches, especially through so-called evangelical fundamentalists.

I consider myself a fundamentalist in many ways. And I consider myself an evangelical. However, the word *fundamentalism* has taken on such negative connotations relative to the political machinations of the *Religious Right* (and its insistence on certain exclusionary views) that I often prefer the word *foundationalism* over *fundamentalism*. To me, a Christian "foundationalist" is someone who has the foundation for his or her belief system in the Holy Bible, not only believing the Bible to be the inspired written Word of God (and acting accordingly), but also holding the whole Bible and its entire message while simultaneously attending to its various parts. To be sure, this holistic approach must be taken to discern the truths necessary for building sound and solid personal theologies as well as church doctrines.

Although Roman Catholicism may view homosexual people as incurably disordered, many Protestant fundamentalists would view homosexual people as *depraved heterosexuals* (that is, perverted versions of God's standard). They think that homosexual people can and should be cured. Because they do not understand the homosexual orientation, they end up thinking that the basic nature of all humankind is heterosexual and, consequently, that homosexual people need to be healed of their homosexuality. When you think about the so-called ex-gay movement, it really did not originate from Judaism or Roman Catholicism but from so-called *evangelical* Protestantism. Those who have bought into the notion of changing one's sexual orientation think that homosexual people can be made "whole" through such things as aversion therapy, hormone therapy, prayer, exorcism, and/or reeducation as well as special opportunities for them to have healthier parental figure nurturing and bonding.

When I was in Uganda in 2003 to do my "Christianity and Homosexuality Reconciled" seminar and workshop, I had to conduct it within a fenced compound into which attendees were admitted only if someone on the premises knew them personally. The climate in Uganda, as well as in many other countries of the world, is still hostile to homosexual people and transgender people and, consequently, to the idea of equal human rights for all people.

In fact, many nations are hostile to equal human rights and civil rights for homosexual people and transgender people. There continues to be a wave of propaganda in some nations that is similar to the propaganda of the Nazi war machine against homosexual people. Citizens of many economically-emerging nations (such as Uganda and Nigeria), as well as nations in the current Russian Federation, are being miseducated to believe that the homosexual agenda is in place in their countries in order to recruit their children into homosexuality and that homosexual people are typically involved in such depraved acts as pedophilia and even ingesting the feces of their sexual partners. In those countries, such vulgar psychopathologic behaviors are erroneously touted as uniquely representative of homosexual people and homosexuality.

The Protestant ministers who promulgate this disinformation fail to mention that all vulgar psychopathologic behaviors — such as child molestation and child pornography as well as bizarre and extreme adult paraphilial sexual practices — are found in both heterosexual and homosexual subpopulations. Examples of such vulgar and extreme sexual behaviors can be found on pornography web sites that appeal to both psychopathologic heterosexual people as well as psychopathologic homosexual people.

People who export their own homophobia and transphobia to economically-emerging nations do not realize that there are insufficiently organized human rights and civil rights initiatives in such countries to protect homosexual people and transgender people from being disemboweled, raped, hanged, mutilated, decapitated, thrown off roofs, and burned alive. People who export their own homophobia and transphobia anywhere are either unwitting tools or willing accomplices of demonic forces. Unfortunately, the systematic extermination of homosexual people and transgender people is desired in some places even in the twenty-first century.

Obviously, heterosexual people who view homosexual people as perverted versions of God's standard have not walked in their shoes. The overwhelming majority of homosexual people would tell them (if they would only ask) that as we were developing, maturing, and "growing up," we would have given anything to be like them. Why? Because no one would actually choose to be despised or looked at as depraved and perverted. Nobody wants to be rejected by the majority of society. And, even though other people have been oppressed and rejected, there is an extra burden for homosexual people because, *for example*, though certain ethnic and racial groups may experience rejection from a prejudiced group with political power, they can generally turn to their own families for nurturance and support. For many homosexual people, nurturance and support are not available. To be sure, many — if not most — homosexual people throughout the world have been rejected even by their own family members. My own parents rejected me, and I am not an exception.

The advice I share with those of you who may have homosexual or transgender family members is that you need to accept them for who and what they are, continue to love them, and serve as a support system for them. Without the support of family members, many homosexual people and transgender people have taken their own lives because they could not bear the emotional and mental pain from the rejection of those they love as well as those whose love they desire and need.

Homosexual people and transgender people learn to deal with their rejection at the same time that the rejection leaves a hole in their heart. Fortunately, Christ Jesus fills that gap through his love and acceptance. It states in Scripture, "When your father and mother reject you, the Lord will take you up" (Psalm 27:10 KJV).

I am seventy years of age at the time of this edition (2017), and I have been socialized by gay and lesbian culture (I am not using the word *lifestyle* but *culture*) since I was a teenager. I have known gay and lesbian people for over half a century. Unfortunately, I have known several people who have committed suicide, including those who found the rejection by their family members to be much too great an emotional pain to endure and burden to bear.

Certainly, I believe that there is individual responsibility for such acts of desperation, but I also believe there is societal and familial responsibility as well. And I believe that many people will be asked by our Lord and Savior, "Why did you try to keep these people from me? "Why did you hinder them from approaching my cross?" "Why did you not share the Gospel with them in nonjudgmental, noncondemning, and loving ways?" I think it will be very difficult for those who hear such questions at God's judgment seat (i.e., at His "Great White Throne"[14]) to answer in a way with which they themselves will be pleased let alone our Lord.

Previously, Christian gay, lesbian, and transgender people who wanted to attend church had only two options: either 1) they could go to a church that accepted them because it watered down Scripture due to theological liberalism and progressivism; or 2) they could go to a church that threatened expulsion if they were honest about who they really are. Today, Christian homosexual people and transgender people need to attend churches whose spiritual culture and climate are conducive to personal growth without compromising the gospel message. I am hopeful that such communities of faith will continue to develop during this third millennium after the birth of Christ Jesus.

---

14   Revelation 20:11, King James Version

The Need for Healing Homophobia

Homophobia is the fear and/or hatred of homosexual people. Sometimes homophobia is based on ignorance. Sometimes homophobia is based on malice. And sometimes homophobia is based on inner fears of being gay or lesbian and not being willing to be identified as such. What follows is a short quiz for homosexual people that might help them determine if they themselves are homophobic:

Quiz for Homosexual People

1. Do you think that it is better when gay and lesbian people are more *straight acting* because "men should be men" and "women should be women?"

2. Do you cringe when a gay or lesbian character is shown on TV or in a movie?

3. Do you wish you were not gay or lesbian?

4. Do you pretend that you are heterosexual?

5. Do you only desire to have shared sexual experiences with others of the same sex and not shared companionship?

6. Are you afraid that others will reject you if they find out that you are gay or lesbian?

7. Do you purposely refrain from speaking with a gay or lesbian person in a work setting or public place because others might conclude that you are homosexual?

8. Do you have indiscriminate sex with others?

A "yes" to more than two of the above eight questions should indicate to a homosexual person that he or she is harboring homophobic attitudes or exhibiting signs and symptoms of homophobia.

It is no wonder that homosexual people become self-loathing due to social pressure from homophobia. To be sure, it is all right to not want to suffer emotional pain from rejection, victimization, harassment, and persecution because of one's sexual orientation. However, it is not all right — from the standpoint of one's own personal emotional health and well-being — to wish not to be homosexual when one is. We should not desire to change a trait that should be viewed as blameless as skin color or as neutral as being right-handed or left-handed. In fact, homosexual people should celebrate that their sexual orientation contributes to their uniqueness since God foreknew what they would be:

{13} You created me: You protected me in my mother's womb. {14} I will praise You; for I am fearfully and wonderfully made: marvelous are Your works; and that my soul knows full well. {15} My substance was not hidden from You when I was made in secret — curiously wrought in the lowest parts of the earth. {16} Your eyes saw my substance before it was finished; and in Your book all my members were written before they were formed.

Psalm 139:13-16 KJV Paraphrase

With regard to additional possible causes, homophobia is sometimes manufactured as a means for going along with the crowd or — in the case of certain televangelists and politicians — as a rationale for asking for money from the crowd. Yes, homophobia has become a political agenda because railing against homosexuality is a money-maker. From World War II up through most of the 1980s, two of the biggest money-making issues that drew huge financial support, especially for the ministries of many televangelists, were: 1) communism and 2) homosexuality.

As communism fell in the former Soviet Union, televangelists lost one way to pull in money from the viewing public who was made to fear communism's potential encroachment, terror, and threat looming on the horizon. However, after the fall of communism, the issue of homosexuality still remained for televangelists and politicians to harp on. The existence of homosexuality became a convenient agenda for many public figures who wanted to enlarge their power base and increase their financial resources. I would submit to you that some people understand and even accept homosexuality in others and, yet, would speak out against it pretentiously because speaking out furthers their own personal, political, and/or social agendas and increases their popularity and public support.

People who fear and/or hate homosexual people need to understand that sexual behavior (meaning, *the sexual act*) does not determine who is straight or gay (i.e., heterosexual or homosexual). As mentioned earlier, behavior does not make a person gay, just as it does not make a person straight. Just as one can be heterosexual and remain celibate, so also can one remain homosexual and never act on his or her sexual orientation. Indeed, one could even be involved in same-sex behaviors and still be heterosexual. *For example*, some individuals in prison are involved in same-sex behaviors although their sexual orientation is definitely not homosexual. Also, many homosexual people get married in order to help avoid the emotional pain from the social stigmatization of being labeled *homosexual*. Even though homosexual people live as if they are heterosexual, they certainly are not heterosexual. Vaginal intercourse with a penis does not make someone heterosexual. Similarly, anal intercourse does not make someone homosexual.

It is my hope that, eventually, society will come to understand that *homosexual* does not mean "one who engages in same-sex behaviors." To be sure, the perspective I share is in agreement with that expressed by the American Psychological Association, which states: "Sexual orientation is different from sexual behavior because it refers to feelings and self-concept. Persons may or may not express their sexual orientation in their behaviors."[15]

Overall, *sexual orientation* is a better phrase to describe heterosexuality or homosexuality than *sexual preference*. *Sexual preference* connotes choice and, for most heterosexual people and homosexual people, there is no choice concerning their personal sexual orientation. The only time an opposite-sex or a same-sex relationship is a choice is when a bisexual person decides to actively, and exclusively, seek a companion of the opposite sex or the same sex. For people who are gay, and not bisexual, the only choice involved in their sexual orientation is whether or not

---

15   "Answers to Your Questions about Sexual Orientation and Homosexuality," American Psychological Association, 750 First Street NE, Washington, DC 20002-4242.

to act on their natural desires. And seeking same-sex companionship and intimacy for gay people is just as natural as seeking opposite-sex companionship and intimacy for straight people.

In a publication from the Oregon Psychological Association (also published and distributed by the Arizona Psychological Association), the following statement is made in response to the question, "Is the homosexual orientation a choice?"

Research indicates that sexual orientation is not a choice and cannot be changed for most people. Sexual orientation involves much more than performing sexual acts. It involves powerful inner feelings, self-concept, and social identity.

Psychologists generally agree that people who accept and integrate their sexual orientation (accept and act in accord with their inner feelings) are psychologically better adjusted then those who don't. Thus, homosexually-oriented people can refrain from acting upon their feelings and from letting others know of their sexual orientation, but only at a substantial cost to their personal well being.[16]

I will now also include an eight-question quiz for heterosexual people. Although I personally authored the previous quiz for homosexual people, the following eight questions are adopted and adapted from a twenty-question "Quiz for Heterosexuals," authored by Dr. Martin Rochlin in the 1970s. This quiz is intended to help heterosexual people think outside of their own sexual orientation as well as challenge them concerning to what degree their own sexual orientation was, or is, a choice.

Quiz for Heterosexual People

1. What do you think caused your heterosexuality?

2. When, and how, did you first decide you were heterosexual?

16 "Answers About Homosexuality," prepared by the Oregon Psychological Association and distributed by the Arizona Psychological Association, 202 East McDowell Road, Suite 170, Phoenix, Arizona, 85004.

3. Is it possible that your heterosexuality is just a phase that you will grow out of?

4. To whom have you disclosed your heterosexual tendencies and how did they react?

5. Why do so many heterosexual people feel compelled to seduce others into their sexual orientation?

6. Because a disproportionate number of child molesters are heterosexual, do you really want to expose your children to heterosexual teachers?

7. Why do heterosexual people place so much emphasis on sex?

8. Why are there so few stable spousal relationships within the heterosexual community?

True heterosexual people should not think of changing their sexual orientation because they cannot. So, too, true homosexual people should not think of changing their sexual orientation. Unfortunately, however, because of the prejudice and bias from a society whose majority is heterosexual, many homosexual people end up closeting themselves and pretending, and even longing, to be heterosexual.

It is unfortunate that many homosexual people have acquiesced to the majority opinion about them and accepted the shame and guilt assigned to them by society. This shame and guilt causes them to feel less than whole and act in terms of a fractured identity and consciousness.

Homosexual people need to have more positive gay role models after whom they might pattern their thinking, feeling, and behavior. As long as society enforces "don't ask, don't tell, don't-be-yourself" policies, gay people will continue to suffer, and even die, needlessly.

Unfortunately, the victims of homophobia are not only gay people. Victims also include heterosexual people who are homophobes. Hate is an insidious thing that — regardless of the outward damage it may do to others — helps to kill the inner self of those who permit it access to their hearts, minds, and souls. In the final analysis, it is somewhat queer to me that so many have abandoned the foundational Christian principle of sacrificial, selfless, and forgiving love in order to judge and condemn others based on traits and characteristics about which they know so little. Perhaps one way that homophobia proves that some people are not really born of God is through the hate and fear engendered by homophobes. Unfortunately, homophobia reproduces itself. Fortunately, there are cures for homophobia.

Deviations from the Norm

On a number of occasions, I have heard the following statement uttered by so-called Christian fundamentalists to combat the possible social acceptance of homosexuality: "God made Adam and Eve, not Adam and Steve." The ignorance of that statement astounds me both as a Christian and as a biologist. Because it is simplistic and reductionist, the statement fails to take into consideration the multivariate nature of diversity throughout this world.

There is a whole faction of Christians who not only want nothing to do with science but also would like to discredit all science that does not fit into their own personal world-view — which world-view is based on their own interpretations of the Holy Bible. It is important to remember that Galileo was convicted of heresy by the Christian Church in 1633 for following the teachings of Nicolaus Copernicus. Both Copernicus and Galileo concluded that the earth revolved around the sun and that our solar system is not the center of the physical universe. After his conviction, Galileo "was placed under house arrest for the rest of his life."[17]

Many unusual phenomena related to male and female *sex identity*[18] occur within the natural world. *For example*: 1) Certain avians and fish undergo spontaneous sex reversals and are even capable of reproduction in their newfound gender. 2) Various unfertilized insect eggs develop into males. 3) The females of specific flying insects possess "XY" sex chromosomes and the males possess "XX" sex chromosomes. 4) An all-female species of fish has been discovered, the Amazon molly, whose eggs develop through parthenogenesis (stimulation of ova to develop without the customary fusion of

---

17 http://en.wikipedia.org/wiki/Nicolaus_Copernicus (as it appeared in 2010)

18 *Sex identity* refers to the biological determination of an organism as asexual, male, female, or hermaphrodite (i.e., *monoecious*) as well as how an individual organism or colony functions biologically relative to the reproductive process.

male and female reproductive cells). And, most importantly, 5) a wide range of human intersexuality exists that fits on a continuum between normal male and female *genital identity*[19] (here, the word *normal* is used in the sense of "population-normed," or "that which occurs most frequently").

The issue of human sex identity is a complex one. There are many legitimate questions regarding an individual's: 1) genetic or chromosome status, 2) phenotypic or anatomic status, 3) psychological or gender identification status, and 4) sociological or society-assigned status of sex identity. In humans, sex identity may be determined by chromosome composition (generally XX for females and XY for males). However, genetic testing is not always the best indicator of sex identity. Why? There are a fair number of individuals who fall into *intersex* categories: *For example*, 1) those with abnormal chromosome composition or genetic code variances; 2) genetic males who differentiate into anatomic females due to low androgen production, androgen inaction, or androgen insensitivity; and 3) genetic females who differentiate into anatomic males because of exposure to abnormally high amounts of androgens either *in utero* from their mothers' hyperactive adrenal glands or *post partum* directly from their own hyperactive adrenal glands. (See Appendix A for a more detailed classification of intersexuality.)

Perhaps you have been taught that the basic human form, or early embryonic appearance, is female. That is not entirely true or accurate. What is true is that it is virtually impossible to determine the sex of a developing human embryo five weeks after conception. At that stage, external genitals include an undifferentiated *glans* area that will eventually become the penis in a male or the clitoris in a female. Undifferentiated *labioscrotal swellings* on either side of a general opening, known as the *urethral groove*, will either eventually fuse on the midline to form the scrotum in a male or remain separate as they develop into the labia majora ("outer lips") in a female. (See Figure One)

---

19 *Genital identity* refers to the presence or absence of external and/or internal genitals, how an organism's genitals are categorized, and in what stage of development or physical condition the genitals are.

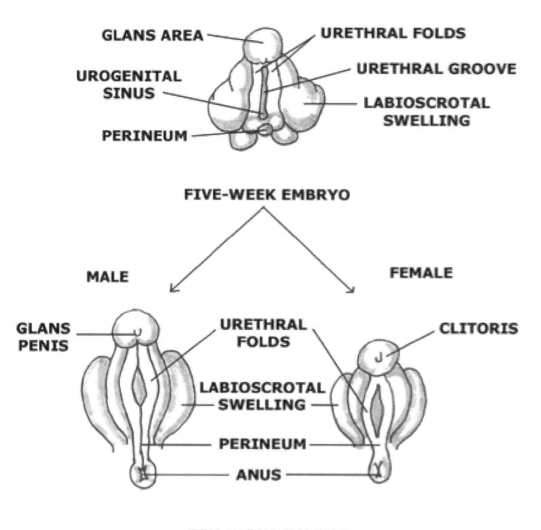

GLANS AREA

URETHRAL FOLDS

UROGENITAL SINUS

URETHRAL GROOVE

LABIOSCROTAL SWELLING

PERINEUM

FIVE-WEEK EMBRYO

MALE

FEMALE

GLANS PENIS

URETHRAL FOLDS

CLITORIS

LABIOSCROTAL SWELLING

PERINEUM

ANUS

TEN-WEEK EMBRYO

Early Development of the External Genitals
Figure One

At five weeks after conception, internal genitals include undifferentiated sex glands, also known as *gonads*, that normally develop into testes in a male or ovaries in a female. In the case of an anatomic male, the testes usually make their descent into the scrotal sac from one to three months before birth. Internal genitals in the five-week-old developing

XX or XY embryo also include two sets of tubes: 1) the paramesonephric, or Müllerian, ducts; and 2) the mesonephric, or Wolffian, ducts. In the case of most developing males, the paramesonephric ducts degenerate and the mesonephric ducts develop into the vasa deferentia (singular: *vas deferens*), or ducti deferentia (singular: *ductus deferens*), the major sperm-carrying tubes that connect the testicles to the urethra. In the case of most developing females, the mesonephric ducts degenerate and the paramesonephric ducts develop into the Fallopian tubes (i.e., oviducts or uterine tubes) as well as the uterus. (See Figure Two)

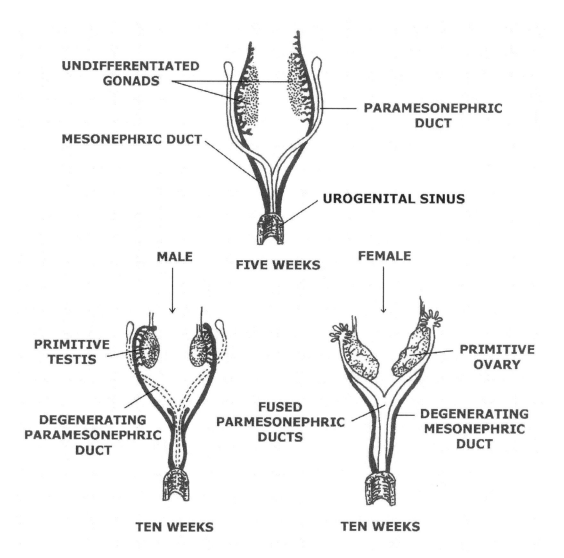

Early Development of the Internal Genitals
Figure Two

The external and internal changes described in the previous paragraphs, and shown in Figures One and Two, are all mediated by various genes that trigger the release and/or inhibition of various sex steroid hormones and related enzymes that convert inactive sex steroid hormone forms into their active forms. In developing males, one of the most important regulating genes in the processes described is known as the SRY gene, — the so-called Sex-determining Region of the Y chromosome.[20] (See Figure Three)

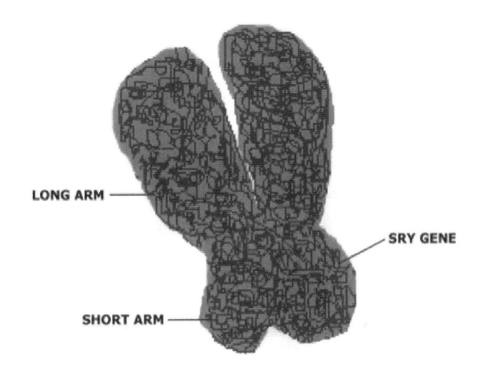

LONG ARM

SRY GENE

SHORT ARM

The Sex-determining Region of the Y Chromosome
Figure Three

In developing males, the SRY gene triggers a cascade of events between the fourth and seventh weeks after conception that results in the production of testosterone by the sex glands as they begin to differentiate into testes. Without the production of testosterone, or its conversion into a special active form known as dihydrotestosterone, internal and external genitals would not virilize — which is to say, they would remain

20   Haqq *et al*. "Molecular Basis of Mammalian Sexual Determination: Activation of Müllerian Inhibiting Substance Gene Expression by SRY." *Science*, Volume 266, December 2, 1994, pages 1494-1500.

somewhat ambiguous, resulting in indeterminate primary and secondary sexual characteristics. (Primary sexual characteristics are those with which you are born, and secondary sexual characteristics are those that you begin to develop at the onset of puberty.)

Generally, the SRY gene is found on the short arm of the Y chromosome in a developing Y sperm. (See Figure Three) By *Y sperm*, I mean a sperm that contains a Y chromosome in addition to 22 non-sex chromosomes (i.e., 22 autosomes). However, sometimes the SRY gene translocates (fragments and moves) and ends up spliced into an X chromosome in a developing X sperm. By *X sperm*, I mean a sperm that contains an X chromosome in addition to 22 non-sex chromosomes (i.e., 22 autosomes).

When the SRY gene is missing from the Y chromosome of a sperm that has fertilized an egg, the resulting XY individual generally develops a female anatomic form. When the SRY gene has translocated and is on the X chromosome of a sperm that has fertilized an egg, the resulting XX individual usually develops a male anatomic form (provided succeeding events, which the SRY gene initiates, proceed as they normally would). Hence, intersexuality includes XY females and XX males as well as individuals with ambiguous external genitals and/ or ambiguous internal genitals.

Since as many as 0.1% of the global population fall into intersex status categories,[21] there may be more than six million people on earth whose sex identities are in question using one basis for classification or another. Because these people are not *real* Adams or *real* Eves in the strictest definitions of *male* and *female*, are we to assume that intersex individuals were not created by God? No, we should never use the following characteristics to classify people as "real" men or "real" women: 1) the presence, absence, or appearance of external and internal genitals; 2) the numbers and kinds of chromosomes and the DNA they contain; 3) the presence or absence of sex hormones in blood, their concentrations, and their proportionalities; and 4) skeletomuscular dimensions.

Although sex identity is neither equivalent to sexual orientation nor equivalent to gender identity (however, from a statistical standpoint, each pair is positively correlated), a major point I am trying to make

---

21   Wilson, Jean D., M.D. "Sex Testing in International Athletics." *Journal of the American Medical Association*, Vol. 267, No. 6, 1992, page 853.

is that not all things are as black and white as some people would like them to be.

Today, within the biological community, there is legitimate debate about the biological basis of homosexuality in the light of recent scientific work: 1) that correlates sexual orientation in males to a locus on the X chromosome;[22] 2) that links brain morphology and sexual orientation;[23] and 3) that demonstrates statistical significance in favor of a genetic contribution to sexual orientation when comparing identical and fraternal twins.[24] Thus, it is more than likely that some seemingly unnatural and sinful behaviors ("unnatural" and "sinful" from the standpoint of judgmentalism) are actually part of nature. Can we assume that God made only some people and not others? Are we to assume that "God made Adam and Eve but not Adam and Steve nor Ada and Eve?" No, simply stated, God created all of humanity. God created each one of us.

In our discussion of what is natural (that is, what occurs in nature), I will share a personal anecdote from my childhood:

My maternal grandmother had a chicken farm and, on that farm, I noticed that once in a while there was a rooster who wanted to be a brooding hen. What he would do was bother the laying hens, trying to steal an egg so he could sit on it. Usually, the hens would not allow that to happen — so, he would often end up finding a smooth stone to sit on. Also, I noted within the chicken coop that, once in a while, there would be a hen that transformed into a rooster. Later, in my biological studies, I came to understand that, although every hen has two gonads (meaning, two sex glands that are both specialized as ovaries in most female vertebrates), only the right gonad in the hen is differentiated into an ovary while the left gonad remains undifferentiated (i.e., nonspecialized). Later in the hen's life, if the right gonad is destroyed by a disease process (or removed surgically), then the left gonad can either develop into an ovary or a testis. If the gonad develops into a testis, the

---

22 Hu, Stella *et al.* "Linkage between Sexual Orientation and Chromosome Xq28 in Males but not in Females." *Nature Genetics* 11, November 1995, pages 248-256.

23 LaVay, Simon. "Brain Structure Difference Between Heterosexual and Homosexual Men." *New England Journal of Medicine*, Vol. 162, Issue 9, 1995, pages 145-167.

24 Whitam, Frederick L, Milton Diamond, and James Martin. "Homosexual Orientation in Twins: A Report on 61 Pairs and Three Triplet Sets." *Archives of Sexual Behavior*, Vol. 22, No. 3, November 3, 1993, pages 187-206.

hen becomes transformed into a fully-functioning rooster that is even capable of fertilizing eggs produced by the other chickens that were born hens.

In order for a human being to be considered a *true hermaphrodite*, the person must have at least some functioning testicular tissue as well as some functioning ovarian tissue. It does not matter what other body parts the individual has or does not have. As long as this criterion is met, then the person is considered a *true hermaphrodite*. To be sure, there are individuals who might appear to be hermaphrodites but are actually *pseudohermaphrodites*.

Interestingly, there is one group of pseudohermaphrodites, known as *guevodoces* in Spanish, who are born appearing as if they are anatomic females. Consequently, they are raised and socialized as females. However, at the onset of puberty, testosterone and dihydrotestosterone surge within them, eventually transforming them into anatomic males. Perhaps the most curious thing is that, although these individuals have been raised and socialized as females, many of them end up functioning as males within society and even fathering children. Again, the point I am trying to make is that sex identity is not as simple as many people would have us believe. Also, it is important to note that, in this case, *nature* takes precedence over *nurture*.

There really is no good legal definition for *gender*. Certainly, one cannot define a male as someone having two testes. Does that person stop being a male if he must have a bilateral orchiectomy (both testes removed) because of cancer? Should that person no longer be considered a male? No, I think you see how ridiculous that would be. Does a woman who has had a total hysterectomy stop being a female? No, from a biological standpoint, maleness or femaleness is, first and foremost, a state of mind.

So much of who we are, and what we are, is provided to us by the brain. Indeed, the brain is actually the primary sexual organ. Sexual differences exist naturally within the brain as a result of varying hormone levels. And hormones impinge upon both the structural and functional development of the brain. *For example*, it is well known within the scientific world that a high concentration of androgens (which category of hormones includes both testosterone and dihydrotestosterone) tends to alter the development of the left cortex of the brain during embryonic and fetal development in males, contributing to population differences between males and females in languaging abilities and spatial conceptualization.[25]

It may come as a surprise to you, but even the so-called "male" and "female" hormone categories are misnomers because both males and females produce both androgens and estrogens. (Just as "androgen" is a category of sex steroid hormones, so, too, is "estrogen" a category of sex steroid hormones, including ß-estradiol, estrone, and estriol.) It is the relative proportions of these two categories of hormones that differ between males and females and not the hormone categories themselves. *For example*, in the adult human population, 90% of the sex steroids in most males are androgens and 10% are estrogens. The reverse is true for females; 90% of the sex steroids in most females are estrogens and 10% are androgens. Even the biochemical pathway for progesterone production in females includes various androgens.

Substantial scientific investigation has been conducted to elucidate the complex differences between males and females relative to hormones and brain functioning. Yes, hormones act on our developing brains as well as our developing genitals. Beginning the fourth week after conception and continuing through the seventh week, a cascade of hormones kicks in, causing a rather unisex-looking little embryo to begin manifestly changing from the fifth through eighth weeks either into the male anatomic form or continuing on (in what might appear to some) as the female anatomic form. Not only is the appearance of external genitals determined hormonally, brain morphology (or brain structure) is also determined by the presence or absence of the same sex steroids and their varying levels of concentration as well as relative proportions. And, because these hormones greatly impact our mental and emotional development, they influence the development of gender identity and sexual orientation during embryonic and fetal life. The evidence leads to the conclusion that how we view ourselves and how we evaluate others as potential sexual partners and spousal companions are biologically predetermined through hormones during embryonic and fetal life.

In a 1995 issue of *Development Psychology*, one article states that, for some women who took diethylstilbistrol, or DES (a synthetic form

---

25   Kimura, Doreen. "Sex Differences in the Brain." *Scientific American*, September 1992, page 124.

of estrogen that was once used to help stabilize pregnancy), there is a statistically-greater incidence of lesbianism within their daughters.[26] That is not to say that all lesbianism is the result of DES. Rather, there may be some biochemical contributing factors to gender identity and sexual orientation relative to maternal hormones that are being produced or artificially administered during pregnancy. The authors of that article emphasize:

> Many investigators see the sex hormones as the likely major biological factor in the development of sexual orientation because sex hormone action underlies {early} sexual differentiation and the {later} development of the secondary sex characteristics. As studies of the association of systemic sex hormone levels during adolescence and adulthood with sexual orientation have yielded largely negative results, especially in men, most of the psychoendocrine research on homosexuality is currently focused on prenatal hormones.[27]

Despite some recent scientific breakthroughs, we still live in a medieval world with regard to understanding the causes of homosexuality and gender identity. Thus, scientific explanations for the causes of sexual orientation and gender identity will not be worked out easily or quickly. Personally, I believe that what happened in my own development is that certain hormones kicked in during my embryonic and fetal life that contributed not only to my outward appearance but also to the anatomy and physiology of my brain — which, in turn, contributed to the formation within my own fetal brain of neural *grids*, or brain *fabrics*, for my specific gender identity and sexual orientation (meaning, who I view myself to be as well as how I view others as potential romantic partners). Consequently, I am homosexual. Interestingly, although I did not have the terminology to describe my innermost feelings as a child, I viewed myself as homosexual as early as the age of six or seven.

What makes each of you heterosexual or homosexual, I do not know. I think it is possible that the cause may vary for different individuals.

26 Meyer-Bahlburg, Heino *et al.* "Prenatal Estrogens and the Development of Homosexual Orientation." *Developmental Psychology*, 31, 1995, pages 12-21.

27 *Ibid.*, page 12. {brackets mine}

Perhaps there are some cases that are environmentally-caused, some psychologically-caused, others genetically- and/or hormonally-caused. However, with some psychotherapeutic exceptions, I do not think that the cause or causes should really matter. Rather, what I do think should really matter is that no one become enslaved to their own sexuality or to fears concerning it. We should seek comfort in pleasing God rather than comfort in carnal pleasures. And we should not be afraid to admit who we are, at the very least, to ourselves.

So, relative to the issue of homosexuality, there still remains a seeming dilemma for many people who are Christian, who would like to be Christian, or who would like to continue in their Christianity. To them, the anomalous condition of homosexuality is considered sinful, perverted, and disgusting. Additionally, they believe the Holy Bible says that the condition is considered an abomination by the Lord God Almighty.

To help understand anomalous conditions from the biological standpoint, I think that we can look to intersexuality to serve as a neutral biological model, or prototype, for the homosexual orientation. Did God not create intersexuals (that is, people for whom biologic sex identity is somewhat hazy)? Of course, God created them. Do others have the right to determine for individual intersexuals which sexual intimacies are normal for them or to whom they should look for a sexual partner or spousal companion? Indeed not! They neither have the moral right nor the requisite knowledge to do so.

Some Christians might think, "Intersexuality is a direct result of the Adamic Fall and intergenerationally-determined iniquity and sin, and that is why intersexual people exist." To counterbalance this thinking, I would point them to John 9:2 (KJV Paraphrase), where it is recorded that the Apostles turned to Christ Jesus and asked, "'Master, who sinned, this man, or his parents, that he was born blind?'" In the Apostles' minds, only a direct link with intergenerational iniquity or personal sin could explain the man's blind condition from birth. Our Lord Jesus answered them clearly by saying, "Neither this man nor his parents sinned, but that the glory of God might be made manifest in his life" (John 9:3 KJV Paraphrase). In other words, Christ Jesus was saying that there are some anomalous conditions that are neither intergenerationally- nor personally-determined by iniquity or sin.

To be sure, there are those who would argue that, because Christ Jesus went on to heal the blind man, so will God heal homosexual people of their homosexuality. The answer to the question of whether or not homosexual people need to be healed of their homosexuality will be carefully considered based on Scripture in the chapters to follow.

In bringing this chapter to a close, I would like to add that, just as most people consider vision the ideal condition in contrast to blindness, so do most people consider heterosexuality the ideal condition in contrast to homosexuality. However, some blind people actually consider their blindness to be a gift from God. Likewise, so do some homosexual people consider their sexual orientation to be a gift from God as well.

As we prepare for study in the following chapters concerning Bible passages that traditionally have been used against homosexual people, homosexuality, and the homosexual orientation as well as the transgender condition, I would like to reiterate the following:

When studying the Holy Bible, we need to hold the whole Bible while simultaneously attending to its various parts. Christians should never translate, interpret, or apply individual Bible verses in isolation! I have emphasized this approach to Bible study already, and I will continue to emphasize it in the chapters to follow because of its significant importance.

When studying the Holy Bible, we need to remember that "pure religion" does not contradict true science and that true science does not contradict pure religion. For the sake of clarification, *science* is not a bad word. *Science* simply includes "objective knowledge" and "factual understanding." Also for the sake of clarification, *religion* is not a bad word. *Religion* is "the practice of one's faith." I particularly like the way the New American Standard Bible (NAS) renders James 1:27:

> Pure and undefiled religion in the sight of *our* God and Father is this: to visit orphans and widows in their distress, *and* to keep oneself unstained by the world.

In other words, we are to share our resources and reserves with those who are the most vulnerable, and we are to resist demonic and fleshly temptations. We are to learn as much as we can about ourselves through science, so that we can correctly apply religious principles ethically and morally — with analysis through deductive and inductive reasoning as well as in good conscience.

When studying the Holy Bible, we need to understand context, because — as every Bible school student has been taught — "to proof text without context is pretext." Not only is it true for real estate that "location, location, location" are the three most important considerations, so is it true in Bible study that "context, context, context" are the three most important considerations. The various segments of the Holy Bible are framed by the contexts in which they were written, including: historical context, social context, cultural context, political context, literary context, etymologic context, and linguistic context. The Holy Bible is inerrant only when its verses are properly contextualized.

The following questions need to be answered during an in-depth Bible study:

1. To whom was a passage written?

2. What kind of people were the original, intended recipients?

3. What was their society like and how was it stratified?

4. What were the daily activities and practices of the original, intended recipients?

5. What type of civil and/or religious government did they have?

6. Why was a particular Bible passage written?

7. What was the intended meaning of the passage?

8. How do cross references within the Bible help to elucidate the truer, deeper, and higher meaning of a passage?

9. What is the etymology, or word origin, of each Hebrew, Aramaic, or Greek word used in a particular Bible passage?

10. What did each word mean when it was written?

11. Do the words have application to contemporary situations and settings?

12. How does the immediate context help us to uncover a word's specific meaning or its multiple meanings?

Taking the answers to all twelve of the previous questions into consideration will help Bible students to better understand the meaning(s) of various Bible verses when they were written as well as correctly apply their principles, or not apply them, to contemporary circumstances and situations.

CHAPTER FOUR

Sodom and Sodomites Revisited

Introduction

In this chapter, the story of Sodom is recounted in order to come to a better understanding of what is represented by it as well as by other Biblical references to it and to the ill-chosen word *sodomite*.

Abraham Pleads for Sodom

Many of you are already familiar with the story of Sodom. Ideally, it would be helpful if you took a few minutes to reread the introduction to it in Genesis 18:20-33 before you continue reading this chapter. In the Eighteenth Chapter of Genesis, you will find that Abraham pleaded with the Lord God Almighty (*Yahweh*, *Yehova*, or *Jehovah*) to spare

Sodom on behalf of his nephew, Lot. He asked the Lord to spare the city if fifty righteous people could be found in it:

> If there are fifty *righteous people* (*Tzaddekeem* {H6662(a)}) within the city, will You still destroy and not spare the place for the sake of *the* fifty *righteous people* (*HaTzaddekeem* {H6662(b)}) that are there?

Genesis 18:24 KJV Paraphrase

Strong's Number	Hebrew Word	Transliteration in Syllables	Word Meaning(s)
H6662(a)	צַדִּיקִם	Tzad·dē·keem'	1. righteous (people) 2. innocent (people)
H6662(b)	הַצַּדִּיקִם	Ha·Tza·dē·keem'	1. the righteous (people) 2. the innocent (people)

Table One

The Lord God Almighty replied to Abraham, "If there are fifty righteous people within the city, then I will spare the city." Abraham was delighted, of course, and quickly moved to ask the Lord to consider forty-five: "Will you spare the city of Sodom if there are only forty-five righteous people in it?" Because the Lord replied, "Yes," Abraham continued to barter with God from forty-five to forty to thirty to twenty and, finally, to ten. Although God's patience may have been tried, He ultimately answered, "For the sake of ten people, I will not destroy Sodom." Thus, the deal that Abraham worked out with the Lord was that the Lord would spare the city if ten righteous people could be found within its walls.

At the time of Abraham's conversation with the Lord, righteousness was not yet contingent on adherence to the rules, regulations, and ordinances of Levitical Law found in the Pentateuch, or Torah (i.e., the first five books of the Bible) because Levitical Law had not yet been given by God to the children of Israel. To be sure, Levitical Law was not put into effect until the time of Moses, more than four centuries after Abraham:

God's covenant with Abraham is not cancelled by the Law of Moses [which includes Levitical Law] that was given four hundred and thirty years after that promise.

Galatians 3:17[28] KJV Paraphrase

Instead of adherence to Levitical Law, righteousness from the time of Abraham until the time of Moses was based entirely on faith in the Lord God Almighty (*Yahweh*) — as it is based in these New Testament times on faith in the Lord God Almighty through His only-begotten Son, Christ Jesus. For the sake of clarity, *faith* is herewith defined as "believing in the Lord God Almighty (*Yahweh*) as the one true and only real God and acting unwaveringly on that belief." From Scripture, we know: 1) that faith is a gift from God (Ephesians 2:8); 2) that faith comes from hearing the good news of salvation through Christ Jesus (Romans 10:17); 3) that it is impossible to please the Lord God Almighty without faith (Hebrews 11:6); and 4) that Christ Jesus is "the author and finisher (or *perfecter*) of our New Testament faith" (Hebrews 12:2 KJV Paraphrase).

Scripture clearly teaches that Abraham had faith in God and that righteousness was imputed to him because of that faith (Romans 4:20-22 and James 2:23). From our knowledge of what happened to Sodom, it should be clear that the city did not even have ten people who had faith — and, thereby, possessed *righteousness* — in the Lord God Almighty. The people of Sodom were considered wicked, or guilty, by the Lord God Almighty. Why? They were considered wicked, or guilty, because they worshiped false gods (i.e., idols).

The Biblical Story of Sodom

Upon reading Genesis 19:1-15, we learn that two angelic visitors came to Sodom and that Lot saw the visitors and beckoned them into his home, cautioning them not to spend the night in the town square. Town squares then were much like downtown areas of many older cities today: They were dangerous and hostile, especially to identifiable strangers. Once the angels were inside Lot's home, it is recorded that

28   See also Genesis 15:1-21 and Exodus 12:40-41.

the people of the city gathered together and called out, "Send us the two visitors so that we may *know* them" (Genesis 19:5 KJV Paraphrase).

The verse immediately preceding Genesis 19:5 states:

But before they lay down, the *men* (*Enosh* {H582}) of Sodom surrounded the house, both old adults and young adults, all the *people* (*Am* {H5971}) from every quarter.

Genesis 19:4 KJV Paraphrase

Strong's Number	Hebrew Word	Transliteration in Syllables	Word Meaning(s)
H582	אֱנוֹשׁ	En·osh′	1. men (males) 2. people (males and females)
H5971	עַם	Am	people

Table Two

If only the Hebrew word *Enosh* {H582} was used in Genesis 19:4, then it might be conceded that only males gathered together outside of Lot's house. But it would only be a concession because the Hebrew word *Enosh* {H582} can mean either "males" or "people." However, since the Hebrew word *Am* {H5971} is used later in the phrase, "all the *people* from every quarter," it can be interpreted that both adult males and adult females, including young adults and older adults, came from all parts of the city to descend on Lot's house.

Let us now focus on a different Hebrew word in Genesis 19:5:

"Send us the two visitors so that we may *know* (*yadaw* {H3045}) them."

Genesis 19:5 KJV Paraphrase

Strong's Number	Hebrew Word	Transliteration in Syllables	Word Meaning(s)
H3045	יָדַע	ya·daw′	1. know 2. have sex with 3. rape

Table Three

The Hebrew word *yadaw* [H3045] is a root word, or base word, that has been incorporated into the Hebrew word translated in the King James Version of Genesis 19:5 as "that we might *know*." You will note in Table Three that *yadaw* [H3045] has multiple meanings when it is read in isolation, including: 1) *to know* (i.e., cognitively, intellectually, or socially); 2) *to have sex with*; and 3) *to rape*. Like many Hebrew words, the reader does not know the intended meaning of *yadaw* [H3045] until it is read in context.

Like the Hebrew language, most words in the English language are *multinyms* — which means they have multiple meanings and/ or different nuances that can only be determined when each word is read or heard in context. *For example*, in English, the word *cleave* can mean "to join together," but it can also mean "to separate." The reader or hearer would not know the meaning of the word *cleave* until it was read or heard in context. The Hebrew word *yadaw* [H3045] is somewhat like the English word *date*, which can mean: 1) "day of the year," 2) "innocent prearranged social engagement," or, more colloquially, 3) a "sexual encounter between a prostitute and his or her client."

Yadaw [H3045] has multiple meanings. *For example*, when *yadaw* [H3045] is used in Genesis 3:22 ("to know good and evil"), its meaning is "to know cognitively, intellectually, or socially." When *yadaw* [H3045] is used in Genesis 4:1 ("Adam knew Eve"), its meaning is "to experience intimacy in consensual sex." And, when *yadaw* [H3045] is used in Genesis 19:5 and Judges 19:25, its meaning is "to rape." As a side note here, *yadaw* [H3045] is translated correctly as "rape" in the New American Standard (NAS) and New Living Translation (NLT) in Judges 19:25 but not in Genesis 19:5 of those versions. Thus, "so that we may *know* them" (Genesis 19:5 KJV) really means "to know *carnally* by brute force" — or, more specifically in this context, "so that we might *rape* them."

Anyone who tries to present the Biblical account of Sodom as just a story about getting to know someone cognitively, intellectually, or socially is doing the written Word of God an injustice. The story of Sodom is not about getting to know people cognitively, intellectually, or socially. The story of Sodom is not even about consensual sex between adults. The story of Sodom is about an intended violent and brutal rape by multiple perpetrators. And the story of Sodom is not about rape among human males but the intended rape of two angelic visitors by all of the adult townspeople. Even if it were conceded that the Biblical account of Sodom may only be referring to the males of the city, the story of Sodom is still referring to rape. How does anyone confuse consensual sex with rape?

Naturally, Lot was horrified by this demand for a number of reasons, including that these visitors were guests within his own home. People at that time respected and honored the Law of Hammurabi, which dictated that, when you extend hospitality to visitors, you agree to provide them protection even at the expense of your own life as well as the lives of your immediate household. As a result, Lot offered his daughters to the townspeople instead of the angelic visitors, but the townspeople refused them.

Anyone who tries to make the story of Sodom solely an issue of hospitality and inhospitality is doing the written Word of God an injustice. The story of Sodom is not just about hospitality and inhospitality. And for those who might interpret that the Lord God Almighty is misogynistic because Lot offered his two daughters, it should be emphasized that the Biblical account of Sodom is a narrative about what happened and not an endorsement by God that women should be viewed and treated as if they are the property of males.

After Lot offered his daughters to the people of the city, the angelic visitors struck them blind, and Lot and his family made haste to leave the city. Sodom was then destroyed. Unfortunately, the story of Sodom is often linked erroneously to modern-day homosexuality.

In order to better understand the events just described, we need to recognize that what was intended by the townspeople of Sodom was not consensual intimacy but, instead, brutal group rape. Fortunately, we are living at a time when rape is understood, not only as a sexual act, but also as a psychopathologic action meant to demean and victimize others by overpowering them. Rape is based on the desire to dominate, or domineer, as well as to demonstrate one's seeming superiority over others who are physically weaker and, therefore, especially vulnerable to such an action. Rape is intended by the psychologically sick and criminal mind to draw attention to the victim's supposed gross vulnerabilities, infirmities, and defects at the same time that it draws attention away from the perpetrator's own feelings of inadequacy, inferiority, and lack of control. Rape is an act of violence, domination, and rage meant to victimize others in order to humiliate and control them. The issue in the story of Sodom is not an issue of consensual sexual activity, or intimacy between two people, but an issue of violent victimization through group rape.

If there is anyone reading this book who has been the victim of rape, let us pray, right now, in the Name of Christ Jesus, for our Lord Jesus to take away any guilt or shame that you may have unwittingly accepted and that he imbue you with the perfect love that will enable you to eventually forgive the perpetrator of this horrible and heinous crime against you. Please know that your forgiveness of the perpetrator is a process and may take a long time. Don't be too hard on yourself if you have not yet found forgiveness in your heart for the perpetrator of the crime. This perpetrator committed a crime, not only against you, but also against the loved ones who grieve for you. In addition to praying, I encourage you to talk with your pastor, with your loved ones, and with a trained psychotherapist to help you sort through your traumatized emotions for the purpose of healing them.

In addition to what I have just described relative to a contemporary understanding of rape, it is also essential for us to know that warring peoples (in this case, barbarians) throughout most of ancient history commonly raped the conquered — men as well as women. They did this in order: 1) to indicate that they (i.e., the conquerors) had complete statutory control over the vanquished; and 2) to warn enemies and potential aggressors of their (i.e., the conquerors') ferocity.

Many insights to the Genesis 19 account of Sodom are provided by a very similar set of circumstances within the Bible that begins in Judges 19:1 and ends at Judges 20:5. Although I will now share some of the parallels between the two accounts and draw some analogies, I encourage you to read the two accounts for yourself before you continue to the next paragraph.

In the Nineteenth Chapter of Judges, we find a Levite (i.e., a male from the tribe of Levi) traveling with his concubine. In today's language, and in this context, a *concubine* would be considered a married man's *secondary wife* (perhaps a member of a harem of women), a *mistress*, and/or a *sex slave*. Regardless of these categories, the concubine had no spousal legal rights or entitlements because she was viewed as the man's property.

As the Levite and his concubine were traveling, they happened upon the city of Gibeah. Like the angels who visited Sodom, the Levite and his concubine were cautioned not to stay in the town square. An old man who lived in Gibeah told them, "Please do not stay in this dangerous place. Instead, come to my home, where I will provide for you and protect you." So, the Levite and his concubine ended up going home with the old man of Gibeah.

Then, as in Sodom, Scripture reports that the people of Gibeah — described in Judges 19 as the "offspring of Belial" — gathered around the residence where the Levite and his concubine were staying, demanding that the host send out the Levite in order that they might *know* him (*know* having been translated from *yadaw* [H3045]) — or, as indicated previously, that they might *rape* him. In response, the old man of Gibeah replied, "Oh, no, please do not do so; take, instead, his concubine and my daughter and use them accordingly, but do not do so to my male visitor." (Remember, the old man of Gibeah promised to protect the Levite.) Eventually, they sent out the Levite's concubine, and the men of the city raped and ravaged her until she swaggered to the doorstep of the home of the old man from Gibeah and fell down dead.

To be hermeneutically sound, an accurate interpretation of the Nineteenth Chapter of Genesis must consider the Nineteenth Chapter of Judges. For the sake of clarification, *hermeneutics* is defined by *Webster's II New Riverside Dictionary* as "the science and methodology of interpretation, especially of the Bible."[29]

---

29 *Webster's II New Riverside Dictionary*, Riverside Publishing Company, 1984, page 577.

The parallels that exist between Genesis 19:1-15 and Judges 19:1-20:5 are summarized in Table Four:

Sodom Account	Gibeah Account
two visitors or travelers:	
two angels	a Levite and his concubine
cautioned not to spend the night in the town square:	
by Lot	by an old man of Gibeah
demands of group rape by the men or people of the city and two women offered instead	
Lot's two virgin daughters	old man's virgin daughter and the Levite's concubine
same Hebrew word (ya·daw' [H3045]) used in:	
Genesis 19:5	Judges 19:25

Parallels between Genesis 19 and Judges 19
Table Four

A very important principle in understanding difficult passages in the Bible is expressed by the statement, "Scripture interprets Scripture." In other words, as we read and study a difficult passage in the Holy Bible, we will eventually discover that there are helpful explanations, keys, and/or hints to unlock its meaning provided by other passages located elsewhere in the Bible. Thus, it is very important that Christians read and study the entire written Word of God or they may fall into the same trap that many people fall into by stopping short of a full understanding and, then, sharing that incomplete and imperfect understanding with others. However, if we study God's entire written Word, the Holy Spirit will guide us to the whole truth that is to be found within the wholeness of Scripture. Remember, there is great continuity in the Holy Bible from its beginning to its end, and we must hold the whole Bible while we simultaneously attend to its various parts.

In Judges 20:5, tremendous insight is provided relative to the intentions of the men of Gibeah and, also, transferably so, to the intended rape of the two angelic visitors in Sodom. In retelling the story when he returned home, the Levite states:

> And the men of Gibeah rose against me and encircled the house at night, thinking to have me slain: my concubine was sexually abused by them until she died.

> Judges 20:5 KJV Paraphrase

Historians would consider the Levite a *primary source* (i.e., a most credible witness) because he was there when it happened. When the Levite himself described what would have happened to him, he said, "The men of the city encircled the old man's residence, *thinking to have me slain*." The Levite's statement tells us that the men of Gibeah had fully intended to kill him by brutally raping him. That they had succeeded in doing this to his concubine is proof of their evil intentions. We also need to understand that this intended raping of a man — especially in the case of Judges 19:1-20:5 — was not by homosexual males. There are no homosexual males who would desire to rape a female; simply stated, they would have no interest in doing so. That the people of

Gibeah stepped out of their heterosexual "nature" (that is, out of their personal instinctual predisposition toward heterosexuality) to victimize the Levite should be clear, much like modern-day male prisoners step outside of their heterosexual nature to rape fellow male inmates. What is also provided by the Biblical story of Gibeah is that the intended group rape in the Nineteenth Chapter of Genesis was not an isolated incident specific to Sodom but, instead, representative of a more widespread activity throughout the land at that time.

Relative to the depiction of women in the Sodom and Gibeah stories, I think it important to emphasize that most ancient societies subscribed to the notion of female inferiority and subordinancy. Women were regarded as no better than property or chattel — as they still are in many places throughout the world today. That the Bible recounts these stories does not mean that God condones, or that Scripture endorses. the foul treatment of women. As stated earlier in this chapter, the Bible is simply retelling events that occurred and what happened when they occurred.

Consider the narratives in the Nineteenth Chapters of Genesis and Judges in their historical and literary contexts and not in the context of the desperately-needed, current social movements toward equality and fairness for women. Also, remember that most of the great strides that women have made in modern-day societies were really not made until the twentieth century and that women are still treated as property in many economically-emerging nations and unenlightened (indeed, primitive) societies throughout the world today. Even women in the United States did not receive the right to vote until August 18, 1920. For many countries in the West, women made the greatest progress when they entered the workforce in droves to replace the males who were fighting during World War II.

In comparison to murder, whether rape is the ultimate or penultimate act of contempt for another person, the reader must decide for himself or herself. Regardless of your conclusion, neither murder nor rape takes into consideration a victim's desires, wants, or needs; and both acts are intended to brutalize others. It should be obvious to the reader that the story of the intended brutal rape in Sodom has nothing to do with loving, monogamous, and committed relationships between consenting adults of the same sex or even opposite sex.

Canaanite Pagan Deities

I would now like to introduce the reader to a few Canaanite pagan deities that played a major role in shaping the culture of Sodom and its surrounding areas, including Gomorrah.

Genesis 10:19 indicates that the borders of Canaan included Sodom and Gomorrah. Sodom and Gomorrah, then, were part of Canaan, the land that was eventually conquered by the children of Israel. And these cities were not only part of Canaan geographically but also part of Canaan culturally. This is especially germane to our story because Canaanite fertility cults played a particularly important role in the day-to-day activities of the indigenous peoples who inhabited this general region as well as many people who migrated there. Not surprisingly, "Canaanite fertility cults, which were more lewd and influential than any other nature cults of the Middle East, made incursions into the austere, wilderness-born faith of Israel."[30]

In order to consider further the topic of Sodom, we need to cover some historical background relative to a few of the more popular fertility pagan deities that were worshiped during much of the two millennia preceding the birth of Christ Jesus.

Although there were other pagan deities worshiped in Canaan, major fertility deities included the gods Molech and Baal as well as the goddess Ashtoreth (see Table Five).

Molech

In Old Testament times, Molech was a male fertility god to whom devotees sacrificed the lives of their "seed," or children, in ritualistic burning (see Leviticus 18:21 and 20:2-5). The transliterated word *Molech* is derived from the Hebrew word *Molek* [H4432], which means "king:"

{1} The Lord said to Moses, {2} "Say to the children of Israel, 'Anyone of the children of Israel, or of the strangers that sojourn in Israel that gives of his seed to Molech shall be put to death: the people of the land shall stone him. {3} And I will set my face against that man, and will cut him off from among his people because he has given of his

---

30   Miller, Madeleine S. and J. Lane. *The New Harper's Bible Dictionary*. Harper and Row, New York, 1973, page 89.

seed to Molech to defile my sanctuary and to profane my holy name. {4} And if the people of the land ignore the man when he gives of his seed to Molech, and they do not kill him, {5} Then I will set my face against that man, and against his family, and will cut him off, and all that commit adultery with Molech, from among their people.'"

Leviticus 20:1-5 KJV Paraphrase

Baal/Baalim

Customarily, each Baal god was specific to a different city-state that existed within the Canaanite region. At times, the word *Baal* {H1168} was used as an umbrella term for all *Baalim* (the Hebrew "-im" ending here denoting the masculine plural) — or *Baal gods* — of the region. Variant forms of the name *Baal* include "Bel" and "Beel." The name *Baal*, or one of its variant forms, was often incorporated into the names of pagan people who worshiped Baal — *for example*, Jeze*bal*, who was a devotee, or temple cult priestess, of *Baal*, and her father, Eth*baal*:

{29} And in the thirty-eighth year of Asa, king of Judah, Ahab the son of Omri began to reign over Israel: and Ahab the son of Omri reigned over Israel in Samaria for twenty-two years. {30} And Ahab the son of Omri did greater evil in the sight of the Lord than all who were before him. {31} And it came to pass, as if it had been a light thing for him to walk in the sins of Jeroboam the son of Nebat, that he married Jezebel, the daughter of Ethbaal, king of the Zidonians, and went and served Baal, and worshiped him. {32} And he raised an altar for Baal in the temple of Baal that he had built in Samaria. {33} And Ahab did more to provoke the Lord God of Israel to anger than all the kings of Israel that were before him.

1 Kings 16:29-33 KJV Paraphrase

It was not by accident that Christ Jesus referred to the Devil as "Beelzebub" (Matthew 12:26-27), which word is derived from "Baal-Zebub, the god of Ekron" (see 2 Kings 1:2). The literal meaning of Baal-Zebub, or *Beelzebub*, is "lord of the flies." To be sure, "lord of the flies" is an apt epithet for Satan, who is behind every form of idolatrous worship. Just as dung draws flies to itself here on earth, so does Satan draw unclean spirits, devils, or demons to himself in the world of the unseen.

Although *Baal* represents an evil thing, the word *Baal* itself is not evil; it simply means "lord" or "master" in Hebrew. Although the word means *lord*, *Baal* should not be confused with the Hebrew words *Adonai* or *Shem* (or its variant *HaShem*) that are often used in place of the unpronounceable Hebrew tetragrammaton YHWH, the most holy name of the one true and only real God. *Yahweh*, *Jehovah*, or *Yehova* {H3068} is often translated in the Old Testament, especially in the King James Version, with all upper case letters as *LORD*.

Ashtoreth/Ashtaroth

The singular form for many feminine nouns in Hebrew ends in "-eth." For such nouns, it is the "-oth" (or "-ot") ending that makes the plural form. Thus, although the transliterated word *Ashtaroth* {H6252} looks similar to the transliterated *Ashtoreth*, the former word is the plural form and the latter is the singular form. Just as there were many representations of the god Baal, so, too, were there many representations of the goddess Ashtoreth.

Ashtoreth is the very same goddess referred to in Babylonian and Assyrian times as "Ishtar" and "Ashtar" (or "Astar") and in Greek and Roman times as "Astarte." We even find that the Scandinavian fertility goddess "Easter" (i.e., *Eostre* or *Ostara*) is likely derived, symbolically as well as etymologically, from the Greek word "Astarte" — and, for this reason, the fertility symbols of eggs and rabbits are used during the holiday known by many as *Easter*. (This helps to explain why some Christians prefer using the phrase *Resurrection Sunday* instead of the word *Easter*.)

Ashtoreth, *Ishtar*, *Ashtar*, and *Astarte* all represent the pagan goddess referred to by the appellation "Queen of Heaven" (Jeremiah 7:18; 44:17-19; and 44:25). The *Asherah pole* — mentioned in 1 Kings 16:33 and 2 Kings 23:13-14 — was a huge pole or totem made of stone or wood, erected in honor of one of the manifestations of Ashtoreth (and sometimes Baal) and thought to be in the form of a phallus, or penis.[31]

---

31 Nicoll, Reverend W. Robertson (editor). *The Expositor's Bible*, Volume 6, Funk and Wagnalls, New York, 1900, pages 304 and 389.

And the high places that were before Jerusalem, which were on the right hand of the mount of corruption, which Solomon the king of Israel had built for Ashtoreth the *abomination* {i.e., false god or idol} of the Zidonians, and for Chemosh the *abomination* {i.e., false god or idol} of the Moabites, and for Milcom the *abomination* {i.e., false god or idol} of the children of Ammon, did King Josiah destroy.

2 Kings 23:13 KJV Paraphrase

And the children of Israel did evil again in the sight of the Lord, and served Baalim {plural of Baal}, and Ashtaroth {plural of Ashtoreth}. {brackets mine}

Judges 10:6 KJV

Strong's Number	Hebrew Word	Transliteration in Syllables	Word Meaning(s)
H4432	מֹלֶךְ	Mō'·lek	1. "king" 2. a Canaanite fertility deity, especially of the Ammonites and Phoenicians, to whom infants were sacrificed
H1168	בַּעַל	Ba'·al	1. "lord" 2. a major Canaanite fertility deity
H3068	יְהֹוָה	Yeh·hō·vä'	1. "LORD" 2. the self-existing One 3. the one true and only real God
H6252	עַשְׁתָּרֹת	Ash·tä·rōth' or As·tä·rōth'	1. plural of Ashtoreth ("star") 2. Canaanite female fertility deities 3. fertility goddesses

Table Five

The pagan deities worshiped in Canaanite times — including Molech, Baal, and Ashtoreth — were attributed special powers of fertility. In order to curry favor from these gods and receive their blessings of abundance for crops, livestock, and human progeny, the ways that they were served by their acolytes included orgies as well as partnered sexual activities between worshipers and their so-called priests and priestesses. The sexual activities were considered forms of sacrifice to, and worship of, each fertility deity. From the standpoint of contemporary society, it may sound absurd to you that people would confuse sexual activity with worship. However, the temple cult priests and priestesses of these fertility religions were considered *sacred* and *holy* because they were functionaries of the fertility gods and goddesses they served. In effect, they functioned as *stand-ins* for them.

Fertility cults is an appropriate descriptive noun phrase for these religions. In order to honor their pagan deities, worshipers either: 1) offered their seed (that is, their "life") through masturbation and/or the sacrifice of their children; or 2) committed sexual *sacrificial* acts with the priests and priestesses who worked as cult prostitutes either in the temples constructed to these false gods or in quarters adjacent to them. To be sure, there were many different cult priests and priestesses who functioned as temple prostitutes throughout antiquity in lands that bordered the Mediterranean Sea, including Canaan — the land of Sodom and Gomorrah.

Idolatry is what the children of Israel were faced with when they entered into the Promised Land (i.e., the land of Canaan). One of the reasons that the Lord God Almighty had told them to slay everyone and get rid of all of the people who were occupying the land of Canaan was to prevent the children of Israel from gradually being influenced by idolatrous worship practices and, consequently, ending up estranged from the Lord God Almighty by adopting such profane behaviors. Hence, the Lord God Almighty gave the following directives to the children of Israel:

> And you must kill all people that the Lord your God delivers to you; You must not have pity on them: neither shall you serve their gods; for that will be a snare to you.
>
> Deuteronomy 7:16 KJV Paraphrase

> The graven images of their gods you must burn with fire: you must not desire or take the silver or gold that is on them so that you are not profaned by them because they are

abominations (*Toevot* {H8441 plural}) to the Lord your God. Neither shall you bring an abomination (*Toevah* {H8441 singular}) into your house, to avoid being cursed like it: but you shall utterly detest it, and you shall utterly abhor it; for it is a cursed thing.

Deuteronomy 7:25-26 KJV Paraphrase

Strong's Number	Hebrew Word	Transliteration in Syllables	Word Meaning(s)
H8441 (singular)	תּוֹעֵבָה	Tō·ā·vä′	1. abomination, idol, or idolatry 2. abominable, detestable, unclean, or idolatrous thing 3. abominable, detestable, unclean, or idolatrous practice
H8441 (plural)	תּוֹעֲבֹת	Tō·e·vot′	1. abominations, idols, or idolatries 2. abominable, detestable, unclean, or idolatrous things 3. abominable, detestable, unclean, or idolatrous practices

Table Six

The Lord God Almighty gave this warning to the children of Israel:

If you in any way go back, and embrace the remnant of these nations, even those that remain among you, and shall participate in marriages with them: Know for a certainty that the Lord your God will cease to drive out any of these nations from before you; but they shall be snares and traps to you, and scourges in your sides, and thorns in your eyes, until you perish from off this good land which the Lord your God has given to you.

Joshua 23:12-13 KJV Paraphrase

Unfortunately, in the end, "the Israelites lived among the Canaanites, Hittites, Amorites, Perizzites, Hivites, and Jebusites; and their sons took their daughters in marriage and the Israelites gave their own daughters to their sons, and they served their gods. Thus, the children of Israel did evil in the sight of the Lord, and forgot the Lord their God, and served Baalim and the Asherah-idols" (Judges 3:5-7 KJV Paraphrase).

Even King Solomon, son of King David, fell to idolatrous worship:

{1} But king Solomon loved many foreign women, together with the daughter of Pharaoh, women of the Moabites, Ammonites, Edomites, Zidonians, and Hittites; {2} Of the nations which the Lord God Almighty said unto the children of Israel, "You must not intermarry because they will surely turn away your heart after their gods," Solomon held to them in lust. {3} And he had seven hundred wives and three hundred concubines: and his wives turned away his heart from serving the Lord. {4} For it came to pass, when Solomon was old, that his wives turned his heart toward other gods: and his heart was not perfect with the Lord his God as the heart of David his father had been. {5} For Solomon went after Ashtoreth the goddess of the Zidonians, and after Milcom {a variant of Molech} the abomination of the Ammonites. {6} And Solomon did evil in the sight of the Lord, and did not devote himself completely to the Lord, as David his father had done. {7} Then, Solomon built a high place for Chemosh, the *abomination* of Moab, in the hill that is before Jerusalem, and for Molech, the *abomination* of the children of Ammon.

1 Kings 11:1-7 KJV Paraphrase

During Old Testament times, the hearts of the children of Israel often turned in the direction of idolatrous worship and practices. They were regularly pulled in the direction of offering sexual "sacrifices" to fertility gods and goddesses as well as to other pagan deities. Finally, just like those who later indulged the common idolatrous practices of the Roman Empire during early New Testament times, "God gave them up to uncleanness through the lusts of their own hearts to dishonor their own bodies among themselves" (Romans 1:24 KJV Paraphrase).

Idolatry, or *abomination*, always brings confusion and destruction to those who practice it.

The Role of Temple Cult Prostitution

The historical background concerning Canaanite pagan deities is of particular significance concerning the word *sodomite*. In the King James Version of the Bible, first published in 1611, the word *sodomite* exists in its singular form only once, and that is in Deuteronomy 23:17; its plural form, *sodomites*, is found in four additional references that include 1 Kings 14:24, 15:12, and 22:46 as well as 2 Kings 23:7:

> There shall be no whore of the daughters of Israel nor a *sodomite* of the sons of Israel. [italics mine]
>
> Deuteronomy 23:17 KJV

> And there were also *sodomites* in the land; and they did according to all the abominations of the nations which the Lord cast out before the children of Israel. [italics mine]
>
> 1 Kings 14:24 KJV

> And he took away the *sodomites* out of the land, and removed all of the idols that his fathers had made. [italics mine]
>
> 1 Kings 15:12 KJV

> And the remnant of the *sodomites*, which remained in the days of his father Asa, he took out of the land. [italics mine]
>
> 1 Kings 22:46 KJV

> And he [King Josiah] brake down the houses of the *sodomites*, that were by the house of the Lord, where the women wove

hangings for the grove {*grove* translated here from the Hebrew *Asherah*, which is an idol dedicated to the fertility cult goddess *Ashtoreth*}. {brackets and italics mine}

2 Kings 23:7 KJV

The five times that the singular and plural forms of the word *sodomite* are used are particularly significant because most people (even most people who are not Christian) view the words *homosexual* (i.e., homosexual person) and *sodomite* as synonyms — which is to say, that they are interchangeable.

Unfortunately, even when most students of the Bible read or hear the words *sodomite* and *sodomites*, they automatically assume the words to mean "homosexual person" and "homosexual people." However, relative to etymology (i.e., word origin), *sodomite* and *homosexual person* are *not* synonyms and, therefore, not interchangeable. In other words, relative to the Hebrew noun from which the words *sodomite* and *sodomites* have been translated, the word *sodomite* does not mean "homosexual person." Anyone who insists that it does is a revisionist with an anti-gay agenda.

If we go back to the original Hebrew, we find that the word *sodomite* has been translated from the Hebrew noun *Qadashe* {H6945}. There are three different characters (or alphabet letters) found in this Hebrew word (see Table Seven). In Hebrew, one reads from right to left: 1) the first character (called "kof") on the right roughly represents the "q," "k," or "g" sound of the English alphabet ("qadeshe," "kawdeshe," or "gadeshe"); 2) the second character (called "dalet") represents the "d" sound; and 3) the third character (called "shin") represents the "sh" sound. The plural of the masculine form *Qadashe* {H6945} is *Qadashim*, or *Qadasheem* (see Table Seven) — which, of course, refers to more than one "male temple cult prostitute." Female counterparts are *Qedasha*, or *Qedashah* {H6948 singular}, and *Qedashoth*, or *Qedashot* {H6948 plural} — the "-oth" (or "-ot") ending indicating the feminine plural form (just as "Ashtar*oth*," or "Ashtar*ot*," is the plural form of "Ashtor*eth*").

There shall be no *Qedasha* (female temple cult prostitute {H6948 singular}) of the daughters of Israel, neither shall there be a

Qadashe (male temple cult prostitute {H6945 singular}) of the sons of Israel. {italics and parentheses mine}

Deuteronomy 23:17 KJV Paraphrase

Strong's Number	Hebrew Word	Transliteration in Syllables	Word Meaning(s)
H6945 (singular)	קָדֵשׁ	Qä·dashe'	1. holy, sacred, or consecrated male 2. male temple cult prostitute 3. male shrine prostitute 4. male fertility cult prostitute
H6945 (plural)	קְדֵשִׁים	Qä·dash·eem'	1. holy, sacred, or consecrated males 2. male temple cult prostitutes 3. male shrine prostitutes 4. male fertility cult prostitutes
H6948 (singular)	קְדֵשָׁה	Qed·ā·shä'	1. holy, sacred, or consecrated female 2. female temple cult prostitute 3. female shrine prostitute 4. female fertility cult prostitute
H6948 (plural)	קְדֵשׁוֹת	Qed·ā·shōt'	1. holy, sacred, or consecrated females 2. female temple cult prostitutes 3. female shrine prostitutes 4. female fertility cult prostitutes

Table Seven

Like the word *Baal,* the word *Qadashe* {H6945} is not an evil word, but the word *Qadashe* {H6945} represents an evil thing. Actually, in contexts different from that currently considered, the word *Qadashe* {H6945} simply means "sacred, "holy," "consecrated," or "set apart." However, the true Hebrew meaning of "sodomite" in these particular literary contexts (that is, in the indicated five verses in which the word *sodomite/sodomites* are found) refers to males consecrated to idolatrous worship through sacrificial prostitution. *Qadashe* {H6945} has a significantly different meaning from "homosexual person." Basically, what the word means in these five KJV contexts is "a quasi-sacred person — that is, technically, a male devotee by prostitution to licentious idolatry."[32] In this case, the male devotee was *devoted* in idolatrous worship to one of the Canaanite fertility deities — *for example,* Molech, Baal, or Ashtoreth.

Thus, the word *sodomite* is an unfortunate word choice representing *Qadashe* {H6945} in the King James Version of the Bible for two reasons: 1) *sodomite* does not specifically represent someone from Sodom; and 2) the word *sodomite* is erroneously associated with modern-day homosexual people. Actually, by implication and through extension, the word could mean "someone from Sodom" — but only from the standpoint of the licentious idolatry that people in Sodom practiced, and from the standpoint of the "priestly" temple cult prostitutes who served pagan deities found in the Canaanite cities of Sodom and Gomorrah. But that is not what the overwhelming majority of people think when they hear or read the word *sodomite*; they do not understand that the original Hebrew term translated into English as *sodomite* means "male temple cult prostitute" and not "homosexual person."

Many Bible scholars have easy access to what *Qadashe* {H6945} means. Yet, despite its true meaning, we find that in all five citations in the King James Version of the Bible, the translated form is "sodomite" or "sodomites" rather than "male temple cult prostitute" or "male temple cult prostitutes." Some renderings of *Qadashe* {H6945 singular} and *Qadasheem* {H6945 plural} in other translations and paraphrases of the Bible are even worse.

In the Modern Language Version (ML) of the Bible, we find that *Qadashe* {H6945} in Deuteronomy 23:17 is translated as "temple prostitute," which is certainly more accurate than "sodomite," but the plural form for the other four verses is translated only as "male prostitutes." This is unfortunate because the translation "male prostitutes" is just not accurate enough. To be sure, there are male prostitutes that exist in every major city in the world today, but that does not mean that they are idolaters to the extent that they are involved in temple cult prostitution. Though the noun phrase "male prostitutes" is closer to the true meaning than "sodomites," that translation still does not accurately represent the meaning intended by the original Hebrew.

---

32   Strong, James. "Hebrew and Chaldee Dictionary of the Bible" in *Strong's Exhaustive Concordance of the Bible*. World Bible Publishers, 1973, page 135. {The original was published in 1890.}

Although one might expect the Hebrew translation of the Bible to be executed more precisely by the Jewish Publication Society (JPS), the plural word *Qadasheem* is also translated in the Hebrew-English *Tanakh* as "male prostitutes" rather than the more accurate "male temple cult prostitutes." (The Hebrew *Tanakh* is what Christians refer to as the *Old Testament*.)

If we consider *The Holy Bible, New International Version®*, "shrine prostitute" is used in place of "sodomite" and, in the majority of the verses that use the plural form, "male shrine prostitutes" is used in place of "sodomites." Although these renderings are accurate, the preferred translation relative to ideal clarity concerning this particular issue (that is, the issue of temple cult prostitution versus homosexuality) happens to be in the Revised Standard Version (RSV) of the Bible. In the RSV, the majority of the references is given as "male cult prostitutes."

Unfortunately, the New King James Version (NKJV) of the Bible does not do a very good job. It translates *Qadashe* [H6945 singular] and *Qadasheem* [H6945 plural] as "perverted person" and "perverted persons," respectively. So, if readers are already biased (that is, believing homosexual persons to be perverted versions of God's standard), there would be no reason for them to question the accuracy of the New King James Version relative to its particular rendering.

The absolutely worst rendering is in the Living Bible (LB), which is very popular. Many of you may know or recall that the Living Bible is not a word-for-word translation of the Bible but, rather, a paraphrase. It is an attempt to make concepts more understandable by using modern common language. The writers took a fair measure of liberty from the original in order to contemporize the language, intending for readers to be more easily engaged. *For example*, the phrase in 1 Samuel 25:22 that reads in the King James Version as "...pisseth against the wall" is rendered "...went to the bathroom" in the Living Bible. Obviously, the "bathroom" that we know today did not exist back then, but that is the rendering used by the Living Bible paraphrasers because most people today use the expressions "*go* to the bathroom" and "*went* to the bathroom" to represent elimination of waste products (even to describe the activity of their housepets).

Compare Deuteronomy 23:17-18 in the Revised Standard Version with that in the Living Bible:

There shall be no *cult prostitute* of the daughters of Israel, neither shall there be a *cult prostitute* of the sons of Israel. You shall not bring the hire of a harlot, or the wages of a dog, into the house of the Lord your God in payment for any vow; for both of these are an *abomination* (*Toevot* {H8441 plural}) to the Lord your God. {italics and parentheses mine}

Deuteronomy 23:17-18 RS

No prostitutes are permitted in Israel, either men or women; you must not bring the earnings of a prostitute or a homosexual, for both are *detestable* (*Toevot* {H8441 plural}) to the Lord your God. {italics and parentheses mine}

Deuteronomy 23:17-18 LB

The writers of the Living Bible have promoted the error that all male homosexual people are prostitutes. It would be just as inaccurate for us to conclude that all female heterosexual people are prostitutes because we have seen one female heterosexual prostitute on the street. How unfair would that be?

Now, let us compare 1 Kings 14:24 in the Revised Standard Version with that in the Living Bible:

And there were also *male cult prostitutes* in the land. They did according to the *abominations* (*Toevot* {H8441 plural}, or idolatries) of the nations which the Lord drove out before the people of Israel. {italics and parentheses mine}

1 Kings 14:24 RS

There was *homosexuality* throughout the land, and the people of Judah became as *depraved* as the heathen nations which the Lord drove out to make room for His people. {italics mine}

1 Kings 14:24 LB

To be most accurate, 1 Kings 14:24 should be translated:

And there were also male temple cult prostitutes throughout the land. They practiced the idolatries of the nations that the Lord God Almighty had driven out before the people of Israel.

If you are a an average Christian heterosexual person — or average Christian homosexual person, for that matter — and, if you are studying the Holy Bible, there would be no reason for you to scrutinize every single word and, in this case, wonder: "Did the translators, writers, or paraphrasers get this particular translation, word, or paraphrase right?" Or, if you are not doing analytical Bible study, and you come across the rendering in the Living Bible that states, "There was homosexuality throughout the land" (I Kings 14:24 LB), you are not going to pause and say, "*Maybe* this is inaccurate. *Maybe* there really *wasn't* homosexuality in the land." To be sure, the average reader generally gives credence to what he or she is reading, especially when it is in the Holy Bible. The average church-goer believes that the translators of the Holy Bible applied the highest standards in translating their various versions from the original.

This misunderstanding is especially reinforced if you regularly listen to a pastor or televangelist who harps on how immoral and wrong homosexuality is. All of this just ends up further supporting the average reader's idea that the Bible *must* be speaking about *those perverted people* known as homosexual people and that "abominations" must be referring to the sexual acts in which *those people* engage.

When most Christian heterosexual people imagine intimate acts between two homosexual people, they think of the intimacies as the *detestable practices*, *abominations*, or *abhorrences* spoken of in the Holy Bible about temple cult prostitutes. They are unaware that these are imprecise translations of *Toevot* {H8441}, the plural form of *Toevah* {H8441}.

Consider 1 Kings 14:24 (KJV):

And there were also sodomites in the land. They did according to the abominations (*Toevot* {H8441 plural}) of the nations which the Lord cast out before the children of Israel. {parentheses mine}

Translating *Toevot* {H8441 plural} as *abominations*, *detestable practices*, or *abborrences* is just not good enough. *Toevot* {H8441 plural} are not just *abominable practices* but, more specifically, *idolatrous practices*. Thus, 1 Kings 14:24 would be more accurately rendered as:

And there were also male temple cult prostitutes in the land. They did according to the idolatrous customs of the nations that the Lord God Almighty had driven out before the people of Israel.

Imagining intimacies between homosexual people provides no clue to heterosexual people about the companionship and sharing that might exist between two people of the same sex in a committed, monogamous relationship. To be sure, there is a reason why intimate acts are called *intimate*; they are supposed to remain private. It should be disgusting for any of us to imagine sexual acts between any other people because it is prurient (that is, of unhealthy interest) as well as none of our business. In the final analysis, thinking about sexual intimacies between any two people other than yourself and your committed partner should be just as disgusting to you as thinking about sex between your parents.

Perhaps the most damning of all idolatrous practices adopted by the children of Israel relative to male temple cult prostitution is that indicated in 2 Kings 23:7.

Here are four different translations of 2 Kings 23:7:

[King Josiah] tore down the houses of the male prostitutes {"male prostitutes" translated from *Qadasheem*} in the area of the house of the Lord, where the women wove robes for the shame image. {"Shame image" is translated from the Hebrew word *Asherah*, the wooden or stone totem dedicated to pleasing Ashtoreth.} {brackets mine}

2 Kings 23:7 ML

[King Josiah] broke down the houses of the male cult prostitutes which were in the house of the Lord, where the women wove hangings for the Asherah. {brackets mine}

2 Kings 23:7 RS

{King Josiah} tore down the ritual booths of the perverted persons that were in the house of the Lord, where the women wove hangings for the wooden image. {brackets mine}

2 Kings 23:7 NKJV

{King Josiah} also tore down the houses of male prostitution around the Temple {i.e., the Jerusalem Temple}, where the women wove robes for the Asherah-idol. {brackets mine}

2 Kings 23:7 LB

It is especially clear in the Revised Standard Version that the Asherah-idol was "in the house of the Lord" (that is, in the Jerusalem Temple built for *Yahweh* by King Solomon). The idolatrous image was indeed *detestable* because it was a pole, stone, or totem carved in the shape of a giant phallus, or penis. It was dedicated to the goddess Ashtoreth (that is why it was called an "Asherah"). It was this image for which the women wove "hangings" or "robes" — which may have been pulled down to represent the foreskin being pulled back during a penile erection. In the minds of fertility cult worshipers, the giant phallus was erected to please the sexual desires of their goddess, Ashtoreth.

Though you may think it absolutely unbelievable that the form of the penis was worshiped, all you have to do is wander past the display cases in most museums that house antiquities. Once there, take a look at the artifacts that have survived from both ancient Greek and Roman societies as well as from many earlier cultures and civilizations. In a majority of these pagan societies, the penis was idolized.

Today, the penis is still idolized and worshiped in many cultures around the world. *For example*, all you need to do is type in the words "Hounen Penis Fertility Festival" into your internet search engine and you will easily find pictures of people worshiping the penis today — even engraving their prayers on the sides of plastic and ceramic penises (i.e., *penes*).

I was fortunate to have lived in Chicago at the time that the Pompeii Exhibit was brought to that city's Art Institute. As I looked at the artifacts from Pompeii, it was absolutely amazing to me that a major focus was on external genitals, specifically the phallus. Truly, the ancient Roman Empire was a decadent, depraved, and immoral society.

Decadent, depraved, and immoral thoughts regularly crept into the consciousness of the children of Israel and encroached on their relationship with the Lord God Almighty — even going so far as to introduce phallus worship (vis-à-vis the worship of the Asherah pole) at the Holy Temple of the Lord God Almighty in Jerusalem. Yes, such practices should always be considered "detestable," "disgusting," "abominable," and "abhorrent."

In summary, the pagan deities that were worshiped — including Molech, Baal, and Ashtoreth — had a significant impact, not only on the Canaanite people, but also on the children of Israel. Though reforms were introduced at various times, they did not seem to do a lot of good relative to keeping the children of Israel from regularly abandoning their worship of Yahweh. However, it should be noted that, after their exile from Israel due to their Babylonian captivity, the remnant of Jews who returned to the Promised Land never again returned to idolatry *en masse*. The *Book of Maccabees* relates how some Jews even preferred martyrdom rather than eating ceremonially unclean food (that is, food from animals sacrificed to idols).

Lest you think that food sacrificed to idols is just an activity from the ancient past, when I was in Salvador, Brazil conducting my seminar and workshop entitled *Christianity and Homosexuality Reconciled*, I found a plethora of vendors on street corners and throughout the streets who belonged to the *Candomblé* religion, selling meat that had been sacrificed to pagan gods and goddesses. Similar practices happen today in many other countries of the world.

Concerning the Jews after their Babylonian captivity, it is their renewed commitment to Yahweh and resolve to eschew idolatry that helps us to understand: 1) the psychological profile of first century Jews as well as 2) the historical context for the Apostle Paul's horror and anger concerning sexual idolatry in the worship of fertility gods and goddesses. Indeed, the Apostle Paul was aware of these practices during his own lifetime and reacted contemptuously to them in various epistles.

Dogs are Male Cult Prostitutes and not Homosexual People

In 1990, David H. Stern, who is a Messianic Jew, translated the New Testament from its original Greek in an attempt to bring out its *Jewishness* linguistically, culturally, religiously, and theologically. For the most part, he did an excellent job in producing a work that is extremely valuable for students of the New Testament who need to better recognize its Jewish roots. I write, "for the most part," because of his mistranslation of the word "dogs" from the following verse:

> For outside are *dogs*, and sorcerers, and whoremongers, and murderers, and idolaters, and whoever loves and tells a lie. [For God, "telling lies" is devising a system of worship for anything other than the Lord God Almighty.] [italics and brackets mine]

> Revelation 22:15 KJV Paraphrase

Literally, the original Greek word *kunes* [G2968] in Revelation 22:15 means "hounds" or "dogs" (see Table Eight). Figuratively, this Greek word means: 1) unclean, or ungodly, people; 2) pagans or barbarians; 3) the categories of people who practiced the unclean activities listed in the verse; or 4) male temple cult prostitutes. However, Stern renders the word as follows in the *Jewish New Testament* (JNT):

> Outside are the *homosexuals*, those who misuse drugs in connection with the occult, the sexually immoral, murderers, idol worshipers, and everyone who loves and practices falsehood. [italics mine]

> Revelation 22:15 JNT

To be sure, there is a basis in the Old Testament for connecting "dogs" to sexual acts involving male temple cult prostitutes but not to homosexual people. This connection is established in Deuteronomy 23:17-18:

There shall be no cult prostitute (*Qedasha* {H6948 singular}) of the daughters of Israel, neither shall there be a cult prostitute (*Qadashe* {H6945 singular}) of the sons of Israel. You shall not bring the hire of a harlot {Zonah} or the wages of a dog (*Kehlev* {H 3611}) into the house of the Lord your God in payment for any vow; for both of these {idolatrous practices} are an abomination (*Toevot* {H8441 plural}) unto the Lord your God. {parentheses and brackets mine}

Deuteronomy 23:17-18 RS

Strong's Number	Hebrew or Greek Word	Transliteration in Syllables	Word Meaning(s)
H3611 (singular)	כֶּלֶב	keh'·lev	1. dog or hound 2. ceremonially, or ritually, unclean person 3. Gentile, pagan, or barbarous person 4. male temple cult prostitute
G2965 (plural)	κύνες	kü'·nes	1. dogs or hounds 2. ceremonially, or ritually, unclean people 3. Gentile, pagan, or barbarous people 4. male temple cult prostitutes

Table Eight

Clearly, the use of *dogs* in the two previously-quoted verses are referring to male temple cult prostitution and not homosexuality. The interchangeability of male temple cult prostitutes and "dogs" has been noted by David F. Greenberg in his book, *The Construction of Homosexuality*:

The words *zonah* and *qadeshah* were sometimes used interchangeably, as in the story of Judah and Tamar {Genesis 38:15

and 24]. The parallel construction in Deuteronomy {23:17-18} identifies *qadesh* {i.e., *qadashe*} and *kelev* as a male counterpart.[33]

Further, Greenberg states:

A Phoenician inscription on Cyprus dating from the fourth century B.C., referring to a category of temple personnel who played a role in the sacred service of Astarte {Ashtoreth in the Old Testament}, identifies the *kelev* {"dog"} as a religious functionary.[34]

Revelation 22:15 *in toto* describes pseudo-sacred cultic behaviors and delineates who is excluded from the heavenly city known as New Jerusalem. That "dogs" are excluded from this holy city is not referring to either canines or homosexual people but to male temple cult prostitutes and all who prostitute themselves by serving false gods. Remember, God hates idolatry, and idolatry is the practice of falsehood.

Interestingly, when Christ Jesus spoke of "dogs" (Matthew 15:26), he was referring to the Gentiles of his day, most of whom were idolaters and pagans. He was not referring to homosexual people.

It is important to note that Stern's inaccurate translation of the Greek word for *dogs* as "homosexuals" illustrates that cultural and personal biases play an important role even when well-intentioned and intelligent people translate Scripture from its original languages. It is difficult for all of us to erase the "recorded tapes" that are playing in our minds because of what we have been taught to think by highly-respected role models (*for example*, parents, teachers, professors, pastors, and rabbis — all people to be respected but who have gotten the issue of homosexuality wrong and have taught us incorrectly concerning it). Many, most, or all of them (depending on your life experiences) have incorrectly taught us that homosexual people are outside of the Kingdom of God. Of course, we must forgive them for this false teaching, but we also must disbelieve its lie.

---

33 Greenberg, David F. *The Construction of Homosexuality*. University of Chicago Press, Chicago, 1988, page 965. {brackets mine}

34 *Ibid.*, page 965. {first set of brackets mine}

Additional Biblical References to Sodom

In order to make our study of the Biblical use of the word *Sodom* more complete, let us now turn to the four additional times that the city of Sodom is referred to in the Old Testament.

In Isaiah 1:10-11, Israel's degenerate condition is figuratively compared to Sodom and Gomorrah:

Hear the word of the Lord, you rulers of Sodom; give ear to the law of our God, you people of Gomorrah. "To what purpose is the multitude of your sacrifices to me?" says the Lord: "I am full of the burnt offerings of rams, and the fat of fed beasts; and I do not delight in the blood of bullocks, or of lambs, or of rams."

Isaiah 1:10-11 KJV Paraphrase

In Isaiah 3:8-9, the sinful conditions of both Judah and Jerusalem are compared to the sinful condition of Sodom by the Lord God Almighty:

For Jerusalem is ruined, and Judah is fallen because their words and actions are against the Lord and provoke His wrath. Their very appearance bears witness against them, and they declare their sin as Sodom because they do not even try to hide it. Woe to their souls for they have brought evil on themselves.

Isaiah 3:8-9 KJV Paraphrase

Jeremiah 23:13-14 specifically refers to how the children of Israel were lead astray by followers of Baal. Keep in mind as you read the word *adultery* in the following passage that it is referring to idolatrous worship practices; and also keep in mind as you read the word *Baal* that it is referring to a fertility god and the idolatrous practices associated with worshiping that god:

And I have seen folly in the prophets of Samaria; they prophesied in the name of Baal, and caused my people Israel to err. I have seen also in the prophets of Jerusalem a horrible thing: they commit adultery, and walk in lies: they strengthen the hands of evildoers so that no one repents of his wickedness: all of them are like Sodom to me, and their inhabitants are like Gomorrah.

Jeremiah 23:13-14 KJV Paraphrase

In Ezekiel 16:47-50, the Lord specifically identifies the sin of Sodom and her "daughters." (Here, the word *daughters* refers to adjacent urban areas that originated from the city of Sodom.) The phrase "practiced their abominations" in the passage should not trigger "homosexual acts" within your mind unless your mind is playing recordings from old mental tapes. In other words, if you go to the Holy Bible with the preconceived notion that God is referring to homosexual people as inhabitants of the city of Sodom, then you will naturally interpret "practiced their abomination" to be homosexual acts. However, the abominations were the pagan orgies and ritualistic "consecrated" sexual acts that occurred within the temples erected to honor Baal, Ashtoreth, and Molech — which detestable things included anal intercourse with both male and female temple prostitutes as well as with animals. (Yes, bestiality occurred within the pagan temples and their adjacent houses of cult prostitution, too.)

{47} You not only followed their ways, you practiced their abominations (*Toevot* {H8441 plural}, or "idolatrous practices"); however, as if that were not enough, you became more corrupted than they in all of your ways. {48} As I live, says the Lord God, your sister Sodom and her daughters have not done as you and your daughters have done. {49} Behold, this was the iniquity of your sister Sodom: pride, gluttony, and abundance of idleness was in her and in her daughters. Neither did she strengthen the hand of the poor and needy. {50} And they were haughty, and committed abomination before me {"committed abomination" is translated from the Hebrew that they "committed *Toevah* {H8441 singular}, or "practiced idolatry"). Therefore I did away with them.

Ezekiel 16:47-50 KJV Paraphrase

93

Naturally, we have a tendency to interpret things from a modern-day standpoint. I write *naturally* because that is our referent. Because we do not see such pagan activities, and because we do not have temples built to honor fertility gods and goddesses or any of the other deities mentioned in the Old and New Testaments, we do not comprehend that sexual acts occurred in the context of worship. Most people today cannot even imagine such practices. They do not really have a good sense of what it meant, or means, to worship fertility gods and goddesses, or what so-called religious practices constituted pagan worship.

As stated previously, God is against idolatry. The first of the Ten Commandments condemns it. In the eyes of the Lord, idolatry *is* spiritual adultery. Another way to put it is that, if someone is an idolater, he or she is worshiping for God what is *not* God. We understand today that idolatry goes well beyond worshiping graven images, poles, stones, totems, and icons. We also understand that idolatry can include the worship of possessions or the practice of materialism and other such vain philosophies that are, generally speaking, not identified with particular figurines, statues, or icons.

Yes, God hates idolatry. Idolatry was, is, and always will be "abominable," "abhorrent," and "detestable" (*Toevah* {H8441 singular}) to Him. Idolatrous practices will always be *Toevot* {H8441 plural} to Him:

{1} And God spoke all these words, saying, {2} "I am the Lord your God, who has brought you out of the land of Egypt and out of the house of bondage. {3} You must not have any gods before Me. {4} You must not make for yourselves any graven image, or any likeness of anything that is in heaven above, that is on the earth beneath, or that is in the water under the earth: {5} You must not bow down to them, nor serve them: for I the Lord your God am a jealous God, visiting the iniquity of the fathers upon the children to the third and fourth generations after those who hate Me."

Exodus 20:1-5 KJV Paraphrase

Idolatry — taken together with the detestable things that people did, and still do, in different parts of the world today (that is, integrating sexual activities into the worship of false gods and goddesses) — is what God hates. Idolaters are identified in Exodus 20:5 as "those who hate" the Creator-God.

As one studies the entirety of Scripture, it becomes increasingly clear that Bible verses commonly used to condemn homosexual people are not speaking about them but about temple cult prostitutes, or what is known in Hebrew as *Qadasheem* {H6945 plural}. The Bible is not speaking about homosexuality but *Toevah* {H8441 singular} or, in other words, idolatry. *Qadasheem* {H6945 plural} are not homosexual people but temple cult prostitutes. And *Toevah* {H8441 singular} is not just something disgusting but something disgustingly idolatrous.

If Martin Luther understood that *Qadasheem* {H6945 plural} should be translated into German as "die Tempelhurer" (that is, "the male temple whores"), then why has that meaning been lost to contemporary society? Why is *Qadasheem* now translated as "homosexuals?" Please explain why this is to homosexual men, women, and young people who have been: 1) persecuted by bullies, 2) despised by those who fear what is different, 3) condemned by society, 4) rejected by family members, 5) excommunicated from churches, and 6) even murdered by xenophobes because of their sexual orientation.

In the next Chapter, I will spend considerably more time in discussion of fertility cults (*Toevot* {H8441 plural}) and temple cult prostitutes (*Qadasheem* {H6945 plural}).

Interestingly, when we come to passages in the New Testament in which Christ Jesus refers to Sodom, we find that he refers to the city of Sodom in the context of hospitality to the gospel (that is, receptivity to the good news of salvation through Christ Jesus). This is especially interesting because we find that there was also an issue of hospitality in the original story of Sodom, too. The Messiah told his itinerant disciples that, if the cities they would visit were inhospitable to the message of salvation, then it would be more bearable for Sodom on Judgment Day. In other words, God's wrath will visit the cities that have rejected His gospel to an even greater extent than the wrath He visited on Sodom.

Christ Jesus said:

To be sure, I say to you that it will be more tolerable for the land of Sodom and Gomorrah in the day of judgment than for the city that rejects the gospel.

Matthew 10:15 KJV Paraphrase

And you, city of Capernaum, which is exalted unto heaven, will be brought down to hell: for if the mighty works that have been done in you had been done in Sodom, that city would have remained until this very day. But I say to you that it will be more tolerable for the land of Sodom in the day of judgment than for you.

Matthew 11:23-24 KJV Paraphrase

As part of the Great Commission, Christ Jesus tells his followers to "go," "preach," "make disciples," "teach," and "baptize in his name" (Matthew 28:19-20). However, Christ Jesus also tells us what to do when we have done our part and the hearers reject the truth:

And whoever will not receive you nor hear you, when you depart from there, shake off the dust under your feet for a testimony against them. Indeed, I say to you, It will be more tolerable for Sodom and Gomorrah on the day of judgment than for that city.

Mark 6:11 KJV Paraphrase

Those of us who carry a message that God has asked us to deliver should not take it personally if we are rejected. Rather, we should remember what the Lord said to Samuel: "'They have not rejected you, but they have rejected me'" (1 Samuel 8:7 KJV Paraphrase).

The Lord Jesus, when referring to Sodom, did so relative to the hospitality of cities concerning the preached Gospel, or "evangel." So, basically, our Lord was saying to those who preach salvation through the *only-begotten* Son of God that, if the inhabitants of a city are inhospitable to the gospel message, then leave the city, and it will be far worse for its inhabitants than it was for the inhabitants of Sodom when that city was destroyed. In other words, when the two types of inhospitality are compared, it will be worse to be judged inhospitable to the evangel rather than being judged inhospitable to an angel (referring to the two angels who visited the city of Sodom).

By the way, Christ Jesus nowhere in the Bible addresses the issue of homosexuality. Not once. He was as silent about homosexuality as he was about electricity. Indeed, our Lord Jesus was, and is, aware of everything because he is omniscient. He was certainly aware that electricity (as we know it today) would develop, but he made no mention of it. And, without a doubt, he was aware that there would be homosexuality as we know it today, but he made no direct comment about it. (We will see in Chapter Five of this book how he may have made an indirect comment about homosexual people when he referred to *eunuchs*.)

Sodomites in the New Testament

In the King James Version of the Bible, the word *sodomite* is not used in the New Testament. In the New King James Version (NKJV), however, it is used to translate the Greek word *arsenokoitai* (ἀρσενοκοῖται {G733}) regarding those who will *not* inherit the Kingdom of God:

> Do you not know that the unrighteous will not inherit the kingdom of God? Do not be deceived. Neither fornicators, nor idolaters, nor adulterers, nor *homosexuals*, nor *sodomites*, nor thieves, nor covetous, nor drunkards, nor revilers, nor extortioners will inherit the kingdom of God. [italics mine]
>
> 1 Corinthians 6:9-10 NKJV

Upon first glance, it would appear that there is some redundancy in the previously-quoted passage (specifically in the list that contains both "homosexuals" and "sodomites"). The use of these two words together is somewhat puzzling, especially when homosexual people and sodomites are supposed to be one and the same. Actually, there is no redundancy in the Greek, just inconsistency and inaccuracy in the English translations of the two words *malakoi* (translated in the NKJV as "homosexuals") and *arsenokoitai* (translated in the NKJV as "sodomites").

Relevant to the issue of Christianity and homosexuality, the two important Greek words *malakoi* and *arsenokoitai* in 1 Corinthians 6:9 are often inaccurately rendered by Bible translators who really do not know exactly what to do with these two words. This inability to accurately translate them is underscored by the variety of ways in which each word has been rendered (or avoided) in various translations, versions, and paraphrases of the Holy Bible.

Malakoi

For example, in *The Holy Bible, New International Version®*, the Greek word *malakoi* (μαλακοὶ {G3432}) is interpreted as "male prostitutes." In the Modern Language Version, both *malakoi* and *arsenokoitai* are rendered together as "partakers in homosexuality." The Revised Standard Version translates *malakoi* as "sexual perverts;" and the Living Bible combines both *malakoi* and *arsenokoitai* in the appellation "homosexuals" (as reported earlier in this chapter).

In the King James Version of the Bible, *malakoi* is translated as "effeminate." As we relate "effeminate" to modern English, it is very easy for many people (especially those who think that the average profile for homosexual males includes so-called feminine tendencies, mannerisms, and characteristics) to assume that the word is referring to gay males. To be sure, this is stereotypic and not representative of all male homosexual people (and certainly not the majority of male homosexual people with whom I have been acquainted over the past fifty years).

Please do not misinterpret here that I think something is wrong with a male being nurturing, dramatic, or even flamboyant. Please do not misinterpret here that I think something is wrong with a male being effusive and/or passionate in displaying emotion. It is perfectly alright for each one of us to exhibit the personalities that God has given to us and that have been shaped by nurture as well as nature.

The word *malakoi* — as we relate it to various modern English word forms — has a portion in common with the root of the English word *malleable*, which refers to something "soft" or "pliable." Consequently, some translators prefer to render the word *malakoi* as "soft ones" (which, in fact, is its truest literal meaning in classical Greek). However, because the literal meaning of *malakoi* does not fit exactly within the literary context of 1 Corinthians 6:9, the word *malakoi* most likely had another connotation in the colloquial speech of the Apostle Paul's day. This is especially likely because the Apostle Paul wrote his epistles in *Koine,* or common, Greek (i.e., street vernacular) rather than classical Greek.

There are those who would argue that *malakoi*, by extension, might be referring to "lazy people," "indolent ones," or "the pampered rich" — which message would not be so far afield from this statement by Christ Jesus:

> Then Jesus said to his disciples, "Indeed, I say to you that a rich person shall enter into the kingdom of heaven with great difficulty." Moreover, I say to you, "It is easier for a camel to go through the eye of a needle than for a rich person to enter the kingdom of God."
>
> Matthew 19:23-24 KJV Paraphrase

However, *malakoi* referring to the pampered rich in 1 Corinthians 6:9 is really quite a stretch. Because the word is sandwiched between sexual sins in 1 Corinthians 6:9, *malakoi* is probably referring to moral weakness or a particular type of immorality.

In *The Zondervan Parallel New Testament in Greek and English*, the word *malakoi* has been translated as "voluptuous persons."[35] Who are *voluptuous persons*? Voluptuous persons are those who have a "come hither" look — which is to say, those who are trying to sell their sexual "wares," or sexual favors, in the most provocative of ways.

---

35 *The Zondervan Parallel New Testament in Greek and English*. Zondervan Bible Publishers, Grand Rapids, 1975, page 495.

Some scholars might prefer to translate *malakoi* as "abusers of themselves as women" (that is, persons deceptively presenting themselves as women because they dress in the soft clothing of women — although they are *not* women), which is most revealing. To be sure, such a perspective is in agreement with that of Robin Scroggs,[36] who argues that, by the time of the Apostle Paul, the word *malakoi* had assumed a pejorative slang meaning in reference to young *call boys* (i.e., *catamites*) who actively sought sexual encounters with men for money — something considered quite distasteful in the majority of both Greek and Roman societies. Robin Scroggs' interpretation is in agreement with the *Catholic Study Bible*, which explains *malakoi* as catamite "boy prostitutes"[37] who dressed in feminine attire to attract their male customers (i.e., the *sodomites*).

The most substantive clue for the meaning of *malakoi* can be found in Saint Jerome's Latin Vulgate version of the Bible, which was published in 405 AD. In order to translate the Hebrew Old Testament and Greek New Testament into Latin, Saint Jerome (c. 345 - 420 AD) had to be a scholar of Hebrew, Aramaic, Greek, and Latin. What he tried to do was translate the Old Testament Hebrew and Aramaic and the New Testament Greek into an overall Latin version of the Bible that could be used within the developing Roman Catholic Church. Interestingly, Saint Jerome chose to translate *Qadasheem* {H6945 plural} in the Old Testament using the Latin word *effeminati*. Saint Jerome understood that the *effeminati* (which is the plural form of the Latin word *effeminatus*) were not people who were just "effeminate" (that is, "sissified" or "mollified"), but people who donned female clothing in order to serve as the male transvestite temple cult prostitutes who were an integral part of temple cult prostitution in many Canaanite religions as well as many Greek and Roman religions (some of the latter having been derived from the former). In place of the Greek word *malakoi*, Saint Jerome used a Latin synonym of *effeminati* (singular *effeminatus*) — which is to say, St. Jerome used the Latin word *molles* (singular *mollis*). Thus, like the "effeminati,"

36 Scroggs, Robin. *The New Testament and Homosexuality*. Augsburg Fortress Publications, 1994.

37 *The Catholic Study Bible* (Second Edition). Oxford University Press, New York, 2006, page 1523.

the "molles" (in Latin) or "malakoi" (in Greek) are also transvestite male temple cult prostitutes. This helps to explain the King James Version scholars' choice of "effeminate" in 1611. To be sure, *malakoi* and *molles* are from the same base, or root, word and, thus, have the same etymology (i.e., word origin).

Interestingly, the scholars who translated the 1611 version of the King James Version of the New Testament often adopted the same Latin-based terminology found in the 1582 Catholic New Testament translation known to Roman Catholics as the Douay-Rheims Bible (see Table Nine). Although the King James scholars were expressly forbidden from drawing words from the Douay-Rheims Bible, it is clear that they did so in preference over slightly less erudite Bible translations such as the Tyndale Bible, the Coverdale Bible, or the Geneva Bible (see Table Ten). The Douay-Rheims Bible is a direct translation of the Latin Vulgate version of the Bible completed by St. Jerome in 405 A.D.

Tracing the Historical Basis for the Incorrect Usage of *effeminate* in Two of the Earliest English Translations of 1 Corinthians		
Latin Vulgate (405 AD) Verse 6:10	**Douay-Rheims (1582 AD) Verse 6:10**	**King James (1611 AD) Verse 6:9**
molles **Molles** is a Latin synonym for the Latin word *effeminati*. *Effeminati was* used by St. Jerome as a translation of *Qadasheem* [H6945 plural] in 1 King 14:24.	*effeminate* **The English word** *effeminate* is used in the Douay-Rheims Bible as a translation of both *Qadasheem* [H6945 plural] in 1 King 14:24 and *malakoi* in 1 Corinthians 6:10.	*effeminate* **The English word** *effeminate* was taken from the Douay-Rheims Bible and used by the King James' scholars as a translation of the Greek word *malakoi* in 1 Corinthians 6:9.

Table Nine

Translations of "malakoi" in 1 Corinthians 6:9			
Tyndale (1524 AD)	Coverdale (1535 AD)	Luther (1545 AD)	Geneva (1560 AD)
"weaklinges"	"weaklinges"	"die Weichlinge"	"wantons"

Table Ten

In summary, the King James Version's use of the word "effeminate" is not from the Germanic-based words used in the Tyndale Bible (published in 1524 AD) or the Coverdale Bible (published in 1535 AD). Both of these versions translate *malakoi* into the Germanic-based Early Modern English word *weaklinges*. "Weaklinges" is in keeping with Martin Luther's German translation of *malakoi* as "die Weichlinge" (that is, "the weaklings," or so-called *sissies*). Instead, the King James Version takes the Latin-based word *effeminate* from the Douay-Rheims Bible, published in 1582 AD. The Douay-Rheims scholars used the Latin word *effeminate*, which is derived from the Latin word *effeminati*, a synonym for the Latin word *molles* that St. Jerome used. Again, St. Jerome used the Latin word *effeminati* to translate the Hebrew *Qadasheem* {H6945 plural}, or male temple cult prostitutes, into Latin.

All things taken together, the most accurate rendering of *malakoi* is "young male transvestite temple cult prostitutes."

David Greenberg states:

More plausibly, the term in this context {meaning, in 1 Corinthians 6:9} referred to... cult prostitutes. Corinth and Ephesus, where Timothy was stationed, were strongholds of the Mother Goddess {cults} and had long-established religious prostitution.[38]

Many fertility Mother-Goddess cults existed in ancient Greek and Roman societies. Those attended by transvestite and/or castrated male

38 Greenberg, *op cit.*, page 213. {brackets mine}

priests and boy prostitutes who engaged in same-sex ritualistic practices included cults devoted to Cybele, Aphrodite, Hecate, Artemis, Magna Mater, Ma, Anaitis, and Astarte.[39] (Remember, "Astarte" is essentially the same goddess known as "Ashtoreth," "Ashtar," and "Ishtar" during Old Testament times.) Indeed, these perverted "shriners" were common during the Apostle Paul's lifetime. In *The Life of Constantine*, the Church historian Eusebius Pamphili, who lived *circa* 260 - 360 AD, and who was Bishop of Caesarea, indicates that the effeminate priests {that is, the "effeminati"} of the goddess Cybele still engaged in temple cult prostitution during his own lifetime (thus, as late as the fourth century A.D.).

Arsenokoitai

Although *malakoi* is only used once in the New Testament, *arsenokoitai* is used twice. In addition to its use in 1 Corinthians 6:9, it is also used in 1 Timothy 1:10, where it, too, is translated as "sodomites" in the New King James Version of the Bible:

> ...the law {including "Levitical Law"} is not made for a righteous person, but for the lawless and insubordinate, for the ungodly and for sinners, for the unholy and profane, for murderers of fathers and murderers of mothers, for manslayers, for fornicators, for *sodomites*, for kidnappers, for liars, for perjurers, and if there is any other thing that is contrary to sound doctrine. {brackets and italics mine}

> 1 Timothy 1:9-10 NKJV

Because *arsenokoitai* is not a classical Greek word, it has no clearly translatable modern-day meaning. Either the Apostle Paul coined the word himself or it had already been coined by the society of his day. Simply stated, there is no extant literature that contains this specific word before its recorded use[40] by the Apostle Paul.

---

39   Greenberg, *op cit.*, page 98.

40   Boswell, John. *Christianity, Social Tolerance, and Homosexuality*. The University of Chicago Press, Chicago, 1980, page 345.

Koine Greek was the language of the streets, or conventional vernacular, that the Apostle Paul used for writing and dictating his now-famous letters to the Christian peoples of his day. Rather than use the language of the more literate elements of ancient society, *Koine* Greek is the language that the Apostle Paul used to try to reach the common person. Unfortunately, little has survived that provides a clear understanding of the word *arsenokoitai* as it was used then. Indeed, the exact meaning of this word is unknown today. This helps to account for the wide range of interpretations and translations provided by various Bible scholars.

Arsenokoitai can be divided into two portions: 1) The base, or root, *koitai* — which refers either to sexual intercourse (the Latin past participle *coitus* is derived from this Greek word) or to active sexual partners who provide sexual service. And 2) the prefix *arseno-*, which simply means "male." It is unclear if the *arseno-* prefix is used here in a qualifying or objective sense — which is to say, that it is in question if those providing the sexual service were themselves male or if they were servicing males. This uncertainty is especially germane because, in ancient societies that predate Greece and Rome, male temple cult prostitutes existed who sexually serviced both male and female temple-worshipers participating in pagan rituals. It is also important to note that they serviced both male and female worshipers *anally*. In contrast, during Greek and Roman times, it was the male worshipers who actively engaged in anal sex with both female and male temple cult prostitutes. In summary, anal sex was characteristic of both male and female temple cult prostitutes who were recipients and of male temple cult prostitutes who serviced both male and female clients, customers, or worshipers.

Relative to the word *arsenokoitai*, John Boswell states:

In no [Greek] words coined and generally written with the form "arseno-" is the prefix demonstrably objective… [brackets mine]

"Arsenokoitai," then, means male sexual agents, i.e., active male prostitutes, who were common throughout the Hellenistic world in the time of Paul. That such a designation existed in the Latin of the time is well known: [these were] male prostitutes capable of the active role with either men or women. [brackets mine]

"Arsenokoitai" was the most explicit word available to Paul for a male prostitute.[41]

Some Bible scholars have argued that the Apostle Paul or the Hellenistic Jewish society of his day coined the word *arsenokoitai* from the Septuagint Greek translation of Leviticus 18:22 and 20:13 — where the uncompounded Greek phrase αρσενος ... κοιτην (*arsenos ... koitun*) is used to translate the original Hebrew of "lying with a male." This view helps show Paul's intended meaning because the historical and literary contexts for Leviticus 18:22 and 20:13 are idolatrous and prostitutional in nature. This interpretation is supported by cross-referencing Leviticus 18:22 with 1 Kings 14:24. (I will address this cross-referencing issue in greater detail in Chapter Five.)

To translate *arsenokoitai* into Latin, St. Jerome used *"masculorum concubitores."* "Concubitor" denotes an active sexual partner just as "concubine" denotes its female passive counterpart. In the case of "concubitor" or "concubine," the implication is a sexual partner who has been bought and paid for, either on a one-time basis or for an extended period of time. Thus, St. Jerome's Latin rendering could be translated as "the male *prostitutor* of men (i.e., a male who solicits and accepts payment for sex from other males)." This is certainly in keeping with the types of male-male sex with which the Apostle Paul was familiar.

To be sure, the Apostle Paul was not exposed to homosexual people who pursued committed monogamous relationships. And he was not writing about Christian homosexual people. He simply did not know any. Indeed, the Apostle Paul did not write about what he did not know.

In the final analysis, the *arsenokoitai* are either 1) the male temple cult prostitutes who provided sexual service to both male and female temple-worshipers participating in pagan fertility rituals, or 2) the male purchasers of sexual service from other males. In either case, *arsenokoitai* does not represent Christian people who happen to be homosexual.

The four types of male-male sexual practices that were common in ancient Greece and Rome are summarized as follows:

---

41 *Ibid.*, page 344.

1. Sex between elite and powerful citizens and *statutory minors*. (Statutory minors are those who did not have full legal rights, including slaves and youth.)

2. Ambisexual encounters where participants were ambivalent about, or indifferent to, the gender identity or genital identity of their individual sex partners. (Such indifference was especially common during orgiastic sex.)

3. Male prostitution in male brothels. (Male brothels were especially numerous in seaport cities like Rome and Corinth.)

4. Male temple cult prostitution in pagan temples or in quarters adjacent to them. (Pagan temples were common and numerous in every Greek and Roman city.)

During his own lifetime, the Apostle Paul was exposed to all four of the previously-mentioned types of male-male sexual practices. Here, again, it is important for the reader to remember that there is a distinction between "same-sex practices" and "the homosexual orientation." Romantic involvement between people of a homosexual orientation are different from same-sex sexual activities that occur between people of an unresolved sexual orientation. I write "unresolved" not to describe their internal emotional conflict or the uncertainty of how they viewed themselves but, rather, to describe that it is indeterminate whether the same-sex practices in the Bible — often used to condemn homosexual people — are really between obligate homosexual people (that is, people who have no choice in their attraction) or between heterosexual people simply involved in ambisexual activity.

The word *ambisexual* here refers to a "complete indifference to the gender identity or genital identity of a sexual partner." *For example*, Julius Caesar was described by the Roman historian Cato as "every woman's husband" as well as "every man's wife." Julius Caesar was completely indifferent concerning with whom he had sexual intercourse. That Julius Caesar had sex with everyone and anyone best represents the ambisexual mindset common during the Apostle Paul's day. Certainly, the plural sex, group sex, or orgiastic sex that took place in Roman bath houses, at lavish Roman feasts and festivals, and in pagan Roman temples involved ambisexual sex. Ambisexuality represents the primary type of sexual relations with which the Apostle Paul was acquainted when males had sex with other males.

The Apostle Paul did not know any monogamous homosexual partners. The Apostle Paul did not know any Christian homosexual people. The Apostle Paul did not write about people whom he did not know or about that to which he was not exposed.

Another type of male-male sexual relations with which the Apostle Paul was acquainted occurred between elite and powerful Roman citizens and statutory minors. In this usage, "statutory minors" were those who did not possess full legal rights as Roman citizens and included slaves and youth.

The Roman society of the Apostle Paul's time was a slave-based society. *For example*, the city of Corinth had 400,000 inhabitants, 150,000 of whom were free-born citizens and 250,000 of whom were slaves. Some of the slaves held by Roman citizens were sex slaves. Sex slaves included both young females as well as young males. The Latin word *concubini*, which is the plural form of *concubinus*, was used during the Apostle Paul's lifetime to refer to "slave boys acting as bedroom partners."[42]

Youth involved in male-male sexual relations also included the transvestite *call boys*, or catamites, that were referred to by the Greek word *malakoi* in 1 Corinthians 6:9, also known in Latin as *effeminati* or *molles* and referred to as such by St. Jerome in his Latin translation of the Holy Bible. *The Catholic Study Bible* clearly and accurately translates the Greek word *malakoi* in 1 Corinthians 6:9 as "call boys" and uses these transvestite "catamites" in its footnote to help explain not only the male-male sex reference in 1 Corinthians 6:9 but also the male-male sex reference in Romans, Chapter One, as well.[43]

The Apostle Paul did not know any monogamous homosexual partners. The Apostle Paul did not know any Christian homosexual people. The Apostle Paul did not write about people whom he did not know or about that to which he was not exposed.

The Apostle Paul was also acquainted with sex between male prostitutes and the procurers of their sexual services, especially in

---

42   From *The Arapanacana Press*. In 2010: www.arapacana.com/glossary/co.html

43   *The Catholic Study Bible* (Second Edition). Oxford University Press, New York, 2006, page 1523.

seaport cities like Corinth and Rome. The Apostle Paul wrote epistles to Christian residents of both Corinth and Rome and included in them references to male temple cult prostitution and male brothel prostitution. Male prostitution was so common in the city of Corinth and the city of Rome that male prostitutes were taxed. In fact, April 24th was the legal holiday for male prostitutes in ancient Rome.

The Greek word *arsenokoitai,* used by the Apostle Paul in 1 Corinthians 6:9, is a coined Greek word that St. Jerome translated into Latin as "masculorum concubitores," which literally means "the purchased male sex slaves of men."[44] Although the Latin word *concubitor* "may be used to denote a male lover," more often than not it "connotes an *exoletus,* or an active male prostitute who sexually services both females and males anally."[45] The Apostle Paul was not referring to homosexual people joined in holy union but to people who were involved in prostitutional sexual activity and/or slave-based sexual activity. *The Catholic Study Bible* is partly correct in referring to the *arsenokoitai* in its footnote to 1 Corinthians 6:9 as the procurers of the sexual services of transvestite *call boys,* or catamites (and denoted by the Greek word *malakoi*). I wrote "partly correct" because the *arsenokoitai* included, not only the procurers of the sexual services provided by *call boys* (or catamites), but also male prostitutes who serviced both men and women anally. It is important to note that the role of altar boys in the early Roman Catholic Church representing a stable of *call boys* has been unwittingly perpetuated in modern-day pedophilia by some Roman Catholic priests.

It is also important to note that the type of male-male sexual relations with which the Apostle Paul was acquainted occurred between both transvestite and non-transvestite male temple cult prostitutes who dedicated male-male anal intercourse to the fertility gods and goddesses they served. *For example,* fertility mother goddess cults were attended by castrated and/or transvestite priests who engaged in same-sex practices. These so-called priests could be found in pagan

---

44 The Greek word *arsenokoitai* also used by the Apostle Paul in 1 Timothy 1:10 is translated by St. Jerome into Latin as "masculorum concubitoribus." "Concubitoribus" is a Latin synonym for "concubitores."

45 From *The Arapanacana Press.* In 2010: www.arapacana.com/glossary/co.html

temples and quarters adjacent to them; they were *consecrated* to serve various fertility goddesses.

Again, the Apostle Paul did not know any monogamous homosexual partners. The Apostle Paul did not know any Christian homosexual people. The Apostle Paul did not write about people whom he did not know or about that to which he was not exposed.

There were other Greek words that the Apostle Paul could have used, whose meanings today would be much clearer than the two Greek words, *malakoi* and *arsenokoitai*, that he used in 1 Corinthians 6:9. *For example*, the Apostle Paul could have used the word pair *philerastes* and *pederastes*, or the word pair *philetor* and *eromenos*, both of which indicated males who were involved in same-sex relationships, some of which were transgenerational and some of which were not. Here, "transgenerational" refers to the sexual relationship between an older soldier or mentor and a younger male in his teens or early twenties. Their temporary sexual pairing was really quite common in some segments of both ancient Greek and Roman societies. In ancient Greece, there was even a god of such unions, called *Eros*. Regardless, the Greek words *malakoi* and *arsenokoitai*, used in 1 Corinthians 6:9, do not mean "modern-day Christian homosexual people." Christian homosexual society did not exist at the time that Paul lived.

Paradoxically, committed monogamous relationships between members of the same sex who were of the same social standing and age were derided in both ancient Greek and Roman societies. Such relationships were avoided because they suggested weakness in those who were so paired. Although you may have heard or read that the Greek and Roman empires fell because of homosexuality, that simply is not true. Those empires may have fallen because of their pagan idolatry and their commitment to satisfying pleasure-driven lusts but not because of homosexuality. Lifelong unions between same-sex couples were virtually nonexistent in ancient Greece and ancient Rome. Committed monogamous relationships between people of the same sex were rare and considered distasteful, unnecessary, and even laughable.

With the exception of committed monogamous unions, the panoply of *same-sex* relationships in ancient Greek and Roman societies paralleled the panoply of *opposite-sex* relationships that existed then, just as they are paralleled today. Simply stated, whatever exists in the world of homosexual people also exists in the world of heterosexual people and vice versa. What is psychopathologic in the heterosexual community is also psychopathologic in the homosexual community.

Translating various Hebrew and Greek words in the Holy Bible as *homosexual* is not accurate. Such translations remind me of this statement by the renowned theologian, John Calvin: "I consider looseness with words no less of a defect than looseness of the bowels."

What three words best describe the Bible passages commonly used against Christian homosexual people? *Mistranslation*, *misinterpretation*, and *misapplication*!

Is temple cult prostitution "abominable," "abhorrent," and "detestable" to the Lord God Almighty? Of course, it is. And it should be. To be sure, in some ways, it is even worse than simple prostitution since it was not done just for money or to satisfy an unhealthy sexual addiction but was an attempt to "worship" pagan deities as part of Satan's overall design to rob the Creator-God of His glory, honor, and praise.

Chapter One of the Apostle Paul's Epistle to the Romans helps make this recurring magnetic pull toward pagan cultism crystal clear because it speaks of the tendency of worshipers to turn from God toward idolatry.

Paul's Letter to the Christians in Rome

Let us now consider Romans 1:18-34, paying particular attention to the words and phrases that have been italicized for emphasis:

{18} For the wrath of God is revealed from heaven against the ungodliness and unrighteousness of all people who conceal God's truth because of their unrighteousness, {19} even though that which may be known about God has been clear to them because God has shown it to them. {20} Indeed, the invisible things of God have been clearly seen from the time that the world was created, being understood in the things that were created, which demonstrate God's eternal power and Godhead, so that no one is without excuse {21} because, although they recognized the Creator, they did not glorify Him as God, neither were they thankful, but became vain in their imaginations, and their foolish hearts became darkened. {22} Professing themselves to be wise, they became fools {23} *by changing the glory of the incorruptible God to images made to look like corruptible man, and birds, and mammals, and reptiles.* [italics mine]

Romans 1:18-23 KJV Paraphrase

It should be clear to anyone who can read with comprehension that those who changed the glory of the incorruptible and invisible God into images made to look like corruptible and visible beings — including human beings, birds, mammals, and reptiles — were pagan idolaters. Although somewhat redundant, I am using the words "pagan idolaters" together to give added emphasis as to who were actually involved in the acts described in the additional verses of Chapter One that follow. Wherever the words "they," "them," and "their" occur in the following verses, I have replaced them with the words "the pagan idolaters" or added "pagan and idolatrous" to continually remind the reader about whom the Apostle Paul was referring.

Romans, Chapter One continues…

{24} Therefore, God gave *the pagan idolaters* up to uncleanness through the lusts of their own *pagan and idolatrous* hearts to dishonor their own *pagan and idolatrous* bodies with one another: {25} The *pagan idolaters* changed the truth of God into a lie, and worshiped and served created things more than their Creator, who is blessed forever. Amen. {26} For this reason, God gave *the pagan idolaters* up to their sexual addictions: for even the *pagan and idolatrous* women exchanged conventional relations for unconventional relations [by having anal sex with men]. [italics and brackets mine]

Romans 1:24-26 KJV Paraphrase

Although many people like to quote Romans 1:26 as if it reads, "women with women," that is *not* how it reads in the original Greek. The Greek does not imply that women were having sexual relations with other women but that they were being sexually serviced anally rather than vaginally (*unconventionally* rather than *conventionally*).

In Romans 1:26, the Greek words *para phusin* [G3844 and G5449] — *phusin* derived from *phusis* — are translated as "against nature" in the King James Version and as "unnatural" in *The Holy Bible, New International Version®*. However, *para phusin* can also be translated as "unconventional" or "nontraditional," just as *phusikin* [G5446] — derived from *phusikos* — can also be translated as "conventional" or "traditional" in Romans 1:27. (See Table Eleven.)

Strong's Number	Greek Word(s)	Transliteration in Syllables	Word Meaning(s)
G3844	παρὰ	pä·rä′	1. against 2. beside 3. along side of
G5449	φύσιν φύσις	phü′·sin phü′·sis	1. nature 2. convention 3. tradition
G5446	φυσικὴν φυσικός	phü·sē·kin′ phü·sē·kos′	1. natural 2. conventional 3. traditional

Table Eleven

When the Apostle Paul referred to men's hair length in 1 Corinthians 11:14, he was not referring to *biological* nature but to the traditional and conventional styling of his day. In the King James Version of the Bible, 1 Corinthians 11:14 states:

Does not even *nature* (phusis [G5449]) itself teach you that, if a man has long hair, it is a shame to him? [italics and parentheses mine]

The word "nature" in 1 Corinthians 11:14 (KJV) has been imprecisely translated from the Greek word *phusis* [G5449]. The Apostle Paul certainly did not intend for the Greek word *phusis* [G5449] to be translated as "nature" in 1 Corinthians 11:14 since nature itself *does show* that hair length grows continuously in both males and females. Indeed, nature — that is, *biological* nature — shows that both men and women grow long hair when it is not cut. In writing about hair length, the Apostle Paul was commenting about what was conventional or traditional in cultural customs at that time and not what is "against nature" or "in agreement with nature." (Please understand that the Creator-God has no preferred hair length for either males or females.)

Similarly, in the King James Version of Romans 1:26, the words "against nature" have been imprecisely translated from the Greek words *para phusin* {G3844 and G5449}. Although the Greek word *para* can be translated as "against," it can also be translated as "beside," or "along side of." To illustrate this, the English word *paratroopers* indicates those who are sent out in war, not to fight "against" the troops or foot soldiers, but to fight "beside," or "along side of," the troops. The word "unconventional" is important here because it does not conjure up the judgmentalism or condemnation that is invoked by the phrase "against nature." By using "unconventional" instead of "against nature," Chapter One of Romans becomes more of the report, retelling, or narrative that the Apostle Paul intended it to be.

The fact that Romans 1:26 is not about sex between women, coupled with the complete absence of a reference to women in Leviticus 18:22 in the Old Testament, should make it clear, compelling, and convincing to the reader that the Holy Bible does not address female same-sex relationships. That the Holy Bible never addresses lesbianism nor the female homosexual orientation *should* be problematic for those who believe that the Holy Bible gives a blanket condemnation against all homosexual people. In other words, if you must believe that homosexual people are condemned by the Holy Bible, then you can only believe that male homosexual people are condemned. And, if you must believe that only male homosexual people are condemned, then the contradiction should begin to tear away at your misconceptions of what the Bible does say, and does not say, about homosexual people, homosexuality, and the homosexual orientation.

Romans, Chapter One continues...

{27} And, similarly, the *pagan and idolatrous* men, leaving the conventional (*phusikin* {G5446}) use of the woman, burned in their lust one toward another; *pagan and idolatrous* men committed indecent acts with *pagan and idolatrous* men, and the *pagan and idolatrous* men received in themselves the consequences of their error that were fitting. {italics mine}

Romans 1:27 KJV Paraphrase

That pagan and idolatrous men abandoned vaginal intercourse for anal intercourse with both women and men in idolatrous and orgiastic settings was, indeed, "perverted," "indecent," and "reprobate." And it is understandable that the pagan and idolatrous men received in themselves "the fitting consequences" of their promiscuous sex in diseases and disorders — venereal disease and prolapsed rectums (i.e., *recta*).

Romans, Chapter One continues...

{28} And even as the *pagan idolaters* did not like to retain God in their knowledge, God gave them over to a reprobate mind, to do those things that are unseemly. {29} *The pagan idolaters* were filled with all kinds of unrighteousness, fornication, wickedness, covetousness, maliciousness, and the *pagan idolaters* were full of envy, murder, contentiousness, deceit, and malignity; the *pagan idolaters* were gossips {30} backbiters, haters of God, spiteful, proud, boasters, inventors of evil things, and disobedient to parents. {31} The *pagan idolaters* were without understanding, covenant-breakers, hard-hearted, implacable, and unmerciful. {32} Although the *pagan idolaters* knew the judgment of God (that they which commit such things are worthy of death), the *pagan idolaters* not only do these things, but also take pleasure when others do them, too. {italics mine}

Romans 1:28-32 KJV Paraphrase

That the Bible states in verse 32 that the pagan idolaters "knew the judgment of God, that they which commit such things are worthy of death," implies that these people were not simply pagan barbarians but people who had once understood the Law of God in Torah relative to the Creator-God's hatred of idolatry, idolatrous religious practices, and sexual promiscuity — because they understood that such idolatrous practices were worthy of God's curse (i.e., the death penalty and permanent separation from God). That they knew idolatry was sinful and still participated in idolatrous practices indicates that they were not only sinful but also evil.

It should be clear from its historical context that the people described in Chapter One of Romans are those who turned away from worshiping the one true and only real God. As verses 21 and 28 imply, they once knew God but chose not to obey Him. These same people turned toward, or returned to, worshiping pagan idols. As stated in verse 23, they worshiped images that looked like mortal man and birds and mammals and reptiles. That these idolatrous people were "reprobate" means that they had failed the test of remaining true to God. And it was not that they had been worshiping God only as the "Unknown God," whom the Apostle Paul had referenced in his address to the people of Athens and recorded in Acts 17:23. No, in Chapter One of his Epistle to the Romans, the Apostle Paul describes people who had known God but refused to live their lives in consecration to Him. As a result, they were deemed "illegitimate children and not true heirs" (Hebrews 12:8 KJV Paraphrase). They were reprobate because they had failed to pass God's test of faithfulness to Him. These people fell to the social ills of their day as well as their own unbridled lust to practice promiscuous sexual activities common at the time.

What does the historical context of the Apostle Paul's writings require us to understand?

1. The historical context of the Apostle Paul's writings requires us to understand that the Apostle Paul was familiar with sex for the purpose of "worshiping" fertility gods and goddesses. This so-called worship included pseudo-sacred ritualistic sexual offerings of anal intercourse with both male and female temple cult prostitutes.

2. The historical context of the Apostle Paul's writings requires us to understand that the Apostle Paul was familiar with group sex in which individuals had sex with multiple partners, male

and female, and multiple times (*for example*, in "orgies" at Bacchanalian-type feasts and festivals as well as in bath houses and during fertility cult worship).

3. The historical context of the Apostle Paul's writings requires us to understand that the Apostle Paul was familiar with sex for the sake of unbridled, inflamed lust that was indulged promiscuously and often resulted in venereal disease and/or prolapsed rectums (i.e., *recta*) in males and females and prolapsed rectums, vaginas, and uteruses (i.e., *uteri*) in females.

The Apostle Paul did not know any monogamous homosexual partners. The Apostle Paul did not know any Christian homosexual people. The Apostle Paul did not write about people whom he did not know or about that to which he was not exposed.

In verses 22 through 26 of Romans, Chapter One, are found at least three pairs of parallel constructions all referring to people who exchanged one thing for another: 1) verse 24 describes people who exchanged the glory of God for graven images; 2) verse 25 describes people who exchanged the truth of God for a lie; and 3) verse 26 describes people who exchanged conventional sexual relations for unconventional ones. All three verses are describing the same idol-worshiping people. In other words, the Apostle Paul is not speaking of homosexual people seeking to live their lives in consecrated monogamous relationships. Rather, the Apostle Paul is describing people who were involved in sexual activity within the context of pagan idolatry.

Regarding verses 24, 26, and 27 of Chapter One in Romans, the *Life Application Bible Commentary: Romans,* which is a theologically-conservative expository work accepted by many mainstream Christian educators, confirms the context of the sexual impurity addressed:

Here [in verse 24] Paul introduces the subject of *sexual impurity*. He returns to it in verses 26 and 27. The context indicates that he is referring in part to cultic prostitution and the fertility cults that made use of temple prostitutes in their rites… Paul, writing from Corinth, the home of the temple of Aphrodite, was surrounded by evidences of the horrible evil of such belief (see also 1 Corinthians 6:9-10; 2 Corinthians 12:21).[46]

In summary, the "they," "them," and "their" of Romans, Chapter One, verses 18 through 34, all refer to pagan idolaters — specifically, those who reverted back to idolatry after having known the one true and only real Creator-God. Again, what kind of idolaters, and what kind of idolatry existed during Paul's time? The same kind that existed during Canaanite times and throughout the entirety of Old Testament history, when the worship of fertility gods and goddesses was the order of the day.

In his book, *History of Orgies*, author Burgo Partridge details the sado-masochistic orgiastic debaucheries that occurred throughout the Roman empire, where participants reveled in animal instincts in frenzied group sexual activities:

> The worship of Cybele, besides involving self-castration in a state of frenzy, and dedication of the severed organs to the goddess, had also, as an important part of the ritual, a baptism by blood which came, appropriately enough, from a bull or ram. Banquets were given in honour of this goddess at private houses, but the actual consummation of her worship appears to have been performed by the priests alone. According to Apuleius, the priests of Cybele also indulged in {idolatrous same-sex} practices with strong young peasants.[47]

Partridge then gives example after example of this utterly contemptible society in which same-sex and opposite-sex temple cult and brothel prostitution abounded and where huge phallic symbols were worshiped on almost every street corner by emperor and subject alike. Indeed, people were "inflamed" in depraved lust for one another.

In the following section, I will spend time commenting about what is biologically natural as well as what has been observed in nature.

---

46   Barton, Bruce B., David R. Veerman and Neil Wilson. *Life Application Bible Commentary: Romans*. Tyndale House Publishers, Inc., Wheaton, 1992, page 32.

47   Partridge, Burgo. *A History of Orgies*. Bonanza Books, New York, 1960, page 59. {brackets mine}

What does *Natural* mean in Romans 1:26-27?

If you still believe that Scripture is unequivocally against modern-day Christian homosexual people, then you need to understand the mind of God relative to this issue. To this end, you need to understand that true science does not contradict the Holy Bible nor does the Holy Bible contradict true science. True science shows that there are exceptions to the so-called absolute scriptural rule of "male and female" referred to Genesis 1:27 in the form of intersexuals as well as in same-sex pair bonding throughout much of the animal kingdom. And the Holy Bible shows that there are exceptions to the so-called "absolute" scriptural rule of "male and female" in the form of eunuchs — of whom Christ Jesus said, "some were so born from their mother's womb" (Matthew 19:12 KJV).

In an article entitled "Brain Differences in Sheep Linked to Sexual Partner Preference," published in November, 2002, the Oregon Health and Science University states:

> Research conducted at Oregon Health & Science University (OHSU) has demonstrated structural brain differences associated with naturally occurring variations in sexual partner preferences. These are the first findings to demonstrate such a correlation in research animals, in this case sheep.

The article continues…

> Domestic rams were used as an animal model for this research because they display distinct, natural variations in sexual attraction, making them valuable in studying the biological basis for sexual partner preference. Previous studies documented that approximately 6 percent to 8 percent of domestic rams court and mate with other rams exclusively.[48]

Yes, both intersexuals and same-sex pair bonds throughout the animal kingdom serve as biological examples of what is natural and

---

48 *Oregon Health Science & University (OHSU) News Release*, November 4, 2002, "Brain Differences in Sheep Linked to Sexual Partner Preference," Portland, Oregon.

what occurs in nature. And eunuchs "born that way" serve as Biblical examples of deviations from the norm in nature. Thus, God accounts for exceptions to supposed rules of sexual orientation and gender identity both naturally (that is, biologically) and scripturally.

From a biological standpoint, the presence or absence of genitals is a state of nature, and gender is a state of mind. These combined states are ultimately responsible for an individual's instincts. If you think that the homosexual orientation is a perverted instinct, then you have made heterosexuality a law unto itself (in other words, a universal law), which law is contradictory to the full spectrum of what occurs in nature. Indeed, such an absolute fails to take into consideration the myriad departures in nature that deviate from the norm (*norm* defined here as "that which occurs most frequently"). It also fails to take into consideration spiritual law, which states in Galatians 3:28 that in Christ Jesus there is neither "male nor female."

Through science as well as Scripture, we now know that: 1) intersexuals are "born that way," 2) animals that court and mate exclusively with other animals of the same sex are "born that way," and 3) some eunuchs, as Christ Jesus said, are "born that way." Can we deny the existence of any of these? No, of course not.

Given the context of idolatry and pagan sexual ritual orgies that included group sex as well as sex without commitment, Chapter One of Paul's Epistle to the Romans is referring to what is, in essence, spiritual adultery. Spiritual adultery should be foreign and repugnant to the children of God: 1) because God hates idolatry; and 2) because, as stated in Hebrews 13:4, God's ideal requires monogamous covenant ties between individuals before they consummate their unions sexually. I will say more concerning this ideal in Chapter Six of this book.

In Romans 1:27, it says that the men were inflamed with lust for one another. Does this describe unholy thinking, unholy behavior, and unholy union? Of course, it does. Unbridled lust with multiple partners is sexual obsession and addiction. Depraved, or reprobate, lust is the reduction of another individual to an object for one's own self gratification, which is always wrong in the eyes of God — wrong for heterosexual people as well as for homosexual people. That people exchanged committed monogamous relationships for ambisexual orgiastic activities is indeed depraved and appropriately labeled "against God."

Although you have already read my comments that the English word "conventional" (from the Greek word phusikin {G5446}) should have been used in Romans 1:26 and 27, I would now like to offer further commentary on the English word *natural* that has been used in many Bible translations.

For the sake of discussion, if I concede that the term *natural* should have been used, then either the term *natural* in Romans 1:26 and 1:27 only refers to what the Apostle Paul understood of nature (a limited understanding) or it refers to all of nature for all time, and in all situations and circumstances.

On the one hand, most (if not all) Bible scholars and theologians would agree that a Bible word's meaning is limited to the definition of the word in its original language at the time that it was used (that is, its original meaning at the particular time it was used). Therefore, if the word *natural* only refers to what the Apostle Paul understood of nature, was exposed to, and studied personally, then it cannot be all-inclusive and, therefore, must not include contemporary homosexual people for whom the homosexual orientation is innate, or instinctual. *For example*, the Apostle Paul was neither an animal behaviorist nor a practitioner of animal husbandry and, therefore, was not aware of animals who exclusively court and sexually couple with others of the same sex. And the Apostle Paul did not know any Christian homosexual people. The Apostle Paul did not write about people whom he did not know and about that to which he was not exposed.

On the other hand, if the English word *natural* is all-inclusive (and refers to all of nature for all time, in all situations and circumstances), then the inclusivity itself opens the door for the traditionally-inferred meaning in Romans 1:26 and 1:27 to be counterbalanced by modern scientific contributions to the meaning of sex, gender, and sexual orientation through an understanding of developmental biology and cognitive psychology.

Either way, an intelligent understanding of the homosexual orientation wins out. To be sure, God does not want us to be stuck on stupidity or remain in ignorance.

Here, it is important to again reiterate that there is a distinction between "same-sex behaviors" and "homosexual practices." Romantic involvement between people of a homosexual orientation are different from same-sex sexual activities that may occur between people of an unresolved sexual orientation. I write "unresolved" not to describe their internal conflict or the uncertainty of how they view themselves but, rather, to describe that it is indeterminate if the same-sex behaviors in Chapter One of Romans are between obligate homosexual people (that is, people who have no choice in their attraction) or between heterosexual people simply involved in ambisexual activity that included sex with anyone and, in some settings, *everyone*.

It is also important to note that, in the Apostle Paul's mind, lifelong homosexual pair bonding was not an option for anybody. That it was not an option colored his interpretation of what is "natural" and "unnatural," just as the role of women in the society of his day colored his interpretation of roles for women in church leadership. The Apostle Paul's perspectives on these issues of gender and sex do not have universal application because his perspectives must be interpreted in the historical context of his day.

Concerning the reference to the "depraved" or "reprobate" mind in Romans 1:28, I hope that life experience has already taught you that God only gives us over to a reprobate mind when we are already indulging that mind to begin with. In other words, the indulgence of sinful addictive behaviors results in more of the same until, or unless, we consciously decide to turn, or return, the reins of all aspects of our lives over to God. If you have not yet learned that, and if you belong to God, then you will learn it eventually. Of this, I am certain. Again, God does not turn us over to a sin that we are not already indulging.

As you seek to understand Scripture, it is important, not only to *read the lines* (that is, pay attention to word meanings, grammar, and syntax), but also to *read behind the lines* by understanding historical context, word etymology (or origins), and purpose. And, as you seek to understand Scripture, it is important, not only to *read behind the lines*, but also to *read between the lines* by learning to understand implication and inference. And, as you seek to understand Scripture, it is important, not only to *read between the lines*, but also to *read beyond the lines* concerning application as well as misapplication of its truths to events, circumstances, and realities.

It is important for us to come to an understanding that — if we hold the whole Bible as we simultaneously attend to its various parts — the Bible addresses male same-sex behaviors solely from the standpoint of: 1) idolatry, 2) prostitution, 3) unbridled lust, and 4) brutal sexual assault (remember, such assaults were depicted in the intended group rapes recorded in Genesis 19 for the city of Sodom and in Judges 19 for the city of Gibeah). Moreover, the Holy Bible never addresses the issue of homosexual relationships between women, not once. And the Holy Bible never addresses the issue of homosexual relationships between males from the standpoint of committed, monogamous relationships.

The sum of the matter is this: teach homosexual people to be moral because you cannot teach them to be heterosexual. Heterosexuality is unnatural for homosexual people because it is contradictory to what is innate, or instinctual, in them. To help understand this, you must either grasp the multivariate nature of biological life or transcend (which is to say, go beyond) using only a physical referent for meaningful relationships.

Closing the Chapter on *Sodom* and *Sodomites*

The last reference to Sodom in the Bible often used against homosexual people is found in Jude, verse 7 (there are no chapters in Jude):

> Even as Sodom and Gomorrha, and the cities about them in like manner, giving themselves over to fornication, and going after strange flesh (*strange flesh* translated from *heteras sarkos* [G2087 and G4561]), are set forth for an example, suffering the vengeance of eternal fire. [parentheses mine]
>
> Jude 7 KJV

Strong's Number	Greek Word(s)	Transliteration in Syllables	Word Meaning(s)
G2087	ἑτέρας	he'·te·ras	1. strange 2. different 3. unlike
G4561	σαρκὸς	sär'·kos	1. flesh 2. physical substance

Table Twelve

Rather than describing homosexuality, the two Greek words rendered together as "perversion" in *The Holy Bible, New International Version*® and separately as "strange flesh" in the King James Version could just as well be describing the bestiality common to many Canaanite fertility rites as it could be describing the attempt by the townspeople of Sodom to rape the two angelic visitors, whose angelic flesh was indeed "strange," or "different," to them and "unlike" their own. This explanation is especially plausible in view of the verse's comparison ("in like manner") to the fallen angels in the previous verse who had "kept not their first estate" (verse 6). Verse 6 indicates that the fallen angels commingled with human beings by having sex with them (see Genesis 6:1-2):

And the angels who kept not their first estate, but left their own habitation, God has placed in everlasting chains under darkness until the judgment of the great day.

Jude 6 KJV Paraphrase

And it came to pass, when men [that is, human beings] began to multiply on the face of the earth, and daughters were born to them, that the *sons of God* [or angels] saw the daughters of men that they were appealing; and they took wives from them of all whom they chose. [italics and brackets mine]

Genesis 6:1-2 KJV Paraphrase

CHRISTIANITY AND HOMOSEXUALITY RECONCILED

The "giants" (or *nephilim*) referred to in Genesis 6:4 (KJV) have been inferred by some Hebrew scholars to have been the offspring of the fallen angels and human beings because the Hebrew word *nephilim* can mean "fallen ones."

Ironically, the two words translated as "strange flesh" in the KJV of Jude 7 are *heteras sarkos* [G2087 and G4561][49] — which is to say, "hetero[sexual] flesh," and not "homosexual flesh." And, although my use of "hetero[sexual]" in the previous sentence is obvious and intentional hyperbole, it takes one no more far afield than requiring students of the Bible to believe that the perversion written about in verse 7 of Jude is homosexuality.

The *Word Biblical Commentary*, which is a well-respected mainstream expository work, is in agreement with the interpretation of Jude, verses 6 and 7, that I have just given:

> As the angels fell because of their lust for women, so the Sodomites desired sexual relations with angels. The reference is to the incident in Genesis 19:4-11. *Sarkos heteras* [G4561 and G2087], "strange flesh," cannot, as many commentators and most translations assume, refer to homosexual practice, in which the flesh is not "different" (*heteras* [G2087]); [therefore] it must mean the flesh of angels. The sin of the Sodomites (not strictly, of the other towns) reached its zenith in this most extravagant of sexual aberrations, which would have transgressed the order of creation as shockingly as the fallen angels did.[50] [italics and brackets mine]

---

49 I have intentionally reversed the order of the words in Greek for the reader to more easily compare them to their English counterparts.

50 Bauckman, Richard. *Word Biblical Commentary*: Jude-2 Peter (Volume 50), Word Books, Waco, 1983, page 54.

CHAPTER FIVE

Levitical Law and Grace

Introduction

In Chapter One, the need for reconciliation of Christianity and homosexuality was discussed. In Chapter Two, controversial human rights issues throughout the existence of the Christian Church were acknowledged. In Chapter Three, the seeming dilemma that exists between Christianity and homosexuality was considered; and the necessity for holding the whole Bible while simultaneously attending to its various parts was emphasized. In Chapter Four: 1) The story of Sodom was reviewed. 2) The topic of the *Qadashim*, or *Qadasheem* [H6945 plural] — who were incorrectly referred to as "sodomites" by Bible translators but, more correctly, should have been referred to as "male temple cult prostitutes" — was covered. And 3) the historical role of the worship of fertility gods and goddesses in pre-Canaanite times, in Canaanite times, and in ancient Greek and Roman times was also covered. This historical role will be explicated further within this chapter as Levitical Law and grace are discussed.

The Major Question

The major question that we need to consider relative to this chapter is, "Why the seemingly hard-line stance by God concerning same-sex behavior, cross-dressing, and eunuchs?" — as commonly quoted from the following four verses of (the) Torah:

You must not lie with mankind as with womankind because it is an abomination [the Hebrew word translated as *an abomination* has been translated in other Bible versions as *an abhorrence* or *detestable*].

Leviticus 18:22 KJV Paraphrase

If a man lie with mankind as he lies with a woman, both of them have committed an abomination. They both must be put to death; their blood [i.e., guilt] will be upon them. [brackets mine]

Leviticus 20:13 KJV Paraphrase

A woman shall not wear that which pertains to a man, neither shall a man put on a woman's garment: for all that do so are an abomination unto the Lord your God.

Deuteronomy 22:5 KJV Paraphrase

He that is wounded in the stones [i.e., testicles] or has his privy member [i.e., penis] cut off, shall not enter into the congregation of the Lord. [brackets mine]

Deuteronomy 23:1 KJV

Understanding Why Levitical Law was Originally Imposed on the Children of Israel

In order to answer the major question posed in the previous section, I want to remind the reader that "Torah" (or "the Torah") is another word for "Law" (or "the Law"). Though many people might think only of the Ten Commandments found in Exodus 20:1-17 and Deuteronomy 5:6-22 when they read or hear of "the Law," "the Law" is really much more than that. Generally speaking, "the Law," or "Torah," is used synonymously with the first five books of the Bible, often referred to as the Pentateuch: Genesis, Exodus, Leviticus, Numbers, and Deuteronomy. As such, "the Law" includes all of the covenant requirements, commandments, statutes, rules, regulations, and ordinances laid down by the Lord God Almighty throughout the Pentateuch and found in varying degrees in each of those five books (a few of which are more concerned with the narrative retelling of historical events than with actual laws, rules, regulations, and ordinances).

I have chosen to use the phrase "Levitical Law" in this chapter as representative of "the Law" for the following reasons: 1) because Leviticus is the most thoroughly legalistic book of the Pentateuch as well as the entire Bible; 2) because Leviticus serves as the embodiment of the myriad rules, regulations, and ordinances imposed by the Lord God Almighty on those who were about to inhabit the Promised Land; 3) because most of the laws found in the largely legalistic section of Deuteronomy can be viewed as an amplification of those found in Leviticus; 4) because Leviticus is the location for two of the most often used passages against homosexual people; and 5) to help the reader keep religious law (or "Torah") separate from civil, or governmental, law.

The more than six hundred rules, regulations, and ordinances detailed in Leviticus are quite extensive and cover every major aspect of the human condition experienced by the children of Israel. *For example*, Levitical prohibitions included dietary restrictions:

{6} The rabbit chews its cud but does not have cleft hooves; therefore, it is unclean. {7} And the pig has cleft hooves but does not chew its cud; therefore, it is unclean. {8} You must not eat their flesh or touch their dead carcasses because they are unclean.

Leviticus 11:6-8 KJV Paraphrase

{10} All organisms that do not have fins and scales and live in the water must be considered an abomination to you. {11} Indeed, they will be an abomination to you if you eat their flesh. {12} Whatever does not have fins and scales in the waters will be an abomination to you.

Leviticus 11:10-12 KJV Paraphrase

In other words, Levitical Law required the children of Israel to refrain from eating rabbit, pork, shrimp, lobster, clams, oysters, and even catfish.

For the record, the English words "detest," "detestable," "abhor," "abhorrence," "abominable," and "abomination" used in various translations of Leviticus 11:10-12 have not been translated from the Hebrew word *Toevah* [H8441 singular] (see Table Six), which means "idolatrous practice," but from the Hebrew word *Sheqets* [H8263], which means "filthy," "unhealthy," or "scummy."

Levitical Law also restricted the children of Israel in the following ways:

You must keep My statutes. You must not let your cattle mate with other kinds of animals; you must not sow your field with mixed seed; and you must not wear garments made of both cotton and wool.

Leviticus 19:19 KJV Paraphrase

Thus, allowing a horse to mate with a donkey (or "jackass") to produce a *mule* or *hinny* would be against Levitical Law. Planting rye and barley in the same field would be contrary to what is allowed by Levitical Law. And wearing garments made of mixed fiber would be considered by Levitical Law to be a transgression.

Levitical Law provided guidelines for men's haircuts and prohibited the children of Israel from tattooing themselves:

You must not round the corners of the hair on the sides of your head or of your beard.

Leviticus 19:27 KJV Paraphrase

You must not make any cuttings in your flesh for the dead nor print any marks on you: I am the Lord.

Leviticus 19:28 KJV Paraphrase

Penalties for disobeying Levitical Law were quite severe by today's standards:

Anyone who curses his father or his mother must be put to death: he has cursed his father or his mother; his blood {i.e., his guilt} will be upon him. And the man that commits adultery with another man's wife, even with his neighbor's wife, both the adulterer and the adulteress must be put to death. {brackets mine}

Leviticus 20:9-10 KJV Paraphrase

If a man has vaginal intercourse with a woman during her menstrual flow and, in this way, uncovers her nakedness, and she has thus revealed the flow of her blood, both of them shall be cut off from among their people.

Leviticus 20:18 KJV Paraphrase

Please take the time and read through the entire book of Leviticus. It is rather tedious reading, but it will be challenging for you to find that there were some constraints placed upon the Israelites that were not only severe but also next to impossible to observe — including some prohibitions that, from a modern-day standpoint, just do not make sense without a global view of what the Lord God Almighty was trying to instill in the hearts and minds of those He intended to be His chosen people.

Do the hundreds of rules, regulations, and ordinances detailed by Levitical Law pertain to Christians? No, certainly not. Why not? Because the Nation of Israel and the Church of Christ are two distinctly separate entities. To be sure, the Lord God Almighty is not finished with non-Christian Jews, but, collectively, they are not the same as God's Church. The Christian Church did not replace Zion. Here, a distinction should be made between *national* Israel and *spiritual* Israel. "National Israel" includes nonbelieving Jews, and "spiritual Israel" includes all who believe in Christ Jesus, including Messianic Jews (that is, those who believe that Christ Jesus is the prophesied Messiah). Just as God is not finished with *spiritual Israel*, God is not yet finished with *national Israel* either.

So, then, you may ask, why were the rules, regulations, and ordinances of (the) Torah laid down? I think that question is best answered through understanding the following verse:

> You must learn the difference between what is holy and unholy and between what is unclean and clean.

> Leviticus 10:10 KJV Paraphrase

Again, we need to keep historical context in mind. The people whom the Lord God Almighty was trying to regulate and draw closer to Him were a nomadic and, in many ways, primitive people. Perhaps you may gain additional insight through a comment made by Moses to the children of Israel just before they were to enter the Promised Land — when Moses knew that he would never see them again:

> "You have been rebellious against the Lord from the first day that I knew you."

> Deuteronomy 9:24 KJV Paraphrase

Moses did not say, "I have been with you for 40 years. I have walked with you in the wilderness. We have had some good times and some bad times together. I wish you well, and I will miss you!" Instead, he said, "You have been stiff-necked from the very first day that I knew you!" Indeed, the Lord was dealing with a very difficult group of people — just as difficult as you and I are this very day!

Because they were stubborn, and because they originally had barbarous customs, God wanted to instruct them that they had to consecrate even the smallest details of their lives to Him if they were going to truly be His people, and that such consecration would not be easy. Thus, the rules, regulations, and ordinances of (the) Torah were laid down to help this stiff-necked, rebellious, and nomadic group of people come to understand that, in order to become a holy people, they had to learn to separate themselves from barbarous customs and idolatrous practices, discipline themselves, and offer even the smallest of their daily activities up to God as proof of their willingness to be His people. To be sure, in addition to "Law," the word *Torah* means "teaching," "instruction," and "direction." God was teaching, instructing, and directing the children of Israel to be holy by following the practices that He laid down in *Torah*. Lest any of us boast, it is important to state that modern-day Christians are no less stubborn and no less rebellious today than the children of Israel were during ancient times.

Does this mean that Christians should throw out the Ten Commandments? No, however, it does mean that they should pay particular attention to what Christ Jesus said were the greatest commandments, or what sums up the Law of Moses and the Prophets — which is that we should love the Lord our God with all of our heart, all of our soul, and all of our mind (and all of our might); and that we should love our neighbor as much as we individually love ourselves (Matthew 22:36-40). That is what Christ Jesus said summarizes the Law of Moses and upon which all the Law depends. To be sure, as Christians, though we worship every seven days, most of us do not worship on the Jewish Sabbath, which is from Friday sundown to Saturday sundown. So, the overwhelming majority of Christians do not even keep all of the Ten Commandments. Interestingly, even when some Christian denominations keep the Jewish Sabbath as their day of worship, they often end up unnecessarily adhering to many of the other ordinances and restrictions that are written in the Law of Moses, too.

Why should all Christians read, study, and comprehend the Old Testament, including the Law of Moses? There are at least eight reasons:

1. To understand the origin of the universe.

2. To understand the origin of humankind.

3. To learn the history of humankind since Adam and Eve as well as to learn the origin of iniquity and sin.

4. To understand the promises of God to humankind concerning the Jewish Messiah, who is the only Savior of the world.

5. To understand the prophecies of God that have already been fulfilled, that are currently being fulfilled, and that will be fulfilled at a later time.

6. To learn from the journey of the Children of Israel and how it mirrors the personal journey of individual Christians.

7. To learn basic spiritual principles and apply them to daily living today.

8. To better understand Old Testament quotations and imagery used throughout the New Testament. (Bible students cannot really understand the Book of Revelation unless they first understand the symbology that it borrows from the Old Testament.)

Christians should not read, comprehend, and study the Law of Moses in order for them to follow Levitical Law. Levitical Law was written for a different group of people who lived at a different time in history and in a different place. As recorded in Romans 6:14, Christians are not under the Law of Moses but under grace. [See also the discussion of circumcision in Chapter Five of Galatians.] Unfortunately, many Christians often resort to, or revert to, a default condition of legalism in their practice of Christianity. As stated in Chapter Two of this book, legalism is the brain's natural default in order for it (the brain) to more easily interpret its environment. Going beyond this default mechanism requires one to exert time, effort, and energy in order to understand complex issues. (Most brains do not like to do that at all or to do that repetitively.)

Levitical Law required perfection not only in the people who ministered to the Lord but also in the animals that were to be sacrificed to Him:

{16} And the Lord said to Moses, {17} "Speak to Aaron, saying, 'Whoever of your descendants has a blemish must not serve in the capacity of priest. {18} This includes those who are blind or lame as well as anyone who has a deformity, {19} including a deformity of the foot or hand, {20} or those who have deformities of the spine or are dwarves, or that has an impairment in his vision, or is deformed in any way, or has a skin disease, or has his testicles damaged. {21} No man that has a blemish of the descendants of Aaron the priest shall offer a burnt offering to the Lord: he has a blemish; he must not serve in the role of a priest. {22} He may eat the bread of his God, both of the most holy, and of the holy. {23} Only he shall not go into the Holy of Holies nor approach the altar because he has a blemish — in order to not profane My sanctuaries because I the Lord sanctify them Myself.'"

Leviticus 21:16-23 KJV Paraphrase

{17} The Lord said to Moses, {18} "Speak to Aaron, and to his sons, and to all the children of Israel, and say to them, 'Whoever is of the house of Israel or of the foreigners living in the land that will make an offering to honor a vow, and for all his freewill offerings that will be offered to the Lord for a burnt offering: {19} You must offer a male without blemish from the cattle, sheep, or goats. {20} You must not offer any animal that has a blemish because it will not be acceptable.'"

Leviticus 22:17-20 KJV Paraphrase

Centuries later, Jesus spoke of fulfilling the Law:

"Do not think that I have come to destroy the Law, or the Prophets: I have not come to destroy them but to fulfill them."

Matthew 5:17 KJV Paraphrase

Christ Jesus did not mean that he came to reinstate or reinstitute Levitical Law. Christ Jesus meant: 1) that Levitical Law required the offering of an unblemished, or perfect, blood sacrifice as an atonement for iniquity and sin; 2) that he himself was to serve as that offering in the establishment of a New Covenant as the sacrificial "Lamb of God" (John 1:29 and 36); and 3) that he was to fulfill the entirety of Levitical Law by serving as that sacrifice. In his perfect obedience to God the Father, God the Son fulfilled the Law's requirements. That is what Christ Jesus meant when he stated that he had come to fulfill the Law. To be sure, he ended up canceling the entire written code and releasing people from bondage to Levitical Law, as stated in Colossians 2:14:

> Christ Jesus blotted out {i.e., canceled} the written ordinances that were against us and were contrary to us, and he removed them, nailing them to his cross. [brackets mine]
>
> Colossians 2:14 KJV Paraphrase

According to the Holy Bible, the blood sacrifice of Christ Jesus canceled the rules, regulations, and ordinances of Levitical Law, having nailed them to the cross of his crucifixion.

Understanding Levitical Law in Relationship to Grace

Christians need to understand that Levitical Law is something that was put in place in order to help people learn that God requires His people (no matter who they are and no matter in which generation or age) to be "set aside" — which is to say, to be truly consecrated to, and sanctified unto, Him. How can people become sanctified? Well, the ancients were challenged by Levitical Law to live their lives in a way that *approached* true holiness by trying to follow all of the rules, regulations, and ordinances recorded in Torah.

Christians should be careful about trying to live in accordance with Levitical Law or trying to impose on others what they themselves will not, and cannot, fulfill. Concerning hypocritical adherents to Levitical Law, Christ Jesus said many times, "Woe to you teachers of the Law and Pharisees, you hypocrites" (Matthew 23:1-39 KJV Paraphrase). He called these religious legalists "blind guides!" And he said, "You strain at a gnat but swallow a camel" (Matthew 23:24 KJV Paraphrase). In Matthew 23:33 (KJV Paraphrase), he chided them with, "You snakes! You brood of vipers! How will you escape damnation to hell?" Who or what is a *hypocrite*? A hypocrite is an unfaithful servant or someone who, in the name of God, requires someone else to do what he or she cannot do.

To be sure, we can come to a better understanding of Levitical Law through understanding New Testament teachings. Remember, Christians are taught that they "are not under the Law but under grace" (Romans 6:14 KJV Paraphrase). Indeed, Christians are liberated from following the rules, regulations, and ordinances of Levitical Law. Anyone who says that Christians should follow the rules, regulations, and ordinances in Leviticus is deceived and in bondage and seeks to put others in bondage, too. Anyone who says that Christians should follow the rules, regulations, and ordinances in Leviticus has placed himself or herself under a curse and seeks to place others under the same curse (Galatians 3:10).

The Lord God Almighty established a covenant with Abraham because Abraham was a righteous person. Why was Abraham considered a righteous person? Abraham was considered righteous by God because he was a person of faith. The Bible teaches that righteousness was imputed to him because of his faith in Yahweh:

{20} Abraham did not waver in disbelief concerning the promise of God, but was strong in faith, giving glory to God; {21} being fully persuaded that, what God had promised, God was able also to perform. {22} Therefore, Abraham's faith was imputed to him as righteousness. {23} Now it was not written for his sake alone that it was imputed to him {24} but for us also, to whom it is imputed if we believe on God, who raised up Jesus our Lord from the dead. {25} Christ Jesus was delivered to death for our offences, and he was raised again for our justification.

Romans 4:20-25 KJV Paraphrase

So, God recognized that Abraham had faith. Therefore, God established a covenant with Abraham. And it was not until the children of Israel left Egypt, after more than four centuries in bondage, that the various rules, regulations, and ordinances of Levitical Law were put in place. Are we to believe, then, that there were no people who were righteous in God's sight from the time of Abraham up to the time that Levitical Law was imposed? Are we to believe that there were no people who had faith in the Lord God Almighty during that interval of more than four hundred years? Of course not! People of faith existed during that period of time: some of the descendants of Abraham were people of faith and were considered by the Lord God Almighty to be righteous, like Abraham, because of their faith in Him.

The point I am trying to reiterate here is that the Bible teaches, "Without faith it is impossible to please God" (Hebrews 11:6 KJV). In other words, what the Lord looks at is whether or not we have faith. The Bible also teaches that the Lord Jesus himself is the author and finisher, or *perfecter*, of that faith (Hebrews 12:2). Again, it is faith that is crucial to our right standing with the Lord God Almighty. It was faith that was crucial for Abraham as well as for the people who lived in the centuries between the Abrahamic covenant and the imposition of the rules, regulations, and ordinances of Levitical Law. And it is faith that is still crucial after the first Advent of Christ Jesus and the time of his atonement for our iniquity and sin through his crucifixion and death. Even under Levitical Law, this was true because the purpose of Levitical Law was to teach the children of Israel to put their faith and hope in the coming Messiah promised by Moses and, later, by many of the Old Testament prophets.

If Levitical Law could have made the children of Israel righteous, there would have been no need for animal blood sacrifices, and if the sacrifices of unblemished animals had been sufficient, there would have been no need for an unblemished Savior.

Levitical Law and its required sacrifices all pointed to the need for a Redeemer. Having faith has always been, and still is, what the Lord God Almighty holds to be more valuable than adhering to Levitical Law.

Romans 2:25-29 declares that, spiritually speaking, those who are true descendants of Abraham are those who have humbled themselves before the Lord God Almighty and have their faith and, therefore, their righteousness in Him:

{25} For circumcision is indeed profitable if you keep the Law, but if you are a breaker of the Law your circumcision has become uncircumcision. {26} Therefore, if an uncircumcised man keeps the righteous requirements of the Law will not his uncircumcision be counted as circumcision? {27} And will not the physically uncircumcised, if he fulfills the Law, judge you who even with your written code and circumcision are a transgressor of the Law? {28} For he is not a Jew who is one outwardly nor is circumcision that which is outward in the flesh {this describes *national Israel*}, {29} but he is a Jew who is one inwardly and circumcision is that of the heart in the spirit {of sacrificial, selfless, and forgiving love}, not in the letter {of the Law}, whose praise is not from men but from God {this describes *spiritual Israel*}. {capitalization of "Law" and brackets mine}

Romans 2:25-29 NKJV

Romans 2:25-29 reminds me of a personal story. One of my good Christian friends, Steve, who happens to be heterosexual, is someone with whom I had worked for a long time. He was in a quandary because he recognized that my life demonstrated the principles of Christ Jesus and yet, at the same time, he knew that I was homosexual. However, no matter how often we discussed this issue, he could not reconcile my homosexuality with my Christianity based on his understanding of the Holy Bible. To be sure, we had discussed this issue for hours and hours. I was willing to do that because he was an analytical person and willing to listen as well as to share his comments in non-judgmental and non-condemning ways.

Steve and I went through all Scriptural aspects even obliquely related to same-sex behaviors in the Bible but to no avail. The breakthrough in understanding did not come for Steve until (thinking of the previously-quoted Romans 2:25-29) I asked him, "Isn't it possible, Steve, that, if the Lord God Almighty can view uncircumcision as circumcision when the uncircumsized person has faith, then could the Lord God Almighty not also view a homosexual person who has faith, and who is righteous in God's sight as a result of that faith, to be equal with a heterosexual person who has faith? If, as the Bible states, circumcision is God's standard and God treats uncircumcision as equivalent to circumcision when the person has faith, could God not also treat the homosexual orientation as equivalent to the heterosexual orientation if the person has faith?"

In other words, although God at one time viewed circumcision as the sign, token, or standard through which people demonstrated that they had a covenant with Him (Genesis 17:11), in this New Covenant dispensation God views uncircumcision the same as circumcision provided that the uncircumcised person's heart, or intent, is in the right place. Concomitantly, could God not also end up in this dispensation to view the homosexual orientation the same as the heterosexual orientation for those people whose love for God, faith in God, and hope in God are not displaced?

Though Steve and I had discussed this issue for many months, these particular questions and the particular scriptural references just quoted created the turning point in understanding for Steve. The Holy Spirit moved in a special way, and Steve said, "Oh, I understand. That makes sense!"

I have learned that, sometimes, the Holy Spirit uses different verses, different passages, or different phrases from the Bible for different people in order to impinge on their consciousness the same basic truth. Steve was helped by understanding, interpreting, and applying Romans 2:25-29 to how God might view the homosexual person as righteous (that is, because the person has faith in Him). For Steve, it was as if the Scripture was rephrased to say, "Therefore, if a homosexual person has faith in the Lord God Almighty, then will his homosexuality not be counted equivalent to heterosexuality?" This, of course, assumes that heterosexuality is God's ideal type, or standard. And perhaps heterosexuality *was* God's standard relative to reproduction and one of His earliest commandments to "be fruitful, and multiply, and replenish the earth" (Genesis 1:28 KJV). But we also know through Scripture that God has special promises for those who do not reproduce. *For example*, God comforts eunuchs, who do not reproduce, in Isaiah 56:3b-5. (Isaiah 56:3b-5 is provided as a quotation on page 157 of this chapter).

To be sure, the Gospel message is a very simple message; but, when we end up reading verses and passages within the Bible like Romans 2:25-29, it is not until the Holy Spirit illuminates and elucidates those passages that we are able to more fully understand their implications and applications. Indeed, to the human mind, Romans 2:25-29 is somewhat obtuse; so, unless the Holy Spirit resides in us and ministers the specific meaning of its particular verses to us, we really cannot understand them. Without instruction from God's Holy Spirit, some Bible verses might seem like double-talk or doublespeak (i.e., convoluted or ambiguous). We must depend on the Holy Spirit for interpretation and meaning relative to all Scripture:

> The natural man does not comprehend the things of the Spirit of God: for they are foolishness to him; neither can he recognize them because they are spiritually discerned.

> 1 Corinthians 2:14 KJV Paraphrase

The reason that I am spending considerable time on this particular issue of Levitical Law versus grace is that, too often, people would have others live according to Levitical Law when the Lord God Almighty has done away with adhering to it as a criterion for entering heaven. Many Christians, both heterosexual people as well as homosexual people, have been deceived into believing that Levitical Law should be obeyed by Christians. They have been deceived into believing that people of the homosexual orientation cannot inherit the Kingdom of God. It is now time to get rid of such stinking thinking.

It is not God's desire for Christians to live according to Levitical Law. So, do not quote Levitical Law to one another as the ideal standard or measure because that would be very dangerous. Dangerous? Yes, it is dangerous to use Levitical Law in order to evaluate or assess the lives of other individuals or to impose its restrictions on others. Galatians 3:10 (KJV Paraphrase) tells us of that danger, and this is what it says: "All who follow the Law are under its curse because it is written, 'Cursed is everyone who does not continue in all things that are written in the book of the Law to accomplish them.'" So, if you think that other people should live by Levitical Law, you actually put that same measure, or standard, on yourself, and then you are cursed because you cannot ever fulfill or live up to the obligations of all of the rules, regulations, and ordinances that are found in Leviticus or, for that matter, in the rest of the Pentateuch. There is only one thing that fulfills Levitical Law and that is sacrificial, selfless, and forgiving love:

{8} Owe no one anything except to love one another, for he who loves another has fulfilled the law. {9} For the commandments, "You shall not commit adultery," "You shall not murder," "You shall not steal," "You shall not bear false witness," "You shall not covet," and if there is any other commandment, are all summed up in this saying, namely, "You shall love your neighbor as yourself." {10} Love does no harm to a neighbor; therefore love is the fulfillment of the law.

Romans 13:8-10 NKJV

The Apostle Paul also states:

{15} We Jews by nature, and not Gentile sinners, {16} know that a person is not justified by the works of the Law but by the faith of Christ Jesus. We have believed in Christ Jesus that we might be justified by the faith of Christ Jesus and not by the works of the Law: for by the works of the law shall no flesh be justified.

Galatians 2:15-16 KJV Paraphrase

Those who try to apply Levitical Law to the lives of others should also seek to understand the following passages:

If you judge others, then you will be judged. The criteria you use to judge others will be used to judge you; and what penalty you dispense, the same will be dispensed to you in return.

Matthew 7:1-2 KJV Paraphrase

You are inexcusable, O man, whoever you are that judges: because you judge another, you condemn yourself; for you that judge do the same thing.

Romans 2:1 KJV Paraphrase

Scripture shows that Christ Jesus himself broke Levitical Law — according to the legalistic views of the people of his day — by working on the Sabbath in direct violation of Leviticus 23:3:

Six days shall work be done: but the seventh day is the sabbath of rest, a holy convocation; you shall do no work during that day: it is the sabbath of the Lord wherever you live.

Leviticus 23:3 KJV Paraphrase

How did Christ Jesus "work" on the Sabbath day? He healed the sick on the Sabbath (John 7:23). And he permitted his disciples to pick grain on the Sabbath:

At that time, Jesus went on the sabbath day through the cornfield; and his disciples were hungry, and they began to pluck the ears of corn, and to eat them. But when the Pharisees saw this action, they said to Jesus, "Behold, your disciples do that which is not lawful to do on the sabbath day."

Matthew 12:1-2 KJV Paraphrase

Responding to these legalists, Christ Jesus reminded them that even King David also broke Levitical Law when he ate bread that had been consecrated to the Lord (Matthew 12:3-4; see also 1 Samuel 21:6 and Leviticus 24:5 and 9).

Not only did Christ Jesus fail to enforce Levitical Law when he prevented the adulteress from being stoned (John 8:3-7; see also Leviticus 20:10), he changed, or altered, the Law by challenging the crowd to examine themselves first before they judged her. To be sure, Christ Jesus elevated the Law to a higher level, or more spiritual plane, when he taught:

"You have heard that it was said by those of long ago, 'You shall not murder, and whoever murders will be in danger of condemnation.' But I say to you, 'Whoever is angry with his brother without a cause will be in danger of condemnation. And whoever swears at his brother will be in danger of condemnation, and whoever belittles another person will be in danger of the fires of hell.'"

Matthew 5:21-22 KJV Paraphrase

"You have heard that it was said by those of long ago, 'You shall not commit adultery:' But I say to you, 'Whoever looks at a woman to lust after her has already committed adultery with her in his heart.'"

Matthew 5:27-28 KJV Paraphrase

"You have heard that it was said, 'An eye for an eye, and a tooth for a tooth' {from Exodus 21:24; Leviticus 24:20; and Deuteronomy 19:21}. But I say to you, 'You should not resist evil. Instead, when someone hits you on your right cheek, then turn your left cheek to him or her as well.'" {brackets mine}

Matthew 5:38-39 KJV Paraphrase

"You have heard that it was said, 'Love your neighbor and hate your enemy' {from Leviticus 19:18}. But I tell you, 'Love your enemies, bless those who curse you, do good to those who hate you, and pray for those who exploit you so that you may be the children of your Father in heaven.'" {brackets mine}

Matthew 5:43-45a KJV Paraphrase

Relative to the issue of Levitical Law versus faith, the Apostle Paul wrote:

Who can boast? By what law? By the law of works? No, but by the law of faith. Therefore, we conclude that a person is justified by faith {i.e., made righteous in God} without the deeds of the law. {brackets mine}

Romans 3:27-28 KJV Paraphrase

Titus 3:9 (NLT) gives this good advice to Christians: "Do not get involved in foolish discussions about spiritual pedigrees or in quarrels and fights about obedience to Jewish laws. These kinds of things are useless and a waste of time."

Understanding Biblical Contexts for Laws Regarding Forbidden Sexual Liaisons, Gender Norms, and Eunuchs

So, why the seemingly hard-line stance by God in Torah concerning same-sex behavior, cross-dressing (transvestitism), and eunuchs (castrated males)?

As I stated earlier, in the case of both male and female temple cult prostitutes, God is against all activity that is associated with idolatrous worship — no matter what the activity happens to be. All fertility religions during Old Testament times and early New Testament times incorporated ceremonial practices that involved ritualistic sexual immorality (including anal intercourse among members of the same sex as well as opposite sex), cross dressing, and even self-mutilation through castration. Let's now consider further the role that these cult practices had in terms of shaping Levitical Law.

Forbidden Sexual Liaisons

It has already been indicated in the previous chapter that male temple cult prostitution played a substantial role in the worship of fertility gods and goddesses. Let us now consider 1 Kings 14:24. This is an important enough verse to *italicize* a particular key phrase that helps provide an interpretive link to one of the two verses in Leviticus commonly used against homosexuality and homosexual people:

> And there were also sodomites in the land; and they did according to all the abominations of *the nations which the Lord {had} cast out before the children of Israel*. [italics and brackets mine]

> 1 Kings 14:24 KJV

... and male prostitutes were found in the land; they followed all of the abominations of *the peoples which the Lord dispossessed before the Israelites*. {italics mine}

1 Kings 14:24 ML

... and there were also male cult prostitutes in the land. They did according to the abominations of *the nations which the Lord drove out before the people of Israel*.

1 Kings 14:24 RS

There was homosexuality throughout the land, and the people of Judah became as depraved as *the heathen nations which the Lord drove out to make room for His people*.

1 Kings 14:24 LB

Regardless of Bible translation or version, we now know from the foundation provided in Chapter Four of this book that 1 Kings 14:24 really states that "there were male temple cult prostitutes in the land." Any translation or rendering other than "male temple cult prostitutes" or "male shrine prostitutes" is not accurate or precise enough for translating the Hebrew word *Qadeshim*, or *Qadasheem* {H6945 plural} (see Table Seven) — the male temple cult prostitutes who were used in ceremonial sexual rituals for Ashtoreth, Baal, Molech and various other fertility gods and goddesses worshiped throughout Old Testament and early New Testament times (even as late as the fifth century A.D.). So, in looking at 1 Kings 14:24 (KJV Paraphrase), it states, "there were also male temple cult prostitutes in the land who did according to all the *abominations* (Hebrew *Toevot* {H8441 plural}, or the "idolatrous practices") of *the nations which the Lord {had} cast out before the children of Israel*." {italics, parentheses, and brackets mine}

The key phrase in italics in the last sentence of the previous paragraph is "the nations which the Lord {had} cast out before the children of Israel." "{Had} cast out," "dispossessed," "drove out," and "had driven

144

out" from other versions of 1 Kings 14:24 are translated from the past tense of the Hebrew verb *yarash* [H3423]. In other words, there were male temple cult prostitutes in the land who did according to the abominations (i.e., idolatrous practices) of the nations which the Lord God Almighty *had already* — that is, "by then" — cast out from the Promised Land.[51]

The reader will begin to see how important 1 Kings 14:24 is as a link to help interpret the Levitical reference in verse 22 of Chapter Eighteen that many people think applies to modern-day homosexual people, homosexuality, and the homosexual orientation.

Before we turn to Leviticus 18:22, let me remind you that holding the whole Bible while simultaneously attending to its various parts is imperative in order to understand Scripture. Also, when we interpret the Bible, we need to look at the literary context in which a particular verse is found, not only in terms of surrounding verses, but also cross references and links to it in other places within the Bible as well; and, of course, we need to look at each verse relative to its historical context. Why? Because, when taken alone, individual Bible verses often only present part of the truth. It is the entire Bible that imparts the whole truth. That is why we need to cherish and study the entire book. To understand, interpret, and apply Scripture, we need to abide by the dictum, "To proof text without context is pretext."

Do I believe that the Bible is the inspired word of God? Yes, I believe that the Bible is the inspired word of God, but I also believe that we need to attend to everything it says with equal emphasis. Yes, *everything with equal emphasis*, and not just selectively take out of context what we want to take out. One of the reasons that Christianity has so many denominations is because of selective interpretation and selective misinterpretation as well as selective application and selective misapplication. The Bible's truth is inerrant but only when it is properly contextualized.

---

51   1 Kings 14:24 refers to the time of King Rehoboam of Judah, who was Solomon's son. To put this in proper chronology, Solomon reigned from 961 through 922 BC, approximately 350 years after the children of Israel entered the Promised Land in 1273 BC. So, God is speaking, as recorded in 1 Kings 14:24, approximately 400 years after Leviticus 18:21-24 was recorded — at which time (in Leviticus 18:24) the Lord God Almighty prophesied that He would later cast the pagan nations out of the Promised Land that the nation of Israel would enter.

Let's begin by sharing Leviticus 18:22 in its immediate context:

{21} Do not give any of your children to be sacrificed to Molech [a fertility god], for you must not profane the name of your God. I make this pronouncement because I am the Lord [i.e., "I am *Yahweh*"]. {22} Do not lie with a man as one lies with a woman; that is detestable [i.e., "an idolatrous practice"]. {23} Neither shall you lie with any beast to defile yourself therewith: neither shall any woman stand before a beast to lie down thereto: it is confusion. {24} Defile not yourselves in any of these things: for in all these *the nations are defiled which I {am going to} cast out before you.* [brackets and italics mine]

Leviticus 18:21-24 KJV Paraphrase

In reading Leviticus 18:21-24, you can see that it starts with, "You must not profane the name of the Lord God Almighty by sacrificing your children to the fertility god Molech." Remember that Molech is one of the Canaanite fertility gods, and that profaning the Lord's name includes worshiping false gods through sexual acts committed with male temple cult prostitutes dedicated to those false gods (addressed in verse 22) and ritual acts committed with temple cult animals dedicated to fertility as well (addressed in verse 23).

Table Thirteen shows Leviticus 18:22 in Hebrew with its transliteration and corresponding phrase meanings:

Leviticus 18:22

כב וְאֶת-זָכָר--לֹא תִשְׁכַּב, מִשְׁכְּבֵי אִשָּׁה: תּוֹעֵבָה, הִוא.

ve'et zakhar lo tishkav mishkeve ishah toevah hi

HebrewPhrase	Transliteration	Meaning
וְאֶת-זָכָר	*ve'et zakhar*	"and [with] a male"
לֹא תִשְׁכַּב	*lo tishkav*	"do not bed"
מִשְׁכְּבֵי אִשָּׁה	*mishkeve ishah*	"lyings of a woman"
תּוֹעֵבָה הִוא	*toevah hi*	"it [is an] idolatrous practice (or ritual uncleanness)"

Table Thirteen

The phrase *"mishkeve ishah"* is used in the Holy Bible only in Leviticus 18:22 and in Leviticus 20:13. Its precise meaning, given here as "lyings of a woman," is debatable.

How do we know that the male-male sex indicated in verse 22 is with male temple cult prostitutes? First, through the literary shift away from illicit sexual activities with relatives, near relatives, step-relatives, in-laws, and neighbors in verses 6 through 20 of Leviticus 18 to the worship of the fertility god Molech in verse 21. Second, because of the presence of the Hebrew word *Toevah* {H8441 singular} in verse 22 that signals idolatry and practices associated with it (imprecisely translated in the King James Version as "abomination" and in other versions as "detestable" or "abhorrent"). And, third, through the important link that exists between 1 Kings 14:24 and Leviticus 18:24: Leviticus 18:24 reads, "Do not defile yourselves with any of these things (including the idolatrous activities in verses 21, 22, and 23) that defiled the nations *I am going to cast out before you.*" Because this "casting" is future tense, the phrase *I am going to cast out before you* can also be translated "which I will cast out before you," referring to the same Canaanite nations in 1 Kings 12:24 "which the Lord *had cast out* before the children of Israel" (partly because of the idolatrous worship practices of the male temple cult prostitutes, which God specifically refers to in the beginning of 1 Kings 12:24 by using the Hebrew word *Qadeshim*, or *Qadasheem* {H6945 plural}, mistranslated in the KJV as *sodomites*).

Again, what important link exists between 1 Kings 14:24 and Leviticus 18:24? In 1 Kings 14:24, the Lord explains what specifically was included as defiling the nations for which cause in Leviticus 18:24 He promised He was going to cast them out (i.e., *cast the nations out*).

Then, considering the link that exists between 1 Kings 14:24 and Leviticus 18:24, as well as the lead-in of Leviticus 18:21, what is the context of Leviticus 18:22?

The context is that "they {the male temple cult prostitutes} did according to all of the abominations {that is, the idolatrous practices} of the nations which the Lord *had cast out* before the children of Israel" (1 Kings 14:24 NKJV {brackets and italics mine}). This is significant because it gives us insight into what type of male-male sex is signaled in Leviticus 18:22 through its cross-reference to Leviticus 18:24 (". . . for by all these {practices} the nations are defiled which I *am going to cast out* before you").

Had homosexuality been the reason that the Lord cast out the nations before the children of Israel, the Lord would not have referred specifically to male temple cult prostitution in 1 Kings 14:24. Thus are we provided in 1 Kings 14:24 with the important link to Leviticus 18:22 that God is referring to male-male sex in the context of temple cult prostitution. And just because I am using the expression "male-male sex" does not mean that the sexual activity took place between homosexual people. Just because two males share sexual activity does not mean that they each have a homosexual orientation.

Further, in Leviticus 18:21-24, all four verses must be taken together. The phrase ". . . for by *all these things* . . ." in Leviticus 18:24 {italics mine} includes the idolatrous worship of Molech explicitly stated in verse 21 and the pagan practices incorporated into such worship, which practices included the murderous sacrifices of children (verse 21) as well as sexual relations between male idol worshipers and male temple cult prostitutes (verse 22) as well as between both male and female idol worshipers and temple cult animals (verse 23).

So, in reading Leviticus 18:21-24 relative to 1 Kings 14:24, we have gone back to an earlier time, and the Lord God Almighty is saying "these idolatrous people are doing abominable things (that is, involving themselves in idolatrous practices), and, because of the things that they are doing, I am going to cast them out as you enter their land." Thus, the literary and historical contexts provide this most important Biblical link to help us understand God's seemingly hard-line stance against same-sex activities in Leviticus. What's the context for the male-male sex that's mentioned in verse 22? An idolatrous one! Verse 21 is an introductory sentence. Although those verses do not form what we think of as a paragraph in modern-day terms, verse 21 provides a literary shift away from the forbidden sexual liaisons with family and neighbors referred to in the earlier verses of Chapter Eighteen (verses 6 through 20). Verse 21 is an introductory sentence to a discussion of fertility god worship to the same degree that verse 6 is an introductory sentence to a discussion of forbidden sexual liaisons with family members and neighbors.

Although the Bible is not written in paragraph form, verse 21 is an introduction to a subsection that starts with the fertility god Molech. How was Molech worshiped? Molech was worshiped in all sorts of unseemly ways. *For example*, sometimes worshipers went so far as to actually sacrifice their children to Molech by "passing them through the fire" (that is, burning them to death). This is the context in which verses 22 through 24 have been written in Chapter Eighteen of Leviticus. To be sure, male cult prostitution and idolatrous bestiality were common within houses of worship dedicated to Molech as well as in the houses of worship dedicated to other pagan fertility gods and goddesses.

All mainstream Bible scholars have access to what I have just stated. Following is one example using Volume Two of *The Expositors Bible*. I am purposely quoting from its 1900 edition to show the reader that this is not a recently contrived view born of a modern "gay theology" or so-called gay agenda. The 1900 edition is a 25-volume set used as a study tool and reference aid in the libraries of many Bible colleges, schools, seminaries, and institutes in the early twentieth century. *Volume Two* covers Leviticus and Numbers. Here is what was written in 1900 concerning the Levitical references to "abominable" sex:

The inconceivably unnatural crimes prohibited in verses 22, 23 [meaning, the specified male-male sex and bestiality] were in like manner [like verse 21] essentially connected with idolatrous worship; the former [the male-male aspect] with the worship of Astarte or Ashtoreth [remember that it was the high priests and priestesses of Ashtoreth that actually ended up worshiping the Asherah, which was a pole, stone, or totem shaped like a phallus, or penis, by offering up sexual "sacrifices" as temple cult prostitutes] and the latter [in reference to idolatrous bestiality] with the worship of the he-goat at Mendes in Egypt as the symbol of the generative power in nature. What a hideous perversion of the moral sense was involved in these crimes, as thus connected with idolatrous worship, is illustrated strikingly by the fact that men and women, thus prostituted to the service of false gods, were designated by the terms *qadesh* [male], *qadeshah* [female], "sacred" or "holy!" No wonder that the sacred writer brands these horrible crimes, as in a peculiar and almost solitary sense, "abomination" and "confusion."[52]

Regarding these and other unlawful sexual relations, it is recorded that the Lord God Almighty commanded Moses to do the following:

{1} And the Lord spoke to Moses, saying, {2} "Speak to the children of Israel, and say to them, 'I am the Lord your God. {3} After the practices of the land of Egypt, where you dwelt, you must not be involved: and after the practices of the land of Canaan, where I am bringing you, you must not be involved: neither will you obey their ordinances.

Leviticus 18:1-3 KJV Paraphrase

My discourse on the same-sex question in Leviticus 18:22 is summarized in the following table — which is intentionally on one page so that it might be easily photocopied and used as a handout for small or large group discussion purposes.

---

52   Nicoll, Reverend W. Robertson (editor). *The Expositor's Bible*, Volume 2, Funk and Wagnalls, New York, 1900, pages 387-388. [all brackets mine]

The Pearson Amplification and Paraphrase of Leviticus 18:3 & 21-24 with Reference to 1 Kings 14:24

Leviticus 18:3, 21, 22, 23, & 24

{3} You must not do as they do in Egypt, where you used to live, and you must not do as they do in the land of Canaan, where I am bringing you. Do not follow any of their pagan, barbaric, and idolatrous practices.

{21} You should not dedicate your seed [neither sperm nor children] to the fertility god Molech. This profanes the Name of your God. I DECLARE THIS BECAUSE I AM YAHWEH. {22} You men should not dedicate your seed to any fertility god by sowing seed with a male temple cult prostitute as you would sow seed with a woman. This idolatrous practice causes you to be unclean. {23} And both men and women will be ritually unclean if they cross the species barrier and have so-called sacred sex with temple cult animals. {24} Do not make yourselves unclean by any of these practices; for in all these pagan, barbaric, and idolatrous practices the nations are defiled, which nations I *will cast out* before you.

Author's Note: Who were the overseers of all three of the activities described in verses 21, 22, and 23 of Leviticus 18? The answer comes from 1 Kings 14:24. The individuals in question were the *Qadeshim*, the so-called "sacred ones," "holy ones," or "priests" of the fertility religions, more accurately referred to as *temple cult prostitutes*. It was because of the idolatrous practices of these cult prostitutes that the Lord God cast out the pagan nations from the land.

1 Kings 14:24

{24} And there were also temple cult prostitutes in the land: and they involved themselves in all the pagan, barbaric, and idolatrous practices of the nations which the Lord *had cast out* before the children of Israel.

What is most disturbing is that interpretations such as the one just given have been around for more than a century (*for example*, in the 1900 edition of *The Expositor's Bible*), but these explanations are just pushed to the side in order to permit the promulgation of a particular agenda against homosexual people, which, to be sure, is a socio-political agenda born out of religious legalism as well as personal distaste and arrogance.

Yes, some people are ignorant of what it means to be homosexual. And because they are ignorant of what it means to be homosexual, they assume that the homosexual orientation must be unnatural. People who are not homosexual assume that others who are homosexual must be depraved or perverted because thoughts and ideas of companionship with someone of the same sex are abhorrent, distasteful, and foreign to them (i.e., to the people who are not homosexual). Of course, they are abhorrent, distasteful, and foreign to heterosexual people, but that doesn't mean that they are wrong for those people of the homosexual orientation. Nor does it mean that the Bible condemns modern-day homosexual people.

Regarding the promulgation of such a one-sided perspective, I fault less the people who attend church in ignorance of the Bible and who are being fed from the pulpit one perspective and one perspective only regarding homosexuality. On whose shoulders I think the culpability rests are the pastors, teachers, and Bible scholars who allow a certain viewpoint to be presented relative to this particular issue without ever presenting an alternate hypothesis or view. This does a great disservice to the gospel of Christ Jesus. Why is it a disservice? Because many homosexual people — as well as people sympathetic to their plight — are kept from the cross of Christ. Many are kept from accepting the shed blood of the Lamb of God, Christ Jesus. They are hindered because they end up believing either that God doesn't love them or that God cannot be an honorable God if preachers and ministers of His gospel foster such hatred and condemnation in their own perverse anti-gay agenda.

Do you know what it means to be a homosexual person and sit in a church only to hear a pastor or a preacher say that you are depraved and are bound for hell? Indeed, you would not sit in that church for very long. And, if you are not saved, you may exit that church before you ever really hear (that is, understand) the gospel message. As a result of that, you might decide (and I have known people who have decided this), "Well, if I am going to hell, then I am going to hell *real good*." And, they do that exactly! This is not to negate that homosexual people have individual responsibility; it is to remind Christians everywhere that they have the responsibility to reach out to each and every other person in order to bring them to the cross of Christ by demonstrating Christ in their lives through loving others at the same time that they share the gospel message — which is the good news that atonement has been given for us all through the substitutionary offering of the perfect and blameless only-begotten Son of God, Christ Jesus. If you are a heterosexual Christian, you will not be able to effectively minister to homosexual people if you condemn, judge, or disparage them.

Those of you who know the Bible could very well be asking now, "So why the double reference to male-male sex in both Leviticus 18:21 and Leviticus 20:13?"

Leviticus 20:13 states:

If a man lies with mankind as he lies with a woman ["lies with a woman" translated here from *mishkeve ishah*], both of them have committed an abomination [*abomination* translated here from *Toevah* (H8441 singular)]: they shall surely be put to death; their blood [i.e., guilt] shall be upon them. [brackets mine]

Leviticus 20:13 KJV Paraphrase

Simply stated, Chapter Eighteen of Leviticus identifies the "crime" of committing the idolatrous offense and Chapter Twenty of Leviticus prescribes the "punishment" for committing the crime. In other words, the ancient Jews read the nature of the crimes in Chapters Eighteen and Nineteen and, then, looked up their corresponding punishment in Chapter Twenty (the so-called "Penal Code"). Please keep in mind that, although the Bible is inspired by the Holy Spirit, the chapters of the Bible are man-made and, thus, artificial.

As you read, and reread, Chapters Eighteen and Nineteen in Leviticus, you will find that they contain a listing of various crimes against God. Chapter Twenty is the so-called penal code in Leviticus; therefore, it restates most of the crimes from Chapters Eighteen and Nineteen and, in addition, lists the punishment for each particular crime. It is as if you went to court and the judge opened up one book and said, "Well, I see that you have violated section so-and-so of a particular ordinance;" and, then, the judge would take out a different book containing the penal code (that is, the list of punishments) and say, "Since you have violated the law by breaking section so-and-so of the ordinance, hear now the punishment (or possible punishments) for the crime according to our law."

This is the reason there is a double reference to male-male sex in Chapters Eighteen and Twenty of Leviticus. The Chapter Eighteen reference states the so-called crime, and the Chapter Twenty reference indicates the punishment for that particular crime. I recommend that you read, and reread, Chapters Eighteen and Nineteen ("the crimes") and Chapter Twenty ("the punishments") to confirm for yourself the written division between the identified crimes and their prescribed punishments.

The sum of the entire matter of Levitical Law and grace is threefold:

1. Christians are not under Levitical Law; they are under grace.

2. Levitical Law never addresses same-sex relationships between women.

3. Levitical Law does not address Christian male homosexual people who are in committed, monogamous, and covenant-based relationships.

Christians who fail to understand God's grace have either been blinded by Satan or they have blinded themselves because they are arrogant and, therefore, satisfied with their own ignorance. In the final analysis, ignorance on any topic is the lack of an inquiring mind, especially when information is available on the topic.

The Bible and Gender Norms

Biblical quotations often used against exceptions to gender norms include Genesis 1:27 and 28a:

So God created man {humankind} in his own image, in the image of God He created him; He created them male and female. {brackets mine}

Genesis 1:27 KJV Paraphrase

God blessed them, and God said to them, "Be fruitful, and multiply, and replenish the earth, and subdue it…" {brackets mine}

Genesis 1:28a KJV Paraphrase

To be sure, the previously-quoted passages express the general rule but are neither universal nor absolute. Exceptions to this general rule are found both in nature and in Scripture itself.

From a biological standpoint, the presence or absence of genitals is a state of nature, and gender is a state of mind. These two states are ultimately responsible for an individual's instincts. In this work, I refer to the kind of external and internal sexual organs that one possesses as "genital identity," and I refer to the kind of gender one views oneself having as "gender identity."

Considering both *genital identity* and *gender identity*, if you think that people who are transgender[53] are perversions of nature, then you have made "male and female" an absolute or universal law that is contradictory to the full spectrum of what occurs: 1) in nature, 2) in the Holy Bible, and 3) in the realm of the Holy Spirit:

1. In nature, such an absolute fails to take into consideration the myriad departures in biology that deviate from the norm (*norm*

---

53   *Transgender* is a word whose meaning is still in flux. The word is currently used as an umbrella term applied to a variety of individuals, behaviors, and groups that vary from what is traditionally accepted in a particular culture.

defined here as "that which occurs most frequently" as opposed to the connotation of "normal" versus "abnormal").

2. In the Bible, such an absolute also fails to take into consideration departures from males and females in Biblical references to eunuchs.

3. In the realm of the Holy Spirit, such an absolute fails to take into consideration spiritual law stating that in Christ "there is neither male nor female" (Galatians 3:28). Spiritually speaking, God does not discriminate between individuals using the criteria of genital identity and gender identity. Certainly, in heaven such distinctions do not exist. As recorded in Matthew 22:30 (KJV Paraphrase), Christ Jesus said, "In the resurrection, people neither marry nor are given in marriage, but are as the angels of God in heaven."

True science does not contradict pure religion nor does pure religion contradict true science. True science shows that there are exceptions to the so-called absolute Biblical rule (Genesis 1:27) of "male and female" genital identity in the form of intersexuals; and pure religion shows that there are exceptions to that rule in the form of eunuchs — of whom, Christ Jesus said, "[some eunuchs are] so born from their mother's womb" (Matthew 19:12 KJV [brackets mine]). For the sake of clarity, an intersexual is defined here as "a person whose biological sex is ambiguous at the biochemical level, genetic level, chromosomal level, and/or anatomic level.")

In other words, intersexuals serve as biological prototypes for homosexual people and transgender people; and eunuchs serve as scriptural prototypes for homosexual people and transgender people. Thus, God accounts for exceptions to the general rule of "male and female" both naturally (i.e., biologically) and Biblically. The word *prototype* used here means "an original type, form, or instance that is a model on which later stages are based or judged;" it can also mean "an early typical example."[54] In other words, a prototype provides a pattern for understanding because it serves as an example of a future class. For the sake of clarification, I do not mean to imply that Biblical or Talmudic eunuchs are homosexual people and/or transgender people. If

54 Webster's, *op. cit.*, page 947.

you research the criteria used for identifying eunuchs in the Babylonian Talmud, you will find only physical criteria and not psychological or sociological criteria given to identify someone as a eunuch.

The Holy Bible not only acknowledges that there are exceptions to the rule of anatomic males and females, the Holy Bible also acknowledges that there are exceptions to the directive for them to reproduce. In other words, not all human beings are expected by God to "be fruitful and multiply." If anatomic males and anatomic females were a universal law, and the directive to reproduce was an absolute, God would not have consoled eunuchs the way He does in Chapter Fifty-Six of Isaiah:

{3b} The eunuch must not say, "Behold, I am a dry tree" {*dry tree* connoting the inability to reproduce}. {4} For thus says the Lord to the eunuchs who keep My sabbaths, and choose what pleases Me, and abide by My covenant. {5} "I will give to them in My house and within My walls a place and a name better than of sons and of daughters {*sons and daughters* here referring to those who do reproduce}: I will give them an everlasting name that will not be cut off" [the expression *cut off* is *double entendre* because it also alludes to the eunuch who has had something *cut off*}. {brackets mine}

Isaiah 56:3b-5 KJV Paraphrase

So, why the seemingly hard-line stance when God states:

A woman shall not wear anything that pertains to a man, nor shall a man put on a woman's garment, for all who do so are an abomination to the Lord your God.

Deuteronomy 22:5 NKJV

Why did God take such a hard-line stance against cross-dressing, or transvestitism? Surely, God is omniscient; our Creator knows that various cultures and traditions have different forms of dress. And, certainly, since civilization and culture have evolved in the ways that they have, we find there really is less and less distinction concerning different kinds of apparel for males and for females — except, perhaps, in some countries that are just now economically-emerging and/or governed by Sharia, or Islamic law.

Is God really unwavering relative to dresses for women and pants for men? Of course not! The word "abomination" in Deuteronomy 22:5 is imprecisely translated from the plural Hebrew word *Toevot* [H8441 plural], which means "idolatrous practices." This clarifies the context for the reference in Deuteronomy 22:5 concerning female to male cross-dressing and male to female cross-dressing. More precisely translated from the intended Hebrew meaning, Deuteronomy 22:5 should read, "A woman shall not wear anything that pertains to a man nor shall a man put on a woman's garments in idolatrous practices or with the intent to deceive. Such practices are an affront to the Lord your God."

If the King James Version of Deuteronomy 22:5 is taken alone and out of its literary and historical contexts, students of the Bible might easily, albeit incorrectly, fall to condemn transgender people. Certainly, such condemnation is evident in the world today. Again, keep in mind that the word *transgender* has become an umbrella term that often includes both pre-operative and post-operative transsexual people as well as heterosexual cross-dressers and even some performance artists known in Western culture as "drag queens" and "drag kings." Some people in these individual categories have gender dysphoria while others do not. So, the transgender condition is much more complicated than others might have you believe or that you may have concluded for yourself.

It is very unfair to use Deuteronomy 22:5 against transgender people. This verse was written because idolatrous temple practices involved in the worship of fertility cult goddesses included young male prostitutes dressing up as women to emulate the feminine form of their "idol" as well as to more easily attract and better satisfy the procurers of their sexual services. "Procurers" here refers to the males, often heterosexual, who would purchase their services of ritual sexual activity in anal intercourse. So, transvestitism (i.e., cross-dressing) in itself is not bad; it was the ancient context that was evil; it was the idolatrous and deceptive intent of the cross-dressing that God hated.

God does not care about our outer appearance. Instead, what God cares about is what is within our individual hearts. We find this truth provided as a good object lesson in 1 Samuel 16:1-13. As recorded there, the prophet Samuel evaluated the sons of Jesse relative to whom God was going to choose as the second king of the nation of Israel. As the first son, Eliab, passed by, Samuel looked at him and said, "My, this is an impressive individual. Surely, this is the one whom the Lord is going to choose! This must be the one" (1 Samuel 16:6). However, God's Holy Spirit responded to the prophet Samuel by instructing him that God is "no respecter of persons," and that God does not place as much importance on outward appearance as human beings do:

> The Lord said to Samuel, "Do not look at his countenance or at the height of his stature because I have rejected him: for the Lord does not evaluate as a human being evaluates. A human being looks at the outward appearance, but the Lord looks at the heart."

> 1 Samuel 16:7 KJV Paraphrase

In other words, the Lord looks at the inner core of an individual and the intent of his or her heart. According to God, the true stature — or measure — of a person is determined by how much sacrificial, selfless, and forgiving love is in his or her heart. It is very important for us to understand that our human body is merely an outward expression that may or may not reflect our inner core attitudes, desires, or intents accurately. That is why God is not impressed by our outward appearance, and that is why God does not show favoritism based on it.

Indeed, our physical appearance is not impressive to God. Our personality is not impressive to God either. God is not influenced by our genital identity, sexual orientation, or gender identity. God does not really care about any of these things unless, of course, we are not acting in a holy manner in relation to them, or we are not acting in keeping with what it is God would have us to do relative to them. To be sure, abuses related to our physicality — such as vanity, self-loathing, deception (that is, presenting ourselves as other than who or what we are) — are repugnant to the Lord God Almighty. It is alright for homosexual people and transgender people to not disclose who they are to those people: 1) who would physically harm them; 2) who might put them in jeopardy by disclosing who they are to others that, in turn, would endanger their livelihood or well-being; or 3) who will probably remain casual acquaintances to them.

If we took a decontextualized view of Deuteronomy 22:5 and compared it to 1 Samuel 16:7, it would seem that the Lord God of the Bible is schizophrenic because, on one hand, the Lord says in 1 Samuel 16:7, "No, I look at your heart; I do not look at your outer appearance," and then, on the other hand, if you were to take Deuteronomy 22:5 out of context, it seems that the Lord is saying, "I care more about your outer appearance than the intent of your heart." Well, the God of the Bible is not schizophrenic. The one true and only real Creator-God is much brighter, healthier, and more knowledgeable than we can even imagine. In fact, considering the limitations that we have as human beings, we have little understanding of God's omniscience, perfect emotional health, and complete knowledge to be able to come to a basic understanding of the magnificence and the wonder of God's self-existent intelligence. God understands all things, including intents as well as outcomes. Simply stated, ancient temple cult practices included transvestitism. That is the reason why God was against cross-dressing in Deuteronomy 22:5.

Rabbi Jon-Jay Tilsen provides us with his own Jewish perspective:

The Torah's concern in this verse [Deuteronomy 22:5], then, is not with creating or reinforcing gender differences *per se*, but in preventing gender associations of clothing… from being used to deceive others for purposes leading to sexual immorality. The key here seems to be deception for illicit purposes. Indeed, this law appears in Deuteronomy in the context of laws against deceit.

Rabbi Tilsen continues . . .

While the legal interpretations of this verse from Deuteronomy have been diverse, most of Jewish legal discussion has not taken the verse to suggest a blanket ban or condemnation of what today we call "cross dressing."[55]

---

55   Tilsen, Rabbi Jon-Jay. URL in 2000: www.uscj.org/ctvalley/beki/crossdress.html
       URL in 2014: http://www.beki.org/crossdress.html

If Jews believed in the universal applicability of Deuteronomy 22:5, Rabbi Tilsen acknowledges that they would not be permitted to cross-dress on the festival of Purim, which commemorates the deliverance of the Jewish people throughout the Persian Empire that is recorded in the Biblical Book of Esther.

Further, Rabbi Tilsen states, "… the history of legal interpretation in Jewish law is not unlike that of other legal systems in that judges ultimately must apply the laws to real-life situations and are thus forced to define the terms in a way that will make sense within the framework of their codes, case law and social reality."

The rabbis, priests, and judges of ancient Israel examined the relevancy and contexts of situations before they decided the applicability of the written laws of Moses. Such examination demonstrates the significant intelligence and wisdom that can only be provided through the Self-Existent One, the Lord God Almighty. Indeed, any true intelligence or wisdom we have is derived from God's Holy Spirit, who is the teacher of all truth.

If we consider the Apostle Paul's stance relative to this issue of culturally-accepted gender-related roles and appearances, we find that in 1 Corinthians 11:2 (KJV Paraphrase), he states, "I praise you for remembering me in everything and for keeping the *ordinances* {i.e., teachings or traditions} just as I passed them on to you." {italics and brackets mine}

In verse 6 of that chapter, the Apostle Paul states:

{6} If a woman does not have her head covered, cut off the hair from her head. If it is shameful for a woman's hair to be cut off, then her head should be covered.

And, then, in verses 13 through 15, the Apostle Paul states:

{13} Judge for yourselves: is it appropriate that a woman pray to God with her head uncovered? {14} Does not even nature {*nature* translated from the Greek word *phusis* (G5449)} itself teach you that, if a man has long hair, it is shameful? {15} But if a woman has long hair, it is praiseworthy for her: for her {long} hair is given to her for a covering. {brackets mine}

1 Corinthians 11:6,13-15 KJV Paraphrase

It is very curious that many people might refer to what they think are Biblical injunctions against the homosexual orientation or the transgender condition and they pay absolutely no attention to the idea of women's head coverings in church. Am I advocating that women cover their heads when they pray? No, of course not! We just need to understand the literary, cultural, and historical contexts of the Apostle Paul's injunctions, just as we need to understand that many people apply principles for Biblical interpretation arbitrarily or, at least, selectively.

In order to understand the verses just quoted from 1 Corinthians, Chapter Eleven (verses 6 and 13-15), we need to go back to verse 2 in that chapter. The Apostle Paul said, "I praise you for remembering me in everything and for holding to the *ordinances*." The word *ordinances* in the King James Version is rendered "teachings" in the New Living Translation of the Bible and is translated "traditions" in a number of other English versions of the Bible. The words "ordinances," "teachings," and "traditions" have been translated from the Greek word *paradosis* παράδοσις [G3862], which is defined in *Strong's Concordance* as "Jewish traditionary law."

We know that traditions and customs change. The Lord God Almighty understands that traditions and customs change. Do you *really* think that the Lord God Almighty cares whether a woman has short hair or a man has long hair? Do you *really* think that God cares if we wear unisex clothing? I trust you can answer these questions intelligently for yourself. God only cares about the context. There are positive contexts, negative contexts, and neutral contexts for cross-dressing.

When the Apostle Paul wrote about hair length for males, he certainly was not being circumspect or all-inclusive; he did not even take into consideration the Nazarites (from the Hebrew *Nazirim*), who do not cut their hair as a vow to God (as detailed in Numbers 6:1-21). Although the Jewish Nazarite vow was often of a specific duration, it is recorded in the thirteenth chapter of Judges (verses 5, 7, and 17) that Samson was a Nazarite (or *Nazir*) from his dedication at birth and was not supposed to cut his hair throughout his entire life. Moreover, early recorded eyewitness accounts of the external appearance of Christ Jesus (*for example*, the account by the Roman Publius Lentullus[56]) attribute long hair to him. As part of a living history, we can even see the long sidelocks, or *Payot*, of some Orthodox Jewish men and boys worn today.

Whenever we are tempted to judge another on the basis of their apparel and appearance, we need to remind ourselves that "as many of us as have been baptized into Christ have put on Christ" (Galatians 3:27 KJV Paraphrase). In other words, in the reality of God, when we accept the Lord Jesus Christ as the only-begotten Son of God and our own personal Savior, we are *dressed* in God. We need to remember that in heaven we will be clothed in God's glory! Truly, God cares not one whit, iota, or yod about how we are dressed on earth unless we are not dressed properly for inclement weather.

Again, what God cares most about is what is within our individual hearts. Why? The heart is the central core of each soul. Within the heart, we find one's core attitudes, desires, and intents.

Eunuchs

Let us now return to another verse that, if taken out of context, would pose quite a dilemma for males who have had a bilateral orchiectomy (i.e., both testicles surgically removed) or who have had a penectomy (i.e., the penis surgically removed):

> He that is wounded in the stones {i.e., testicles} or has his privy member {i.e., penis} cut off, shall not enter into the congregation of the Lord. {brackets mine}

> Deuteronomy 23:1 KJV

To be sure, some ancient cult practices involved castration. Why would pagan devotees castrate themselves? They did so in order to emulate the fertility goddesses they served, including Ashtoreth, Cybele, Aphrodite, Astarte, Magna Mater, Ma, and others. These fertility goddesses were all catered to by transvestite male temple cult prostitutes who devoted

---

56   *The Oldest Views and Literary Data on the External Appearance of Jesus: The Description of Publius Lentullus*, URL in 2010: http://www.thenazareneway.com/likeness_of_our_saviour.htm

CHRISTIANITY AND HOMOSEXUALITY RECONCILED

themselves to the life-long worship of them. In order to please their goddesses, the transvestite male temple cult prostitutes wanted to make their bodies physically resemble the feminine form of the deity they idolized. To show their extreme devotion, they also presented their severed organs as a coveted offering to them. This they did in order to make a permanent covenant with the goddess they each worshiped.

For these transvestite male temple cult prostitutes, there were two common castration options or practices: One practice was to break a clay pot and, from the shattered pieces, to take a shard and cut the testicles off (and sometimes the penis as well) in honor of the fertility goddess(es) they served. Another practice was to take the testicles and crush them in between two stones or rocks in order to render oneself a physiologic and, to a certain extent (i.e., without the cutting), an anatomic eunuch.

In the King James Version, Deuteronomy 23:1 is translated, "He who is wounded in the stones ["stones" meant "testicles" in Early Modern English] or has his privy member cut off ["privy member" here refers to "private member," or "penis"] shall not enter into the congregation of the Lord." Taken out of literary and historical contexts, that is an extremely harsh punishment — as well as a very puzzling penalty — relative to contemporary thinking. *For example*, there have been accidents in the game of football or soccer in which a player has actually had to have one or both testicles removed because of damage sustained during the accident. Does that mean, based on the Law of Moses, that he should not be a part of the congregation of the Lord? No, the Law of Moses needs to be properly contextualized before it is applied to this or any other situation.

The reason that God did not want a male who had his penis cut off, or his testes crushed or removed, to enter into His congregation at that time was because such mutilation was characteristically done in honor of pagan fertility goddesses. Of course, they were extreme tokens of the personal commitment and covenant vows made by pagan people to their idols. These actions disgusted God — as they should disgust God. They were, and still are, "detestable," "abhorrent," and "abominable" to Him because of their association with idolatry. Indeed, these practices were detestably, abhorrently, and abominably *idolatrous*. God hated this self-mutilation because, though unknown to most of its practitioners, it broke the First Commandment by seeking to bring honor to Satan and not to the Lord God Almighty.

Concerning the damaged testicles referred to in Deuteronomy 23:1, there is a different reference relative to blemishes in general in Leviticus 21:16-20, repeated here for quick reference although it was quoted earlier:

{16} And the Lord said to Moses, {17} "Speak to Aaron, saying, 'Whoever of your descendants has a blemish must not serve in the capacity of priest. {18} This includes those who are blind or lame as well as anyone who has a deformity, {19} including a deformity of the foot or hand, {20} or those who have deformities of the spine or are dwarves, or that has an impairment in his vision, or is deformed in any way, or has a skin disease, or has his testicles damaged.'"

Leviticus 21:16-20 KJV Paraphrase

Doesn't that sound somewhat strange? In terms of contemporary society and the understanding the Lord Jesus has brought through God's Holy Spirit, you know that the Lord God Almighty would not prevent a dwarf from approaching Him in prayer or keep a little person from salvation. Why did it matter in ancient times? It mattered then because the Lord God Almighty was trying to convey to quite unsophisticated people that He is worthy of unblemished and perfect sacrifices. He did not mean that He was rejecting these people forever, just that they were not to serve in priestly roles in Old Testament times if they were disabled or disfigured. So, even though Leviticus 21:20 and Deuteronomy 23:1 both include eunuchs, Deuteronomy 23:1 is really speaking of those who have self-mutilated in order to honor fertility goddesses and Leviticus 21:20 is speaking about those of the children of Israel who were "blemished" accidentally or congenitally. To be sure, at that time the Lord God Almighty was trying to convey that He is worthy of perfect sacrifices, the embodiment of which would later be found in the sacrifice of Christ Jesus on the cross as the pure and perfect "Lamb of God" (John 1:29 and 36).

A blanket statement that eunuchs cannot enter into the congregation of the Lord is definitely not true. It is neither true that Deuteronomy 23:1 has universal application nor that it is relevant to today's dispensation. We do know that, if God were really against eunuchs, they would not have been consoled by Him in Isaiah 56:3b-5 (the full citation is provided earlier in this chapter). In Deuteronomy 23:1, the Lord stated that He didn't want eunuchs to be a part of His congregation and, yet, in Isaiah 56:3b-5, He comforts them, saying "do not lament that you are not able to reproduce because, if you keep My judgments and My precepts, and if you honor My laws, I am going to give you an everlasting name, — a name better than those who do reproduce, and one that will not be cut off!"

It is important for us to note that God clearly signals that He views eunuchs as a third kind, or third gender, by making a distinction between them and "sons and daughters" (Isaiah 56:5 KJV). In the same verse, God tells eunuchs who worship Him that He will give them "a name better than sons and daughters."

"What's in a name?" you might ask. Biblically-speaking, a name embodies the character and identity of an individual. Consider the many Biblical names that incorporate "-el" (meaning, "God") or "-yah" (a shortened form for "Yahweh" that is also spelled "-iah"). Names like "Ezeki-el" and "Dani-el" and "Isa-iah" and "Jerem-iah." Such names speak of dedication to — as well as identity in and through — the Lord God Almighty. The Bible teaches us that, when we are in heaven, we will have a new name given to us:

> To the person that overcomes… I will give a white stone, and in the stone a new name written, which no one knows except the person who receives it.
>
> Revelation 2:17 KJV Paraphrase

As "Lord" and "Savior," Christ Jesus has the best name in heaven. Perhaps people who have better names than others in heaven will be those who stayed faithful to God despite trials, tribulations, persecutions, and spiritual, emotional, and physical assassination. Maybe a blind, quadriplegic Christian lesbian will have a better name in heaven than someone who enjoyed a more privileged and carefree existence. Of course, I do not know. But, based on Scripture, I think it possible — especially since we know that everything is reversed in the Kingdom of God: the *first* here are *last* there; the *last* here are *first* there; those who are humble here are great there; those who are arrogant and proud here are humbled there; those who are poor here are rich there; and, finally, those who are rich and selfish here are poor there (see Matthew 19:30).

In terms of the nomenclature of God, our names really have great significance. Not the earthly or human appellations that we use today. Rather, when we get to heaven, we are going to have names that are representative of who we are in God and what we did for God on earth to further the gospel and, therefore, bring more honor, glory, and praise to His Holy Name. Why should someone who has had an extra burden in life receive a "better name" than someone who has been less burdened? Simply stated, because they have clung to God despite the difficulties they experienced.

To be sure, some people on this planet live more privileged lives than others. And, although God loves everyone the same, and although, when we are made righteous in God's sight, we are all made the same (that is, "justified"), God also recognizes that some people cling to Him despite great adversity (and, perhaps, because of it), and in spite of people telling them that they have no right to cling. Our Lord is both touched emotionally as well as honored spiritually by such dependence on Him. And, because God is honored by it, He chooses to honor them in return (see John 12:26). Although the wages are the same for every authentic Christian believer (*wages* referring to the salvation of our souls), rewards in heaven for individuals are different based on their works of faith.

Sometimes, I am asked questions by people who are struggling with the issue of Christianity and homosexuality relative to the idea that all should reproduce, be fruitful, and stock the earth. I always tell them that the earth is already fully stocked; and, in addition to making that point, I instruct them that, in the Holy Bible, there are eunuchs who represent non-reproducing individuals, whom the Lord specifically blesses — as recorded in Isaiah 56:3b-5.

In addition to those eunuchs blessed by the Lord in Isaiah 56:3b-5, the Lord also blessed a eunuch in the New Testament by granting him repentance through the knowledge of salvation:

{26} The angel of the Lord spoke to Philip, saying, "Arise, and go toward the south to the desert route that goes from Jerusalem to Gaza." {27} Philip arose and went and found a man of Ethiopia, a eunuch of great authority under the Ethiopian Queen, Candace. The eunuch was responsible for all of her treasure, and had come to Jerusalem to worship. {28} At this time, the eunuch was returning to Ethiopia, and sitting in his chariot, reading the book of Isaiah the prophet. {29} The Holy Spirit said to Philip, "Go near, and join the chariot." {30} Philip ran there, and heard the eunuch reading from the book of Isaiah, and asked, "Do you understand what you are reading?" {31} The eunuch replied, "How can I unless someone should guide me?" And the eunuch asked Philip to come up and sit with him. {32} The Scripture {from Isaiah 57:3-8} that the eunuch was reading was, "He was led as a sheep to the slaughter; and like a lamb dumb before his shearer, so he did not open his mouth: {33} In his humiliation he stood in condemnation without cause. Who will declare that he lived because his life is taken from the earth?" {34} The eunuch spoke to Philip, and said, "I humbly ask of whom the prophet speaks? of himself or of some other man?" {35} Then Philip opened his mouth, and began at the same passage, and explained to him about Jesus. {36} As they continued on their way, they came to a certain body of water, and the eunuch said, "See the water; what hinders me from being baptized?" {37} Philip said, "If you believe with all of your heart, you can be baptized." And the eunuch replied, "I believe that Jesus Christ is the Son of God." {38} And the eunuch commanded the chariot to stop: and they went into the water, both Philip and the eunuch; and Philip baptized the eunuch. {39} When they emerged out of the water, the Holy Spirit caught away Philip so that the eunuch no longer saw him: and the eunuch continued on his way rejoicing.

Acts 8:26-39 KJV Paraphrase

If we were very strictly interpreting an isolated scriptural passage literally, as opposed to considering it in context, we would be faced with some enormous contradictions: In Deuteronomy 23:1, we are told that eunuchs should not enter into the congregation of the Lord; and, then, in Isaiah 56:3b-5 the eunuchs themselves are comforted; and, later, in the New Testament a eunuch is actually invited by the Holy Spirit to receive the Lord Jesus Christ as his personal Savior. Quite a dramatic turn around by God if we were just interpreting Scripture in isolation! But, again, I emphasize that context is just as important to this issue as well as it is to the issues of Christianity and modern-day homosexuality, cross-dressing, and the transgender condition.

So, then, what is the context of Deuteronomy 23:1? The context is that some forms of ancient idolatrous worship involved castration in addition to cross-dressing and sexual prostitution. That is why God took such a hard-line stance against some eunuchs as well as some cross-dressers and all temple cult prostitutes. The Lord God Almighty is against everything and anything associated with idolatry. The eunuchs who are comforted in Chapter Fifty-Six of Isaiah are those who definitely are part of the congregation of the Lord; they could not reproduce because 1) they were born that way, 2) they were accident victims, or 3) they were made that way by others through mutilation (i.e., castration). The eunuch called to salvation in Chapter Eight of Acts was seeking to understand prophetic Scripture, indicating that the intent of his heart was directed toward righteousness, and that his gaze was fixed on the Lord God Almighty; hence, he was called by the Lord God Almighty to receive salvation.

Just as I believe that intersexuals serve as biological prototypes for homosexual people, so do I believe that eunuchs serve as scriptural prototypes for modern-day transgender people. In a way, eunuchs, as referred to in the various verses of the Bible, serve as a prototype for understanding how the Lord views modern-day homosexual people, too. If, during the early days of the New Testament, a eunuch (who would have been prohibited by an unwaveringly narrow interpretation of the Law of Moses from approaching the Lord) could receive salvation, then surely, during these latter days, homosexual people (also cut off from the congregation of the Lord by an unwaveringly narrow interpretation of the Law of Moses) can be saved and received by Christ Jesus into his Kingdom.

Although not anatomic eunuchs, homosexual people are, to a certain extent, akin to physiologic eunuchs. 1) Except for those homosexual people who may have felt compelled to enter into relationships with members of the opposite sex in order for society to accept them and, thereby, had children as a result; 2) except for those homosexual people who may have adopted children; and 3) except for those homosexual people who have used artificial insemination (because it is their right to do so), most homosexual people who have lived openly as homosexual (even in lifelong committed spousal relationships) do not have children because reproduction is not possible between members of the same sex. Regardless, the Lord God Almighty, as recorded in Isaiah 56:3b-5, states, "Do not worry if you cannot reproduce because — if you keep My precepts, My judgments, and My laws and do My Will — I am going to give you a name better than those who do reproduce."

To be sure, Christ Jesus used eunuchs figuratively when he responded to a statement from the disciples that it would seem easier to remain celibate than to get married (Matthew 19:10). Christ Jesus replied:

> "For there are some eunuchs that were so born from their mother's womb: and there are some eunuchs that were made eunuchs by men: and there are some people who live like eunuchs for the kingdom of heaven's sake. Those who are called to celibacy will understand this message."

Matthew 19:11-12 KJV Paraphrase

Do not misconstrue the meaning of this section on eunuchs: Biblical eunuchs *per se* are not homosexual people or transgender people. However, Biblical eunuchs figuratively *represent* homosexual people and transgender people. Christ Jesus understood that there are males who do not have intercourse due to a diminished libido — either because they were born without testes or without functioning testes (i.e., "born that way"). Christ Jesus also understood that there are males who do not have intercourse due to a diminished libido because of loss of both testes accidentally or intentionally (i.e., "made that way by men"). Relative to intentional castration in ancient times, some males were forced to have their testes removed so that they could serve in specific roles — *for example*: 1) they could then be trusted not to commit adultery with the women in a harem they were protecting; or 2) they could be trusted not to steal from their masters for the sake of their own children because they would have none. Finally, Christ Jesus understood that there are some people who do not have intercourse because they have responded to a specific heavenly calling to keep themselves chaste. It is these people who renounce marriage for heavenly purposes. Christ Jesus added that only those who are called to celibacy will be able to fully understand and accept their call. He understood that the majority of people are not asked to be celibate and that, even for those who are asked, celibacy can pose quite a difficult challenge. Christ Jesus recognized that not everyone would understand that some people are called, or *elected*, to celibacy. Only those thus called, or elected, can *fully* understand — just as only those Christians who are homosexual or transgender can fully understand their sexual orientation and gender identity at the same time that they understand their saved position relative to the cross of Christ.

I believe that the principle of Matthew 19:12 can be applied to modern-day homosexual people and transgender people through this refocused paraphrase:

> Those who can understand, or who are willing to understand the homosexual orientation or transgender condition should accept their existence without mental or emotional strife. Those who are unable or unwilling to understand the homosexual orientation or transgender condition should get on with their own individual lives and leave the others in peace.

My refocused paraphrase could just as well be saying, "What business is it of yours if God chooses to save and use homosexual people and transgender people?" This echoes what Christ Jesus said to the Apostle Peter concerning that Apostle's speculation about what would happen to "John the beloved" (i.e., "the man whom Jesus loved"). It is recorded in John 21:22 (ML) that Christ Jesus said, "If I want him to remain until I come, what is it to you?" (As a footnote here, anyone who misinterprets "the man whom Jesus loved" to have a sexual connotation has no clue to non-sexual love between two people.)

Throughout the New Testament, we are constantly reminded that Levitical Law was meant for a certain group of people (the children of Israel) and for a specific dispensation and period of time. The Apostle

Paul recognized that the Apostle Peter was in the wrong (Galatians 2:11) because the Apostle Peter was leading other Jews to believe that Gentile Christians should adopt Jewish traditions and customs and even obey certain ritual aspects of the Law of Moses. The Apostle Paul confronted such ignorance by stating:

{15} We who are Jews by nature and not Gentile sinners {16} know that a person is not justified by the works of the Law of Moses but by the faith of Christ Jesus. We have believed in Christ Jesus that we might be justified by the faith of Christ and not by the works of the Law of Moses: for by the works of the Law of Moses shall no flesh be justified.

Galatians 2:15-16 KJV Paraphrase

All who follow the Law are under its curse because it is written, "Cursed is everyone who does not continue in all things that are written in the book of the Law to accomplish them." [Here, the Apostle Paul is quoting Deuteronomy 27:26]. [brackets mine]

Galatians 3:10 KJV Paraphrase

{23} But before faith came, we were kept under the Law of Moses, denied the faith that would later be revealed. {24} The Law of Moses had been our schoolmaster to prepare us for Christ, who would justify us by faith. {25} Because the faith of Christ has arrived, we are no longer under a schoolmaster.

Galatians 3:23-25 KJV Paraphrase

For in Jesus Christ neither circumcision nor uncircumcision satisfies the requirements of God; but faith that works by love does.

Galatians 5:6 KJV Paraphrase

Christ Jesus nailed the Levitical law to the cross. He "canceled the written code" (Colossians 2:14). Understanding this is important for liberating ourselves and others from the doctrinal error of legalism, a recurring nightmare in the history of the Christian Church. A little knowledge is always dangerous for human beings. In trying to understand its environment, the human brain feels comfortable in creating an easily interpretable environment for itself. That is why, if left to their own devices, human beings always default to legalism. A little religious knowledge always results in religious legalism. It is worse for religious people because those captive to their own thoughts think God supports their limited views. The natural man and the natural woman daily default to legalism. In contrast, the spiritual man and the spiritual woman ascend in consciousness to know the mind of God concerning topics they are studying.

Looking at the references in Revelation concerning the churches of Smyrna and Philadelphia, I believe there is a message for modern-day Christian homosexual people and transgender people relative to those who would impose the Law of Moses on them. As recorded in Revelation 2:8-11 (KJV Paraphrase), Christ Jesus stated:

{8} To the angel of the church in Smyrna write, "These things says the first and the last, who was dead and is alive. {9} I know your works, and tribulation, and poverty (but you are rich), and I know the blasphemy of those who say they are Jews, and are not, but belong to the synagogue of Satan. {10} Fear none of those things that you will suffer. Indeed, the devil will cast you into prison so that you may be tried; and you will have tribulation for ten days: be faithful to death, and I will give you a crown of life. {11} They that have an ear for understanding, let them hear what the Holy Spirit says to the churches. They that overcome shall not be hurt of the second death {i.e., shall not be condemned to the Lake of Fire}." {brackets mine}

You may recall that, according to Romans 2:25-29, a Christian is a Jew not outwardly but inwardly (that is, not naturally but spiritually). So, applying this to Revelation 2:8-11, there are many people who say they are spiritually-minded Christians but would reject Christian homosexual people and Christian transgender people as well as keep them from the Lord Jesus because they do not love God as much as they might say and do not love others to the degree that Christ Jesus would have them love. You see, it is very important for us all to demonstrate that we are children of God through sacrificial and selfless love that is, not only forgiving, but also non-condemning. There are some people who have no, or very little, sacrificial, selfless, and forgiving love in their hearts. They say they are Christian and, yet, do not act in a Christian way.

In Revelation 3:7-13 (KJV Paraphrase), Christ Jesus states:

{7} To the angel of the church in Philadelphia write, "These things says he that is holy, he that is true, and he that has the key of David to open what no person can shut and to shut what no person can open. {8} I know your works. Look, I have set before you an open door, and no man can shut it: for you have a little strength, and have kept my word, and have not denied my name. {9} Indeed, I will make those who belong to the synagogue of Satan that say they are Jews and are not, but lie, I will make them come and worship me at your feet in order that they might know that I have loved you. {10} Because you have kept the word of my patience, I also will keep you from the hour of temptation that shall come upon all the world to try those who dwell on the earth. {11} Watch, I will come quickly: hold fast onto that which you have, that no person take your crown. {12} To the people that overcome, I will make each of them a pillar in the temple of my God, and that person shall go no more out: and I will write upon them the name of my God, and the name of the city of my God, *New Jerusalem*, which is coming down out of heaven from my God: and I will write upon them my new name. {13} They that have an ear for understanding, let them hear what the Holy Spirit says to the churches."

In other words, those who say they are spiritually-minded, but are not, may be made to worship our Lord Jesus at the feet of Christian homosexual people and Christian transgender people (that is, on a tier below them)! Amazing, is it not?

To the homosexual people and transgender people who are reading this book, I carry a message from the Lord God Almighty to you: God loves you. God sent His only-begotten Son to die for you just as much as for any other human being. Yes, God loves you. God desires that you have an intimate eternal relationship with Him through His only-begotten Son, Christ Jesus. The Lord Jesus said, "I have come that they might have life, and that they might have life more abundantly" (John 10:10b KJV Paraphrase).

If you are homosexual or transgender and have not accepted the Lord Jesus Christ because other people have told you that the Bible says that you are not entitled to receive salvation or that there is no place in God's Kingdom for you, I tell you, and I have the Holy Spirit on this, that you are being invited, right now, to accept the Lord Jesus Christ as your personal Savior. "Though your sins are as scarlet, they shall be made white as snow; though they are red like crimson, they shall be made like wool" (Isaiah 1:18b KJV Paraphrase).

I am not talking about inviting you to join a particular denomination or specific local church. What I am doing is inviting you to join the Body of Christ, which is a spiritual body. God is inviting you, right now, to join a religion without walls. The truth be told: Christianity is not a religion, Christianity is a reality and a way of life. The Holy Bible, God's only written Word, guarantees that, if you confess your sins before the Lord God Almighty, you are just as entitled to salvation as anyone else. The Holy Bible, God's only written Word, guarantees that, if you confess your sins and tell the Lord that you are sorry for them, and if you ask for forgiveness for them in the name of God's only-begotten Son, Christ Jesus — whom you have accepted as your personal Savior — you will be forgiven by the Creator-God for all of your sins. At that time, you will be made a new creature and have a rebirth (that is, be "born again") and be able to live with God throughout all eternity in heaven.

Does this mean that you will never sin again? No. Does this mean that you will have everything that you want or that you will have all the money that you will ever need for a wonderful earthly life? No, it does not guarantee that. What it guarantees is that you will have an eternity in heaven with the Lord God Almighty.

Accepting the Lord Jesus Christ as your personal Savior will not prevent your exclusion from so-called mainstream Christianity.

Regarding the rejection of some of His sheep by mainstream religion, Christ Jesus taught:

{1} These things I have spoken to you that you should not be offended. {2} They shall put you out of the synagogues: yes, the time is coming that whoever kills you will think that he does God's service. {3} These things will they do to you because they have not known the Father nor me. {4} These things have I told you that, when the time comes, you may remember that I told you of them. And these things I did not say to you at the beginning because I was with you.

John 16:1-4 KJV Paraphrase

Christ Jesus himself wants us to know that persecution is a part of living in this world as a Christian. Despite persecution, however, we need to give our lives up to God to live in ways that bring more honor, glory, and praise to God's Holy Name. With that understanding, we need to trust in God completely as we continue our journey in this physical world.

Owe no one anything. Instead, love one another because the person that loves others has fulfilled the Law of Moses.

Romans 13:8 KJV Paraphrase

Love works no ill toward one's neighbor: therefore, love is the fulfilling of the Law of Moses.

Romans 13:10 KJV Paraphrase

Won't you take the time, right now, to accept the Lord Jesus Christ as your personal Savior? It is not complicated. Like the thief on the cross next to Jesus, acknowledge him as Lord and Savior and confess your sins to him and tell him that you are sorry for them. In response, he will say, "When you die, you will be with me that very day in Paradise."[57]

---

57   Luke 23:40-43

Like the eunuch in Acts who proclaimed that Christ Jesus is the Son of God, nothing prevents you from being spiritually baptized into the Body of Christ.

What the Lord Said to Me Regarding the Law and Grace

Sometime in 1977, while pondering the idea that I had a spiritual message to convey, this malingering thought would press to the forefront of my consciousness: "Who will believe what you have to say? You are homosexual." I was troubled because, although I felt comfortable with my sexual orientation, I knew most mainstream Christians would be uncomfortable with it — to put it mildly. I felt sure that any good that I might try to do would be prefaced by the words, "Dr. Pearson, an acknowledged homosexual…" I knew most mainstream Christians would erroneously use *what* I was to try to define the entirety of *who* I am. I knew that some would use my homosexual orientation against me to discredit anything I had to say about Christ Jesus, Christianity, and the Church.

I was especially frustrated because I knew that most churched Christians would stopper their ears rather than hear me explain how the homosexual orientation is really quite different from the same-sex activities described in the Bible that only relate to brutal group rape, male prostitution, idolatrous pagan fertility cult practices, and plural sex in group orgies.

As a Christian well-acquainted with the Holy Bible, I recognized long ago that most mainstream Christians would label the teaching and preaching of reconcilability between Christianity and homosexuality as heresy or even apostasy. I knew that many mainstream Christians would conclude that I should be excommunicated from the Christian Church based on their interpretation of what the Apostle Paul taught, as recorded in Galatians 1:8:

> But though we, or an angel from heaven, preach any other gospel unto you than that which we have preached unto you, let him be accursed.
>
> Galatians 1:8 KJV

Rather than listen to me, I knew that most mainstream Christians would think of the constraint articulated by the Bible verse just quoted. I knew that faithful Christians would believe that, because I was departing from what they had learned from the pulpit or in traditional Bible classes, I should be "cursed" or "accursed." "Accursed" is translated in the King James Version of Galatians 1:8 from the Greek word *anathema* (ἀνάθεμα {G331}), which also means: 1) "beyond redemption" and 2) "excommunicated."

I remember mentally working out arguments to justify and vindicate my homosexual orientation should I ever come to public or private trial concerning it. Then, one day after earnestly praying to the Lord for an answer to give my then-imagined, and perhaps now-real, detractors — I inwardly heard (writing while hearing) from the Holy Spirit. The Holy Spirit directed me to state the following to anyone who might say that I was cursed (or "accursed"):

> If I am cursed, then I am joined to my Master, who was cursed of all men. In this, then, do I rejoice that I am cursed of men, for in that curse I receive the blessing of God wherewith I am received into the body of Christ: rejected by man but accepted by God, and delivered by Him from the hand of my own iniquity and sin.

Yes, it is true, the Lord God Almighty answered my prayer! Not only that, but the answer swept over and settled in my soul. I understood. I heard. It spoke to me as no biological, psychological, or sociological argument ever could. Later, in Bible study, I came to better understand the Scriptural foundation for God's truth in the answer I received.

In his letter to the Christians in Galatia, the Apostle Paul wrote: "Christ has redeemed us from the curse of the Law of Moses in that he was made a curse for us, for it is written: 'Cursed is everyone that is hanged on a tree'" (Galatians 3:13 KJV Paraphrase). The Apostle Paul was referring to the Old Testament passage that states:

> If a man has committed a sin worthy of death, and he is to be put to death, and you hang him on a tree, his body must not remain all night on the tree because you must bury him that day (for he

that is hanged is cursed of God). You must not defile your land, which the Lord your God has given to you for an inheritance.

Deuteronomy 21:22-23 KJV Paraphrase

While we all know that Christ Jesus was not *hung* by the neck in the now-common sense of that word — and certainly was not lifted up to the limb of any tree — he was hanged in the sense that the ancients understood the word — that is, "hanged up" for all to see. In ancient times, hanging was viewed primarily as a warning to potential wrongdoers. In many instances, bodies were hung up after execution rather than for execution. In addition to the Apostle Paul, the Apostle Peter also affirms his acceptance of that usage through his direct references to the "hanging" of Christ Jesus:

The God of our fathers raised up Jesus, whom you murdered by hanging on a tree.

Acts 5:30 KJV Paraphrase

We are witnesses of all things that he did in the land of the Jews and in Jerusalem; whom they murdered and hanged on a tree.

Acts 10:39 KJV Paraphrase

He bore our sins in his own body on the tree in order that we, being dead to sins, should live unto righteousness. By his wounds, you were healed.

1 Peter 2:24 KJV Paraphrase

In other words, Christ Jesus also — which is to say, *like homosexual people* (as some might interpret Scripture) — had been cursed by the letter of the Law of Moses! Thus, as I now understand it, what the Lord's Holy Spirit said to me is this:

In that Christ Jesus, God's Chosen, was made a mock for us that we might be reconciled to God, and that his crucifixion won us pardon (if we so believe), so then does God's mercy extend to all souls in dust who feel the scorn of the lion (that is, the Devil) through the unkindnesses of humankind. God will not turn His love away from any who suffer — even if they suffer only a fraction of the passion of His firstborn — because they remind God of His only-begotten Son. In other words, in God's sight, all reviled are joined to His firstborn, who suffered the ultimate rejection.

Yes, there was a time when no blemished thing could come before the Lord. However, during Old Covenant times, the Lord God Almighty was trying to establish within the hearts and minds of some very primitive people that He is sovereign and that He is worthy of perfect sacrifice (of which Christ Jesus was to become, and remain, its only embodiment), much the same as the Lord God Almighty established His tabernacle and tabernacular appointments as a figure of things in heaven (see Hebrews, Chapters Nine and Ten). Remember, according to the Old Testament, the people of that day were "stiff-necked" and "rebellious," ungrateful for the things that the Lord God Almighty was doing for them, and gross with regard to spiritual understanding. Thus, in order to help them subdue an unyielding spirit, the Lord God Almighty subjected them to the various rules, regulations, and ordinances of the Law of Moses, including its Levitical Law.

As recorded in Luke 16:16 (KJV Paraphrase), Christ Jesus said, "'The Law and the Prophets were until John the Baptist: since that time the Kingdom of God is preached, and every person presses into it.'" As recorded in John 1:17 (KJV), the Apostle John wrote, "For the law was given by Moses, but grace and truth came by Jesus Christ." As recorded in Romans 14:14 (KJV Paraphrase), the Apostle Paul wrote: "I know, and am persuaded by the Lord Jesus, that there is nothing unclean of itself: but to the person that esteems anything to be unclean, to that person it is unclean." The Apostle Paul also wrote, "For the entire Law of Moses is fulfilled in one saying: 'You shall love your neighbor as yourself'" (Galatians 5:14 KJV Paraphrase). Keep in mind that it was those who were legalistically-minded (that is, strict adherents of the letter of the Law of Moses) that were offended by Christ Jesus' deeds and eventually saw to it that he was condemned to death. Also, those Gentiles who call themselves Christians today should remember that, at one time, Gentiles were not part of God's chosen (refer to Romans, Chapter Nine) and were even referred to as "dogs" by Christ Jesus himself. Unfortunately, like the Apostle Paul and his evangelistic team 2,000 years ago, homosexual Christians and transgender Christians are "genuine although they are regarded as pretenders" (2 Corinthians 6:8 KJV Paraphrase) by many in the Christian Church today.

Why cannot more believers in Christ be like the Apostle Peter, who said, "God has shown me that I should not call any man common or unclean" (Acts 10:28 RS). No one is permitted by the Lord God to judge or condemn another: "You are inexcusable, whoever you are that judges: for, in that you judge another, you condemn yourself because anyone who judges is viewed by God as doing the same things" (Romans 2:1 KJV Paraphrase).

Again, I urge you to read the entire book of Leviticus as well as Deuteronomy. If you are a Christian, you will be hard pressed to find any of its rules, regulations, and ordinances that you yourself follow. Why impose them on anyone else? Why permit anyone else to impose them on you?

What the Lord Says to Us All

Let us, again, consider what the Holy Spirit says to us all in 1 Corinthians 1:27-29 (KJV Paraphrase):

> {27} But God chose the foolish things of the world to shame the wise; God chose the weak things of the world to shame the strong. {28} God chose the lowly things of this world and the despised things — and the things that are not — to nullify the things that are, {29} so that no one in the flesh is able to boast before the Lord.

The few verses just quoted are my favorite verses in the Holy Bible relative to the issue of Christianity and homosexuality. Why? Because they say so much in so little. They say that it is God who chooses to do what He will do and no one can keep Him from doing it. The major idea in these verses is that God can choose base things, and that God can choose things that are despised, and that God can choose things that were, and are, rejected. Why? To confound people who think they know it all — because, not only is pagan idolatry an abomination to God, but also self-pride, false ego, and arrogance are an abomination to Him. By doing the unexpected, God proves the immeasurable nature of His grace. Indeed, both egoism and egotism are forms of idolatry that the Lord God Almighty hates. He hates it when people sit in condemnation and judgment of others. No, we are not to judge. None of us can judge another. As stated earlier, the Bible clearly tells us not to judge because, if we judge others, then we will be judged by the same standard to the same degree. In this way are we cautioned not to judge.

I challenge each reader to evaluate 1 Corinthians 1:27-29 in the context of the homosexual orientation and the transgender condition in today's world. Also, I challenge them to evaluate the relationship of this world to the sphere in which God operates and His true Shekinah glory manifests. The Lord God Almighty does not care that narrow-minded people playing religion might be offended if He accepts homosexual people and transgender people into His Kingdom. In fact, God often chooses to confound people who think they have all of the answers. When applied to the homosexual orientation, the statement that "no flesh should glory (or boast)" includes in its meaning that neither heterosexual people nor homosexual people should proclaim that one sexual orientation is better than the other.

The idea that God chooses to exalt things that are despised reminds me of what the Lord God Almighty said to Moses: "I will be gracious to whom I will be gracious, and will show mercy on whom I will show mercy" (Exodus 33:19 RS). It reminds me of this praise that Nebuchadnezzar offered to God as recorded in Daniel 4:35 (ML): "All the inhabitants of the earth are accounted as nothing; He does according to His will in the army of heaven and among the inhabitants of the earth and none can stay His hand or say to Him, 'What doest Thou?'" It reminds me of the heavenly voice that spoke to the Apostle Peter and said, "'What God has made clean do not call unclean'" (Acts 10:15 KJV Paraphrase) — which is paraphrased delightfully in the Living Bible as "'Don't contradict God! If he says something is kosher, then it is.'" Finally, it reminds me of the Lord's response to the Apostle Paul when that man prayed for God to remove a thorn from his flesh: "My grace is sufficient for you: for my strength is made perfect in weakness" (2 Corinthians 12:9 KJV Paraphrase).

Yes, the homosexual orientation is somewhat analogous to a thorn in the flesh because of all the pain it brings from social and familial rejection. But we are asked by our Lord to turn to God in order that God's strength be within us so that we not become weary or faint. Christ Jesus said:

> {28} "Come to me, all who labor and have heavy burdens, and I will give you rest. {29} Take my yoke upon you, and learn from me; for I am meek and lowly in heart: and you shall find rest for your souls. {30} For my yoke is easy, and my burden is light."

> Matthew 11:28-30 KJV Paraphrase

If the Lord God Almighty has chosen to extend His dispensation to homosexual people and transgender people, then who are mere mortals to tell Him that He cannot or that He should not? The Lord chooses to whom He is merciful. Thank goodness humankind does not choose because no one would have ever become a Christian. Who are any of us to question the authority or the sovereignty of the Lord God Almighty? What audacity! How full of self-pride and self-will that would be!

What is the lesson here? Let one's sexual orientation and gender identity be between the created individual and the Creator. More importantly, do not hinder homosexual people or transgender people from accepting the cross of Christ Jesus. Do not keep them from corporate worship. And do not keep them from Christian ministry simply because they are homosexual or transgender.

If little of what I have written in this book makes sense to you, that is all right. Just remember to keep your judgments and condemnations to yourself, to refrain from unkindness to me and others like me, and to try and not be too surprised when you meet many of us in heaven. And, if the idea of *faggots* (literally, "embers") burning brightly for God is repugnant to you, then perhaps you are not yet fully prepared for the

Kingdom of God. For this reason, I pray that you permit our Lord to change you by healing you.

To Christian homosexual people who have a broken heart because of all of the pain that they have experienced from rejection, my advice to you is to ask the Lord to use that broken heart to help you more fully yield to Him and to better minister to other brokenhearted people in His Holy Name. How can any of us ever expect to minister to the brokenhearted if we have never had a broken heart?

To Christian homosexual people who are struggling to justify to Christian family-of-origin members and Christian friends that they are redeemed, Scripture is clear that "faith justifies," "Jesus Christ justifies," "faith in the Lord Jesus Christ justifies," and "God justifies" (see Romans 5:1 and 8:33; 1 Corinthians 6:11; Galatians 2:16-17; and Titus 3:7). You do not need to justify to anyone that you have been redeemed because God redeems us solely through the shed blood of Christ Jesus! That we testify that the Lord Jesus is our Savior is testimony enough that the Holy Spirit resides in us. The witness of the Holy Spirit in us is an infallible witness that we are saved — regardless of what anyone else says.

If we have God's Holy Spirit in us, then we must be saved because the Holy Spirit cannot dwell in vessels that have not been cleansed by the Lamb of God's shed blood. If we know that the Lord Jesus is the Messiah, our Savior, and the only-begotten Son of God, it is because the Holy Spirit Himself has revealed that to us. As Christ Jesus said to the Apostle Peter, "Blessed are you... for this was not revealed to you by flesh and blood but by my Father in heaven" (Matthew 16:17 KJV Paraphrase).

Regarding salvation, the Holy Spirit wrote through the Apostle Paul:

{11} What human being knows the things of a human being except for the spirit of being human that is resident within him or her? In the same way, so the things of God no human being knows except for the Spirit of God that dwells within him or her. {12} Now we have not received the spirit of the world but the Spirit of God that we might know the things that are freely given to us from God. {13} We speak about these things, not in the words that human wisdom teaches, but in words that the Holy

Spirit teaches, comparing spiritual things with spiritual. {14} But the human being does not receive the things of the Spirit of God because they are foolishness to him and her: neither can the human being know them because they are spiritually discerned. {15} But the person that is spiritual is able to judge all things, yet he or she is judged by no one. {16} "For who has known the mind of the Lord that he may instruct Him?" [The Apostle Paul is quoting from Isaiah 40:13.] But we have the mind of Christ. {brackets mine}

> 1 Corinthians 2:10-16 KJV Paraphrase

If you are homosexual or transgender and unsure of your salvation, all you need to do is ask yourself these five questions: 1) Have you accepted the Lord Jesus as your personal Savior? 2) Do you regularly repent of sinful and addictive thoughts, feelings, attitudes, and behaviors? 3) Have you shared with others that Christ Jesus is your Savior? 4) Can you understand spiritual things (that is, basic Christian concepts and principles)? 5) Are you able to forgive others in the name of Christ Jesus? If you have answered "yes" to all five questions, then you are saved and have God's Holy Spirit indwelling you. Or would you call God a liar? (With regard to forgiving others, please know that sometimes forgiveness is a long process and not instantaneous. Although Christians strive for immediacy in forgiving others, sometimes the trauma sustained from the abuse of others has been too great to do it immediately.)

> All who believe in the Son of God know that this is true. Those who don't believe this are actually calling God a liar because they don't believe what God has testified about his Son.

> 1 John 5:10 NLT

The Holy Bible teaches that "whoever calls on the name of the Lord will be saved" (Acts 2:21 KJV Paraphrase). *Whoever* means "anyone."

Because this chapter has been about the Law of Moses and God's Grace, it is fitting that I close it with the following admonishment in God's written Word for those who want to debate *ad nauseam* about what the Books of Leviticus and Deuteronomy say and do not say about homosexual people and transgender people:

Do not get involved in foolish discussions about spiritual pedigrees or in quarrels and fights about obedience to Jewish laws. These kinds of things are useless and a waste of time.

Titus 3:9 NLT

CHAPTER SIX

Christian Ethics and Homosexual People

Iniquity and Sin and the Need for Forgiveness

Most simply defined, *iniquity* is "turning from God" and *sin* is "action based on that turning." To be sure, iniquity and sin exist within this state of physical being:

> Wash me thoroughly from my iniquity, and cleanse me from my sin.

> Psalm 51:2 KJV Paraphrase

> Behold, I was shaped in iniquity; and in sin did my mother conceive me.

> Psalm 51:5 KJV Paraphrase

From the Bible, we know that iniquity entered into the universe because of the Fall of Lucifer — who is referred to, after his fall, as *Satan* (or "the Adversary of God") — and that sin entered into the world as a result of the Adamic Fall, or fall of humankind. What has happened as a result of sin is that condemnation was brought upon the world and — concomitantly — grief, guilt, and shame upon all individual human beings. Yes, all of us are sinners. We are predisposed to sin because we are born in iniquity. As Scripture teaches, "If we say that we have no sin, we deceive ourselves, and the truth is not in us" (1 John 1:8 KJV). However, Scripture also teaches that Christ Jesus "bore our sins in his own body on the tree in order that we, being dead to sins, should live unto righteousness" (1 Peter 2:24 KJV Paraphrase), and that "if we confess our sins, he is faithful and just to forgive us our sins, and to cleanse us from all unrighteousness" (1 John 1:9 KJV).

The Holy Bible teaches that, as our substitutionary offering, the Lord Jesus himself bore our shame upon the cross (1 Peter 2:24). Such redemptive sacrifice includes all people who believe on him, heterosexual or homosexual. That the Lord Jesus has served as the atonement for our iniquity and sin means that, if we so accept him as our Lord and Savior, the Creator-God views us as sinless (i.e., without blemish) — just as Christ Jesus was sinless and without blemish. I bring this up as the most important issue because it seems that, even within the Christian Church, there are many individuals who do not quite grasp the sinless nature of Christ Jesus or are turned off by the requirement of God for a blood sacrifice. If, for some reason, you do not understand the substitutionary role that the Lord Jesus played on the cross when he offered himself up as the only blood sacrifice acceptable to God the Father — or if you mistakenly believe that he had blemishes, or that he made errors in judgment, or sinned like everyone else — then you are not grasping who Christ Jesus really is. I believe that, if you are still struggling with the sinless nature of Christ Jesus, this work will help to confirm the words of the Holy Bible as well as the certainty of their truth. Also, I believe that if you are homosexual and avoid portions of God's written Word because you think that they condemn you, this work will help you to trust in the certainty of God's truth in its entirety. (Remember, we are to hold the whole Bible as we simultaneously attend to its various parts.)

The forgiveness of others is also an especially important issue for members of the homosexual and transgender communities because many who belong to them have been victimized, abused, rejected, and despised — even by their own family-of-origin members and closest friends. And, for this reason, forgiveness of others has special significance for them because it is difficult for many of them to forgive. However, all of us must look to Christ Jesus as our example and follow his command to forgive others of their trespasses, or sins, against us.

To be sure, our triune God has demonstrated His perfect love in forgiving us of our sins. In fact, the very first thing that our Lord and Savior said on his cross of crucifixion was, "Father, forgive them, for they do not know what they are doing" (Luke 23:24 KJV Paraphrase). That was the very first thing Christ Jesus said on the cross! Can you imagine that? He asked that those who had committed this heinous crime against him (which is to say, his murder) be forgiven of that crime. Following Christ Jesus' lead, the first Christian martyr, Stephen, said as he was being stoned, "Lord, lay not this sin up to their charge" (Acts 7:60 KJV). In other words, Stephen was following the example that the Lord Jesus set for us all whenever we come to know persecution, oppression, victimization, and abuse. Consequently, I urge you to not forget forgiveness, especially because this may be a primary spiritual axis issue for you. Please do not misconclude here that I am advocating that you remain in a threatening situation or an abusive relationship. Although we are to turn our cheek, we need not run up to get it slapped.

An unforgiving spirit leads to bitterness, and bitterness leads to hatred, and hatred really is the antithesis of *agape* love — which is selfless, sacrificial, and forgiving love. And, when a person is in the throes of hatred, then he or she experiences its consequence, which is fear. Just as "perfect love casts out fear" (1 John 4:18 KJV Paraphrase), conversely, unforgiveness, bitterness, and hatred permit Satan to work against us through his spirit of fear. Indeed, the verse just quoted continues, "fear has torment." From a practical standpoint, if you live in fear or experience fear daily, it is important for you to determine if you are indulging Satan's spirit of unforgiveness. You need to know that you will be liberated from fear as soon as you forgive others for their debts, trespasses, or sins against you.

Forgiving others does not mean that you need to become dysfunctional by pretending that others do not have specific faults, flaws, and infirmities. No, perfect love means that you forgive others despite your knowledge of the existence of their specific faults, flaws, and infirmities — just like Christ Jesus. By doing this, you don't become Christ Jesus, you are simply demonstrating a Christlike spirit.

Our Lord also calls upon us to forgive those who have hurt us, or who have been unkind to us, so that we might progress spiritually. It is just absolutely amazing that, unless we forgive people who have wronged us, we remain inextricably linked to them, and, consequently, we move through life in a downward spiral. If we really want to get on with our lives and leave all unnecessary baggage behind, then we must forgive people who have hurt or harmed us.

Relative to forgiveness, this is the command that has been given to us from Christ Jesus:

> If you forgive people their trespasses, your heavenly Father will also forgive you. But if you do not forgive people their trespasses, neither will your heavenly Father forgive your trespasses.

> Matthew 6:14-15 KJV Paraphrase

The previously-cited passage carries a message that is an extension of the Lord's Prayer. Basically, the prayer tells us that unless we forgive those who have sinned against us, our Father in heaven will not forgive us of our sins. If, however, we forgive those who have sinned against us, then our Father in heaven will forgive us of our sins (provided, of course, that we believe that Christ Jesus is His *only-begotten* Son and our Redeemer). Curiously, Matthew 6:14-15 are verses often avoided by Christians, homosexual and heterosexual alike; for some reason, people do not wish to pay attention to the severity of the ramifications if they refuse to forgive someone who has trespassed against them. Certainly, the Lord God Almighty, not only teaches us that we need to forgive, but also has issued the edict (or commandment) for us to do so as well.

Why are we commanded to forgive? To demonstrate that we have the same nature as our Creator-God — which is a selfless, sacrificial, and forgiving one — and to demonstrate that He resides in us through His Holy Spirit.

It is the strangest thing, but our Lord Jesus teaches us that, unless we forgive, we cannot be forgiven. It is also the strangest thing that, as

190

Christians, when people wrong us, we end up having a debt to repay them — the debt of forgiveness. Scripture tells us to demonstrate that we are perfect as our Father in heaven is perfect (Matthew 5:48). How do we demonstrate this perfection? By loving perfectly in forgiveness, sacrifice, and selflessness — just as our heavenly Father does!

Forgiveness is a demonstration of perfect love. This is how we show that we are the children of God and that we have been born again.

For those of you who may have difficulty with forgiving others, you need not do it alone. The Lord Jesus will help you. All you need to do is ask him for his help.

Relative to the seeming dilemma between Christianity and homosexuality, I believe that my ministry is to those persons who are struggling with this issue, heterosexual or homosexual. I do not believe that my ministry is to people who have already made up their minds one way or the other. I do not believe that it is very productive to share, discuss, and/or debate with someone who is already firm in his or her convictions concerning this issue (except, perhaps, in forums using forensic guidelines).

To me, trying to convince others of the reconcilability of Christianity and homosexuality is generally a waste of time, effort, and energy — especially when there are so many people who are genuinely struggling with the issue and, as a result, deserve help in resolving it. To avoid a verbal conflagration, I try to apply the good sound advice found in Matthew 5:37 (KJV Paraphrase) that advises us to sometimes keep our conversation to a minimum: "Simply let your *Yes* be *Yes*, and your *No* be *No*; whatever is more than this comes from the evil one" (see also James 5:12). Besides, we cannot really convince anyone of anything. However, God's Holy Spirit can convict people of the truth as they hear it or after they hear it.

In a way, homosexual people and heterosexual people are like cats and dogs, but I do not mean that from the fighting standpoint. I have a cat and a dog at home, and they coexist. They just do not quite understand one another. To a certain degree, heterosexual people have no clue as to what the homosexual orientation is about and, to a certain extent, homosexual people do not have a clue as to what the heterosexual orientation is about. However, I must say that, generally speaking, there is a greater understanding of heterosexuality by homosexual people than vice versa. Most homosexual people have been thoroughly exposed to, and indoctrinated by, the interests, experiences, and belief systems commonly held by the dominant heterosexual culture.

Relative to dealing with people who have been unkind to us, the Bible offers this additional solid advice in Romans 12:19 (KJV Paraphrase):

> Do not avenge wrongs against you. Instead, let God's wrath prevail: for it is written, "Vengeance is Mine; I will repay," declares the Lord. (See also Leviticus 19:18 and Deuteronomy 32:35.)

So, if someone trespasses against us, we are not to avenge that sin but, rather, forgive the debt (that is, forgive what they owe to us as a result of their trespass). Forgive the debt and, in so doing, get on with our lives. Perhaps the trespass was born of malice. Perhaps it was born of ignorance. Regardless, it is important in following the lead of our Lord Jesus to ask for our heavenly Father to forgive the trespasser as well — just as Christ Jesus said, "Father, forgive them because they do not know what they are doing" (Luke 23:34 KJV Paraphrase).

In Matthew 5:44 (KJV Paraphrase), Christ Jesus teaches us what we need to do: "Love your enemies, bless those who curse you, do good to those who hate you, and pray for those who despitefully use you and persecute you." Yes, we need to love our enemies. We need to pray for those who hate us and despitefully use us. And we need to bless those who curse us. These are definite commands that are given in the Bible relative to what we are to do if we are oppressed or victimized. That does not mean that we should shrink from standing up for our rights or someone else's rights. That does not mean that we should be very passive and give someone *carte blanche* permission to hurt us if we can prevent it. No, what it means is that we need to keep our distance from people who might try to hurt us, but we also need to keep in mind that we have certain responsibilities as Christians to forgive and try to forget. Forget, too? Yes, as Scripture teaches, love "keeps no record of being wronged" (1 Corinthians 13:5 NLT). I have discovered that if you look at others who have wronged you through the shed blood of Christ Jesus, you will see them as God sees them (which is to say, sinless and without fault). Looking at others this way, you will be able to, not only forgive them, but also forget their wrongs against you.

In Matthew 18:21-22 (KJV), it is recorded that the Apostle Peter approached the Lord Jesus and asked, "How often should we forgive?" The Lord Jesus answered, "Seven times seventy," or 490 times. That is a substantial number of times, indeed. I, of course, understand that the Lord Jesus was speaking figuratively. But, even if he were speaking literally, 490 times is a great number of times to forgive one person. My good guess is that even if you spent all day thinking about how many times your greatest enemy has maligned you, you would be hard pressed to come up with 490 separate instances. To be sure, homosexual people need to join the "490 Club" and forgive those who have wronged them even if they continue to wrong them, recognizing that most trespasses against them are born of ignorance — ignorance of the Lord Jesus Christ.

As the truth that God loves and accepts homosexual people and transgender people is revealed to the Christian community (local church by local church, denomination by denomination, tribe by tribe, and nation by nation), those who victimize and bully homosexual people in the name of religion will no longer have a cloak for their trespass. Coming to an understanding that God loves everyone — and that God accepts everyone for who he or she is, and what he or she is relative to sexual orientation — is crucial to countering the lies that have been spread about the irreconcilability of Christianity and homosexuality. Unfortunately, those lies have kept many homosexual people and their loved ones from the cross of Christ Jesus. Yes, there is individual responsibility, but there is social and familial responsibility as well with regard to spreading the gospel of Christ Jesus without condemnation or judgment to all who will listen.

Fulfilling our Commitment to Christ Jesus

The overwhelming majority of people believe that homosexuality is immoral. I do not. I believe that homosexuality is amoral and that homosexual people individually are either moral or immoral. As has been pointed out in Chapter Three of this book, we are informed in the Bible that "God is no respecter of persons" (Acts 10:34 KJV). I believe that. And I believe it applies, not only to earthly appearance, but also to physical expression, personality, and sexual orientation. I believe that our Creator-God cares not one jot, iota, or yod about any aspect of our being human except that we try to reflect Him and His loving ways in all that we do. Spiritually speaking, sacrificial, selfless, and forgiving love is the only real substance that can be multiplied and bear fruit.

I do not believe that any sexuality (neither heterosexuality nor homosexuality) is an expression of God except in the companionship, mutual support, and shared intimacy of two people in a committed, covenant-based, and monogamous relationship that has been blessed by God. Indeed, I believe that sexuality is, at worst, a parody of — or, at best, a parable of — the creative powers of the Lord God Almighty and the communion (i.e., fellowship) His saints have with one another in their *at-one-ment* with Him.

I am saddened that, for many Christians, the issue of AIDS has been turned into an issue of homosexuality. Why am I saddened? I think homosexuality is one area in which the organized Christian Church has given sanction to anti-Christian attitudes of condemnation and judgment as well as behaviors that are offensive to Christ Jesus, all of which turn many away from where they should be looking during their final days. The spirit of condemnation now operates through many who profess that Christ Jesus is their Savior. It runs rampant through their hearts and minds and souls. For some strange reason, it "sets right" with many Christians — at least many that I have heard and seen — to take such a stand.

Once, when visiting a self-identified "Spirit-filled" church, I heard the pastor make a joke about homosexual people during his sermon. It received a good laugh from the congregation; however, it made me feel badly for those homosexual people who may have been sitting in the pews and who had already suffered rejection by many and were seeking the Lord Jesus, only to be made fun of by one of his "servants." Brothers and sisters, believe me, whenever cruelty raises its ugly head, you can be sure that whoever raises it is not testifying of Christ Jesus' love and power to save.

Like King David — who chose to have retribution meted out by pestilence rather than by the hand of man (2 Samuel 24:13-15) — I think that the Human Immunodeficiency Virus (HIV) should be feared less than human beings. Viruses come nowhere near the power of evil that can be generated through human beings who have given themselves over to malice, malevolence, condemnation, and vengeance. Certainly, human beings are responsible for more damage and suffering than any infectious agent. Yes, there are those Christians who would agree that homosexual people may be "saved" but only on the condition that they repent and change their ways (that is, not act on their sexual orientation).

Homosexual people do not need to be saved from their homosexuality unless, of course, they are indulging a hedonistic or sexually-addictive lifestyle, just as any heterosexual person in bondage to lust of the flesh needs to be healed of that appetite. Why? It is spiritually and emotionally unhealthy for anyone to view other people as objects for self-gratification. Active addiction robs us of a productive life that is pleasing to God.

Unfortunately, it is plain that many people (heterosexual people and homosexual people alike) believe corporeal flesh to be the eternal reflection and likeness of the Creator-God as well as believe that the carnal nature, which animates that flesh, to be part of His pure, perfect, and divine nature. These ideas are entirely incongruent with God's truth and, therefore, erroneous. Really, there is little I can say to clarify my views on homosexuality for them because, for as long as they hold to such thinking, their understanding of sexuality, among other things, will remain earthbound. Simply stated, they will not be able to grasp God's indifference to sexual orientation. (Do not misinterpret here that I am saying the Lord God Almighty is indifferent to sinful human behavior.)

For those who are genuinely struggling to reconcile what they feel inside is true concerning homosexuality with the views of mainstream Christianity (such views at variance with those feelings), I need to add the following:

When I pretended that I was heterosexual so others might accept me, I was in effect rejecting God because I was living a lie. It was not until I became honest with myself and others that I was able to come to the real truth, which is to say, to the reality of Christ Jesus. That is not to say that I believe homosexual people have a license to licentiousness. Quite to the contrary, no. Unless one has been called personally to celibacy, I believe in the unadulterated sharing of the life and love of the Savior within the sanctity of a monogamous, covenant-based spousal relationship. I believe that one of the fullest relationships that can be achieved among souls within this earthly flesh is the one attained between two faithful helpmates who have put God first and each other second. My mate and I have been with each other for 40 years at the time of this edition (2017) and neither one of us has been unfaithful to the other. This is one of the so-called secrets to the longevity of our relationship.

The so-called curse of homosexuality can even be turned into a blessing for those homosexual people who do not become involved in a frenetic escape from it through sexual addiction or in unhealthy repression of their own homosexual feelings. How? By the challenge it presents. To perceive that one does not fit into an accepted mold or pattern can help lead one to the conclusion that people who are spiritually-minded are really strangers, foreigners, and pilgrims in this world. Such recognition is necessary before we can be fully returned to our heavenly home, where God expresses Himself in us and through us without measure. In other words, when dealt with correctly, the homosexual life experience can help one yield to Christ Jesus.

With adversity, rejection, and suffering often comes enlightenment; however, generally speaking, the gifts of adversity, rejection, and suffering are not often gratefully received by souls in dust nor are they generally viewed as spiritual gifts. (I am not saying here that we should abrogate our responsibility: 1) to be active politically, 2) to demonstrate publicly, and 3) to stand up for our human rights and civil rights in peaceful protest.)

I do believe that, if I had not been homosexual, I might have rejected the gospel message because I would have been too comfortable and "at home" in this world. For this reason, I believe that my homosexuality has been a gift from God rather than a curse. Because of the challenge it presented, it helped me to turn to Christ Jesus and ask him to be Lord of my life.

To my friends who happen to be homosexual, I write this: Because the world has been afraid of us (it always fears what it does not understand), it has tried to suppress the natural development of our affections and emotions. And, because it has tried to repress the healthy expression of our sexual orientation as well as suppress knowledge of our existence, many of us — without positive role models of any kind — were consigned by society to lead lives in sordid, backroom-type, sinful activities. Because our personalities were fragmented, we were eaten up from the inside by unhealthy (i.e., addictive) sexual desires. However, it is time for us to break from the bondage of such a mental, emotional, and spiritual miasma. We need to resist the unhealthiness and sinfulness engendered by prevailing attitudes and actions propelled by Satan's spirit of condemnation. We need to take charge of our lives by yielding ourselves to God's Holy Spirit and the Will of Christ. We need to understand that our Creator loves us and that He could not care less about our sexual orientation unless, of course, we have not come to terms with it.

What are the responsibilities of homosexual people? They are the same as heterosexual people. The Apostle Paul wrote, "I beg you, therefore, brothers [and sisters], in view of God's mercies, that you present your bodies a living sacrifice, holy and acceptable to God, which is your reasonable service" (Romans 12:1 ML [brackets mine]). Thus, we should accept our rejection by humankind as well as our acceptance by God, taking time to be holy all the while. (Again, this is not to say that we should not peacefully struggle for justice and equality globally.)

When they feel especially sad and lonely, should homosexual people not be able to turn to the one who knew the ultimate rejection, Christ Jesus, so that their burdens might be shared with him? Can Christians who happen to be homosexual not have the same hope as Christians who happen to be heterosexual? Are homosexual people covered by God's grace? Yes, yes, and yes. Believe me, daily I prove God's saving grace and I am a witness of it to you, right now.

What is sexual immorality? Immorality, simply stated, is defined here as "any sexual activity outside of the sanctity of a committed, covenant-based, and monogamous spousal relationship." What does sexual immorality include? It includes orgies, bath house activities, "swinging" sexually with other couples, casual sex, adultery, lust (that is, unchecked sexual desire), pornography, telephone sex, addictive masturbation, lap dancing, voyeurism, and even serial monogamy. Certainly, not one of the activities or behaviors that has just been named are unique to the homosexual community. Such promiscuous behaviors are indulged by the heterosexual community as well. As stated earlier, whatever psychopathologies exist in the homosexual community also exist in the heterosexual community.

For the sake of clarification, "serial monogamy" is periodically passing from one short-term, albeit monogamous, relationship to another. This, too, is displeasing to the Lord. When Christ Jesus met the Samaritan woman by the well and asked her to call her husband, the woman answered, "I have no husband" (John 4:17 KJV). Christ Jesus replied:

> "You have said correctly, 'I have no husband,' because you have had five husbands; and he whom you now have is not your husband."

> John 4:17-18 KJV Paraphrase

The Lord God Almighty is a God of commitment, a God of vows, and a God of promises. He expects the promises and the vows and the commitments that we make — not only to Him but to each other — to be executed and to be brought to full term and fruition. Thus, our God expects us to fulfill our commitments, including commitments to lifelong companionship.

There have been many extra societal pressures placed on homosexual people. Because our relationships are not deemed natural or normal, and because they are not fostered in emotionally-healthy ways (*for example*, there is no real courtship *per se* during middle school and high school for homosexual people), homosexual pair-bondings often get off to a very shaky start. Without the opportunity to experiment in developing healthy relationships during our preteen and teenage years, many of us are *developmentally delayed* — destined to repeat unhealthy relationships because we missed out on that crucial time of experimenting and learning how to develop healthy, lasting, and intimate relationships without running away from the challenges they present. (Certainly this holds true for some heterosexual people, too.)

Because homosexual people have had the added pressure of society frowning upon them for being together, it creates an extra burden for them individually and often takes its toll on their relationships. However, though I am aware of extra pressures on homosexual relationships, I am also aware of the extra responsibilities that we have as individuals in the spousal relationships that we do form. We need to continue on with those relationships — especially when we, in the eyes of God, have been made one. All human beings should refrain from passing from one spousal partner to another. I urge the heterosexual community to consider these words as well because all segments of society need to work on faithfulness and fulfilling commitments. It is just that, for homosexual people, there are some different burdens and added responsibilities that impact on spousal partners remaining together — especially during the periods of difficult testing that all spousal relationships experience.

In 1 Corinthians 6:18-20 (KJV Paraphrase), the Apostle Paul further delineates our responsibilities to God and others. He states:

{18} Flee fornication. Every sin that a person commits is outside of his or her own body except for fornication, which is sin against one's own body. {19} Do you not know that your body is the temple of the Holy Spirit who lives in you, which you received from God, and that you are not your own? {20} You are bought with a price. Therefore, glorify God in your body, and in your spirit, both of which are God's.

Yes, honor God with your body! Both heterosexual people and homosexual people need to flee from sexual immorality. We need to resist temptation by recognizing and affirming Scriptural truth. We need to look for a life-long partner, and if we have a life-long partner, then we need to stay committed to that partner throughout life. Such faithfulness is pleasing to the Lord. We need to continually work at establishing healthy relationships. Both heterosexual people and homosexual people need to investigate why their relationships falter and fail.

Why Marriage or Holy Unions?

Hindering marriage, or holy union, between homosexual people contributes to immorality and not vice versa.

During the time of legalized slavery in the United States, because Blacks were prevented from legally marrying in the slave states, many of them participated in a ceremony of "jumping the broom" to signify that they were mates to one another. Even some of the more benevolent slavemasters came to the "jumping the broom" ceremonies of their slaves. However, the so-called marriage ceremony consisted of the intended partners merely jumping over a broom. Was this ideal? No, of course not. Why? There were no vows exchanged.

To be sure, when laws prevent marriage, we do what we can do in order to present ourselves to each other and to signal that we are committed to one another. However, it is not sufficient either to just jump a broom or simply rent a trailer and move in together. Scripture teaches that:

Marriage is honorable for all, and one's bed should remain undefiled because God will judge fornicators and adulterers.

Hebrews 13:4 KJV Paraphrase

Marriage specifically involves an exchange of vows between two intended spousal partners who desire to live in a committed, lifelong, and monogamous spousal relationship with one another in the sight of God. For those who might say that marriage or holy union between two people of the same sex should not be performed in countries where they are not legal, I would respond that the laws of God are higher than governmental laws. In other words, it is God who desires that we should marry in order to escape sexual immorality. (Read 1 Corinthians, Chapter 7.) Consequently, marriages between homosexual people should not be hindered. Christ Jesus said, "What God has joined together, let no one pull apart" (Matthew 19:6b KJV Paraphrase).

Scripture teaches that sexual intimacy between two people seals the vows that they have made between them so "they are no longer two but one flesh" (Matthew 19:6a KJV Paraphrase). If sexual intimacy takes place without the exchange of vows, then the potential for all sorts of problems is set up. *For example*, the Apostle Paul taught:

Do you not know that one who unites his or her body with a prostitute is one with him or her? "Two who join themselves together sexually," God says, "become one flesh."

1 Corinthians 6:16 KJV Paraphrase

Joining oneself to nonspousal bedpartners produces all sorts of unhealthy consequences — such as shared addictions, shared emotional instabilities, and shared sexually-transmitted diseases. Furthermore, Scripture is quite clear that God is against "fornication" (that is, sex outside of marriage, holy union, or spousal commitment).

Because marriage is God's ideal, homosexual people who profess love for one another should exchange vows. With the exchange of vows comes rights, responsibilities, expectations, and trust that honor the love that two people share. That is why marriage should be honored by all, homosexual people and heterosexual people alike.

When I was Senior Pastor of Healing Waters Ministries in Tempe, Arizona (U.S.A.) from 1998 to 2007, couples would came to me to perform a holy union or marriage ceremony. I counseled them over a period of time and instructed them by discussing the following questions with them:

1. Have both partners accepted the Lord Jesus Christ as their personal Savior?

2. Is the couple seeking to make the relationship permanent through lifelong monogamous commitment?

3. Is the couple willing to stay together, and remain faithful to one another (*for example*, during extended periods of sickness or unemployment) until death separates them?

4. Do the partners have a long term history of mutual love and respect?

5. Have the partners disclosed to each other their respective income, assets, and liabilities and obligations?

6. Is each partner willing to completely share their income and assets with the other; and is each partner willing to jointly assume the debts, liabilities, and obligations of the other?

7. Is the couple willing to demonstrate their commitment legally through joint ownership of property, shared banking and checking accounts, medical powers of attorney, and naming each other as beneficiaries in wills and on insurance policies?

8. Is the couple willing to state their commitments to one another in the form of vows and promises?

9. Is the couple willing to state what would make their commitment to one another null and void?

If the answer to any one of the previous questions was "no," then I would not perform the ceremony until such time as each answer was genuinely "yes." Otherwise, the couple would be unequally yoked together or their relationship based on false assumptions, and their partnership would be headed in the direction of failure.

Spiritual Healing and Restoration

In the broadest sense, spiritual healing and restoration refer to the reunion of God's people and the Lord God Almighty. That spiritual healing and restoration are possible is a gift from the Lord God Almighty and Him alone. It is He who has sought us. It is He who has refused to give His glory — which is to say, His creation — to His Enemy, the Devil. Because of God's love for us, He has restrained His Wrath, or justified Anger, from being poured out on His fallen creation and, at the same time, He has provided a pathway of salvation for us to return to Him:

> I am the Lord [*Yahweh*]: that is My name: and My glory will I not give to another, neither will I give My praise to graven images. [brackets mine]
>
> Isaiah 42:8 KJV Paraphrase

> For My name's sake I defer My anger, for the sake of My praise I restrain it for you, that I may not cut you off. Behold I have refined you, but not like silver; I have tried you in the furnace of affliction. For My own sake, for My own sake, I do it, for how should My name be profaned? My glory I will not give to another.
>
> Isaiah 48:9-11 RS

Our lives are meaningless and without purpose unless they are lived for the glory of God. To be sure, the Lord God Almighty desires humanity to be healed and restored to Him and desires that we be healed and restored to each other in that process as well. Scripture is clear that we are considered by the Lord God Almighty to be parts of a whole through our individual membership in the body of His Christ (1 Corinthians 12:12-31) — as "living stones" in His spiritual temple, which has Christ Jesus as its cornerstone (1 Peter 2:4-8). Indeed, all of us are parts of God's whole.

It is recorded in 1 Corinthians 12:21 (KJV), concerning the body of Christ, that "the eye cannot say to the hand, 'I have no need of you' nor the head to the feet, 'I have no need of you.'" So, also, it is not permissible for Christian heterosexual people and homosexual people to say to each other, "we don't need you."

{24} Our important parts seem to have no need of other parts, but God has tempered all parts of the body together, having given greater honor to the parts that seem less important {25} that there should be no schism in the body, but that the parts should have the same care and concern for another. {26} And, if one member of the body suffers, all other members suffer with it; or if one member is honored, then all other members rejoice with it.

1 Corinthians 12:24-26 KJV Paraphrase

Scripture teaches that, through the wounds of Christ Jesus, all separation from God has already been healed (1 Peter 2:24). To be sure, when souls are added to the body of Christ at the time they accept Christ Jesus as their personal Savior, they are instantly and immediately healed spiritually and restored to God. In other words, saved souls are made whole and perfect in God's sight as soon as they are added to the Church Universal, which consists of the visible church as well as the invisible church (the latter includes those who have already preceded the former in their entrance to Paradise).

Unfortunately, the arms of the visible church are not outstretched to receive homosexual people and transgender people into fellowship with it: Some denominations will not receive Christian homosexual people at all and others will not receive them as full participants. These are the areas where spiritual healing and restoration must yet take place. Since the foundation for such spiritual healing and restoration has already been laid in Christ Jesus at the time of his crucifixion, I anticipate that full healing and restoration will come one day — although not completely until Christ Jesus returns to the earth at his Second Coming.

When asked when he was going to restore the kingdom to Israel (which occurs upon his return to earth), Christ Jesus responded, "'It is not for you to know the times or the seasons that the Father has put under His own power'" (Acts 1:7 KJV Paraphrase). Similarly, we may not know when complete restoration for Christian homosexual people to the visible church will take place until it happens. It is my hope that this book is part of a good beginning for reconciliation and restoration because its message seeks to honor the name of the Lord God Almighty, and influence others toward Good, God. As Christ Jesus teaches us in Matthew 19:17 (KJV), "There is none good but one, that is, God."

Witnessing to GLBT Non-Christians

A short list compiled for those who seek to share the Biblical gospel of Christ Jesus with GLBT non-Christians:

1. Pray that God grants repentance to GLBT non-Christians in the knowledge of salvation through Christ Jesus and Christ Jesus alone. Emphasize to GLBT non-Christians that they are to repent of their sins and not of their sexual orientation or gender identity. Especially pray for those GLBT non-Christians who have been taught to believe that Christ Jesus wants nothing to do with them. It is important to understand that, because of such indoctrination, some GLBT non-Christians have not yet had an opportunity to make a free will choice concerning acceptance or rejection of Christ Jesus as their Personal Savior. It is our job to help explain that Christ Jesus died for everyone. Pray that God reveal the true source of hateful judgmentalism and condemnation (all judgmentalism and condemnation are hateful) from so-called mainstream Christianity and purported fundamental Christians. Pray that God reveal the source of the Christian faith, which is the crucified and resurrected *only-begotten* Son of God, Christ Jesus,

to GLBT non-Christians as well as to nominal GLBT Christians (those who might say that they are Christian but do not accept their rights and responsibilities as authentic Christian believers).

2. Emphasize that God is the God of sacrificial, selfless, and forgiving love and not the god of hatred and accusation (Satan himself is *that* god). Explain the difference between God's righteous judgment through wrath (divine judgment in justified anger) as opposed to Satan's cruelty through fear, intimidation, terrorism, judgmentalism, condemnation, and accusation. Acknowledge that, historically, mainstream Christianity and fundamental Christians have been guilty of ignorance and intolerance of GLBT communities and that mainstream Christianity and fundamental Christians have been guilty of attempting to convert GLBT non-Christians by forcing them to reject what God has created and designed them to be. (A real conversion is an exercise of one's free will choice and not an acquiescence to coercion or peer pressure.) Help new GLBT Christians come to understand how important it is for them to forgive others for abusing, oppressing, and victimizing them. Help them to understand that such forgiveness occurs over time through God's healing their wounded hearts.

3. Emphasize that judgmental and condemning people have distorted, and continue to distort, who God is and what He has said in His written Word, the Holy Bible.

4. Emphasize that the Bible is not a work that has been corrupted over thousands of years: The roles of the ancient Hebrew "lawyers" (Torah scholars) and "scribes" (Tanakh copyists) helped to ensure that the Christian Old Testament (the Hebrew Scripture used in Judaism) was painstakingly copied accurately and correctly. Emphasize that enough scrolls have survived through thousands of years to help substantiate the validity of the individual books of the Old Testament as well as the gospels and letters of the New Testament. Emphasize that the Holy Spirit is responsible for authoring the Holy Bible but not responsible for the mistranslations, misinterpretations, and misapplications of it. (Keep in mind that most GLBT non-Christians have only been

exposed to the Bible through religious ignorance and intolerance of them as well as through error-filled secular television programs with titillating titles such as "The Lost Books of the Bible" and "Was Jesus Married to Mary Magdalene?")

5. Encourage GLBT non-Christians to read the Bible, starting with Genesis and Exodus and then the four gospels (John, Matthew, Mark, and Luke — in that order). Invite them to a home Bible study specifically designed for GLBT non-Christians.

6. Talk about God's requirement of a perfect blood sacrifice for the forgiveness of sins and how the only perfect blood sacrifice was the one He provided through His Son, Y'shua H'Moshiach (Christ Jesus, Jesus Christ, Jesus the Messiah, or Jesus the Christ).

7. Talk about God's goodness as demonstrated through His grace (receiving what we do not deserve) and mercy (not receiving what we do deserve). God's grace is demonstrated through the opportunity to receive forgiveness for our sins, and God's mercy is demonstrated by our not receiving eternal separation from God, which is actually what all people, gay and straight alike, deserve.

8. Talk about how, when we come to Christ Jesus, the burdens of: a) guilt from sin, b) condemnation by God, and c) accompanying shame are palpably removed from us and that then, and only then, do we have the freedom to be who God created and designed us to be, which includes coming to complete terms with God's acceptance of our God-given GLBT natures and personalities.

9. Emphasize that God desires for GLBT people to act responsibly by seeking to live up to His moral and ethical standards as proud GLBT people. Because GLBT non-Christians will be interested in what those moral and ethical standards are, be prepared to talk about God's ideals concerning covenants, commitments, and faithfulness and how learning to live up to His ideals can take an entire lifetime.

10. Be much less concerned about force-feeding your denominational views and personal interpretations of Scripture. Use noncontroversial Scripture to help explain the foundational principles of the Christian faith. Do not undermine someone's salvation because you feel it imperative to discuss what you think is error in another denomination's doctrinal position. Be honest and open about what you believe but not dogmatic.

11. Be patient with new Christians. Don't expect them to understand everything all at once. *For example*, new Christians may have an easy time understanding that Christ Jesus is the "*only-begotten* Son of God" but have a difficult time understanding that Christ Jesus *is* God in the flesh.

12. Use this list (items 1 through 11) as a "talking document" to generate discussion with other Christians concerning additional items to include and how to further refine the ones already listed.

Concluding Remarks

In summary, Christian heterosexual people have no right to call Christian homosexual people *unclean* when God has cleansed them — even under the guise of "hating the sin but loving the sinner." To be sure, the homosexual orientation is no more sinful than the heterosexual orientation. And, if Christian homosexual people want to lay claim to all of the promises of God, then they need to act responsibly — in accordance with the ideal of morality inscribed within God's written Word, the Holy Bible. All who seek to enter the Kingdom of God must take time to be holy, and that includes having holy spousal relationships unless God has called them to be celibate. Those who pursue holiness will not regret it when they hear the Lord Jesus say to them, "Well done, my good and faithful servants.[58] You may now enter the heavenly gates!"

Relative to the artificial division that currently exists between Christian heterosexual people and Christian homosexual people, it is

---

58   Matthew 25:21, KJV Paraphrase

fitting that I close this final chapter with Christ Jesus' prayer to God the Father for all believers, both heterosexual and homosexual:

> "Let me be in them as You are in me, that they may be made perfect in one; and that the world may know that You have sent me and have loved them, just as You have loved me."

John 17:23 KJV Paraphrase

Because this prayer is the prayer of Christ Jesus, it cannot help but be answered because it is in perfect agreement with the Will of God the Father. Therefore, trust that this prayer is being answered and its prophetic elements are being fulfilled right now. Therefore, let us look forward with eager anticipation to the time of its complete fulfillment through our perfect unity.

Christ Jesus is our living hope — not just hope for tomorrow but hope for this very moment on this very day. Christ Jesus is our eternal hope!

Afterword

In providing support for the reconcilability of Christianity and homosexuality, the author of this book has taken a conservative Biblical approach. Although the author is aware of other, additional arguments that have been used to support such reconciliation, he has purposely refrained from using arguments he considers suspect, specious, and revisionist in nature. *For example*, it is the present author's position that: 1) Any author who even suggests that David and Jonathan, Ruth and Naomi, or Christ Jesus and the Apostle John were homosexual or bisexual people has little understanding of the intensity of nonsexual, or platonic, love that can develop between two people of the same sex. 2) Any author who purports that the word *eunuch* is a Biblical code word for a homosexual or transgender person has never carefully studied the Babylonian Talmud. And 3) anyone who teaches that the centurion and his servant from Matthew 8:5-13 (or Luke 7:1-10) were gay lovers is willing to "strain out a gnat while swallowing a camel" (Matthew 23:24 KJV Paraphrase).

In writing this book, the present author has not sought to ingratiate himself to either heterosexual people or homosexual people. Instead, the present author has sought to honor the God of the Holy Bible as well as to help free people who have been held captive by ignorance, fear, and/or hatred.

Jesus Christ is the *only-begotten* Son of God, Savior of the world, and my personal Savior. Won't you, the reader or listener, accept Jesus Christ as your personal Savior, too?

Examples of Intersex Categories

The following list has not been included to try to prepare you for a medical degree but to help you see that the causes for ambiguities in sexual identity and genital identity are complex and varied as well as found in a wide spectrum on a continuum.

I.   XY individuals that feminize or fail to masculinize
    A. Lack SRY gene (normally found on short arm of Y chromosome)
    B. Have SRY gene
        1. Decreased androgen activity due to protein receptor abnormalities
            a. Complete Testicular Feminization
            b. Incomplete (Partial) Testicular Feminization
            c. Reifenstein's Syndrome (presence of enlarged mammary glands and male genitalia)
        2. Increased estrogen activity
            a. Abnormal pituitary hypersecretion of LH (ICSH) that leads to testicular estrogen production
            b. Testicular tumor

c. Increased estrogen-androgen ratio

d. Adrenal/Suprarenal tumor

e. Aromatization (i.e., peripheral conversion) of secreted androgens (sometimes due to liver disease)

f. Decrease in peripheral conversion of testosterone to its active metabolite, dihydrotestosterone

3. Male pseudohermaphroditism (with 5α-reductase deficiency) These individuals are usually raised as girls. However, at puberty, breasts fail to develop, pubic and facial hair develop, menses does not occur, and external genitalia virilize (i.e., masculinize). By standards for girls at puberty, testosterone production is increased. Some of these individuals assume male gender roles after puberty. (In Spanish, this condition is sometimes referred to as *Guevodoces*.)

II. XX individuals that masculinize or fail to feminize

A. Have SRY gene (translocated from Y to X during spermatogenesis)

B. Lack SRY gene

1. Female Pseudohermaphroditism

a. Exogenously-produced androgens (intrauterine exposure during pregnancy)

1) hormone therapy

2) maternal ovarian production

3) maternal adrenal production

b. Endogenously-produced androgens

1) adrenal production (includes Adrenogenital Syndrome and Congenital Adrenal Hyperplasia, or CAH)

2) ovarian production (e.g., polycystic ovarian disease)

2. Sexual Infantilism due to 17-hydroxylase deficiency (which mediates estrogen production)

3. Turner's Syndrome (individual has only 45 chromosomes: lacks a second sex chromosome)

III. Hermaphroditism
   A. Pseudohermaphroditism
   B. True Hermaphroditism (requires the concomitant presence of ovarian as well as testicular tissue)
      1. Mosaicism
         A mosaic is an organism that can arise from abnormal cell division of an XY or XXY individual during embryogenesis.
      2. Chimerism
         A chimera is an offspring that results from fusion of two or more different zygotes (i.e., *fertilized oocytes*).

Appendix B

Question Assignments

Dear Students and Prospective Students:

Although the following pages provide the framework for a "stand-alone" online correspondence course entitled *Christianity and Homosexuality Reconciled*, these course materials may also be used in conjunction with "on-the-ground" classroom instruction. Thus, if you have an in-class instructor, facilitator, or discussion leader, supplementary resources may be used to enhance instruction vis-à-vis lecture, multi-media, and classroom discussion sessions.

Regardless of how you are taking this course, please always consult with the contact person(s) identified to answer your questions. If you are taking this course through an organization other than Christ Evangelical Bible Institute (CEBI), contact the lead person identified by that organization. However, if you have recommendations for change to improve the course materials, always contact CEBI by first visiting www.cebiaz.com or www.christevangelicalbibleinstitute.com to find CEBI contact information there.

Although definite theological and doctrinal positions are presented in CEBI course materials, please know that: 1) there are no real divisions within the Body of Christ, and 2) authentic Christian believers are found in all Christian denominations and persuasions. If your own personal Christian theology differs with any of the positions presented in CEBI course materials, all we ask is that you have a sound Scriptural basis for your position. (The Holy Bible is the only true Scripture. There is no other true Scripture.) The primary position in which authentic Christian believers cannot differ is in personal salvation through the shed blood of Christ Jesus, the *only-begotten* Son of God, and in public confession of one's faith in Christ Jesus as the only Savior of the world. Such faith is what unites all authentic Christian believers not only to Christ Jesus but also to each other.

If you would like feedback as well as a certificate of course completion for "Christianity and Homosexuality Reconciled" from Christ Evangelical Bible Institute, answer the following questions carefully after reading each section of *Christianity and Homosexuality Reconciled: New Thinking for a New Millennium!*

Make sure that you incorporate each question itself into your answer so that each question and its answer present a unified whole. Although typed answers are preferred, a handwritten assignment is permitted if your handwriting is very clear and legible.

If you have already paid correspondence tuition for this course to Christ Evangelical Bible Institute, no additional payment is necessary. If you use postal mail, please send a self-addressed stamped envelope (SASE) for each assignment sent. Assignments sent without an SASE or without sufficient postage will not be returned. Otherwise, email all completed assignments to: Dr. Joseph Pearson at DrJPearson@aol.com or drjosephadampearson@gmail.com. You may send in answers to questions from Chapters One through Three, Chapter Four, Chapter Five, and Chapter Six separately or in any combination.

Questions for Chapters One through Three

1. What five historically-controversial human rights issues have existed within the Christian Church? (one sentence)

2.   In the Old and New Testaments, slavery is both explicitly and implicitly condoned. Give a Scriptural basis as to why slavery should not be permitted by civil law? (four to five sentences)

3.   What does the author mean when he states, "half-truths are presented when the Bible is not taken in its entirety"? (one to two sentences)

4.   Students of the Bible should seek to "hold the _____ Bible while they simultaneously attend to its various _____." (fill-in-the-blanks)

5.   Complete the following by referring to 1 Peter 2:24 (KJV): He himself bore "our _____ in his own _____ on the _____ that we, being dead to sins, should live unto righteousness; by His _____ you have been healed." (fill-in-the-blanks)

6.   Complete the following by referring to 1 John 1:8-9 (KJV): "If we say that we have no _____, we _____ ourselves and the _____ is not in us. If we confess our sins, he is _____ and _____ to forgive us our sins and to _____ us from all unrighteousness." (fill-in-the-blanks)

7.   Does the Lord show favoritism toward — or partiality for — heterosexual people over homosexual people or transgender people? Why or why not? Use scriptural references to back up your answer. (four to five sentences)

8.   Scripture plainly teaches that we will have bodies in heaven but not "flesh and blood" bodies. Which Scriptures help us to understand that we will not be gendered males, gendered females, or sexually active beings in heaven? Please explain. (four to five sentences)

9.   Whom shall we look like when our bodies are redeemed? Give the scriptural basis for your answer. (three to four sentences)

10. According to Rabbi Jacob Milgrom, is it correct to universally apply the Biblical prohibition found in Leviticus 18:22 against same-sex behavior? Why or why not? Has the Rabbi taken into account grace and the role that male temple cult prostitution

played in the Lord God Almighty originally instituting such sexual prohibitions? (five to six sentences)

11. In the *Declaration on Certain Questions Concerning Sexual Ethics*, issued by the Vatican in 1975, it is declared that, for some individuals, homosexuality is an *innate instinct*. What significance should the use of the words *innate instinct* have for someone seeking to condemn homosexual people for their homosexual orientation? (three to four sentences)

12. Define the following terms: *homosexual*, *bisexual*, *transgender*, *intersexual*, *sexual orientation*, *sexual preference*, *sexual identity*, *homophobia* and *transphobia*. (one sentence for each term)

13. Does *homosexual* mean *one who engages in same-sex activity*? Why or why not? (three to four sentences)

14. How do some gay and lesbian people become self-loathing? (four to five sentences)

15. According to the American Psychological Association, is sexual orientation a choice? Please explain. (three to four sentences)

16. Describe how you would respond to the statement, "God created Adam and Eve, not Adam and Steve nor Ada and Eve"? Include in your discussion a possible biological explanation for the phenomenon of homosexuality. (about 100 words)

17. Using John 9:1-3, how might you respond to someone who states that all physical, emotional, and psychosexual anomalies exist because of the Adamic Fall and are, therefore, always caused by iniquity and/or sin? (three to four sentences)

Questions for Chapter Four

18. What were the conditions requested by Abraham under which the Lord God Almighty would spare the city of Sodom? (two to three sentences)

19. What parallels exist between the Genesis 19 account of the two angelic visitors in Sodom and the Judges 19 through 20:1-5 account of the Levite and his concubine in Gibeah? (Construct a table to indicate the parallels.)

20. What insights are provided by the Levite's statement in Judges 20:5 regarding the Sodom account of the intended rape in Genesis 19? (three to four sentences)

21. What is meant by the statement, "Scripture interprets Scripture"? (one to three sentences)

22. a) Give the names of three common Canaanite fertility deities.
b) Which goddess is also referred to as "Ishtar" in ancient Babylon and "Astarte" in ancient Greece? (two sentences)

23. a) How did intermarriage with the Canaanites, Hittites, Amorites, Perizzites, Hivites, Jebusites, Moabites, Ammonites, Edomites, and Sidonians influence the religious practices of the children of Israel?
b) What impact did such intermarriage have on King Solomon's relationship with the Lord God Almighty?
c) Which pagan deities did Solomon end up serving? (three to four sentences)

24. What is a Bible concordance? (one to two sentences)

25. a) How many times does the singular form of the word *sodomite* occur in the King James Version of the Bible? (one sentence)
b) How many times does *sodomite* occur in its plural form? (one sentence)
c) Since *sodomite(s)* in the King James Version is used only in the Old Testament, would you expect to find the original word in a Hebrew lexicon (dictionary) or Greek lexicon (dictionary)? (one sentence)
d) Using *Strong's Exhaustive Concordance of the Bible*, what is the meaning of the original word from which *sodomite* has been translated in the *King James Version of the Bible*? (one sentence)

26. In 1 Kings 14:24, did the Lord really say that the people were removed because of homosexuality? Explain by referring to *Strong's Exhaustive Concordance of the Bible*. (two to three sentences)

27. Compare and contrast the various renderings of 1 Kings 14:24 using at least six different versions of the Holy Bible. Which translations are the most accurate, and which are the least accurate relative to translating the word *Qadeshim*? Please explain. (four to five sentences)

28. What is the difference between a Bible translation and a Bible paraphrase? (two sentences)

29. a) What is the *Asherah* or "shame image" referring to in 2 Kings 23:7? (one sentence)
    b) According to the Revised Standard version of the Bible, where was the Asherah that King Josiah destroyed? (one sentence)

30. a) According to Ezekiel, what were the sins of Sodom? (one sentence)
    b) Were the "detestable practices" or "detestable things" referred to by Ezekiel acts between homosexual people in committed monogamous relationships? (one sentence)

31. a) What is idolatry? (one sentence)
    b) Does the Lord God Almighty condemn idolatry? (one sentence)
    c) Why? Please use scriptural references to back up your explanation. (two to three sentences)

32. a) When Christ Jesus referred to Sodom, what was the context? (two sentences)
    b) What did Christ Jesus have to say about homosexuality in the Bible? (one sentence)

33. a) What are the origins of the Greek words *malakoi* and *arsenokoitai*? (one sentence)
    b) What are their probable meanings? (two to three sentences)

34. a) In what way does St. Jerome's Latin Vulgate translation of the Bible (published circa 405 A.D.) help us to understand the meaning of *malakoi*? (one sentence)

b) Who were the *effeminati* and *molles*? (one sentence)

35. Do the words *malakoi* and *arsenokoitai* refer to modern-day Christian homosexual people? Why or why not? (two to three sentences)

36. What kind of male-male sex was the Apostle Paul knowledgeable about in his day? (i.e., What kinds of male-male sex were common in Greco-Roman societies?) (three to four sentences)

37. What is the context of Romans 1:18-32? (two to three sentences)

38. What kind of idolatry existed during the Apostle Paul's time? (one sentence)

39. What is *lust*? (two sentences)

40. a) In what way does the Bible address same-sex behaviors? (one sentence)
    b) Does the Bible condemn committed monogamous relationships between homosexual people? (one sentence)

Questions for Chapter Five

41. What is (the) *Torah*, or the *Pentateuch*? (one sentence)

42. Where in the Bible is *the Law* found? (one to four sentences)

43. Find twelve examples of prohibitions in Leviticus that Christians regularly break. Include scriptural references. (In other words, create a list with related scriptural references.)

44. Do the laws of Leviticus appertain to Christians? (two sentences)

45. Why were Levitical laws laid down? (two sentences)

46. What did Christ Jesus say was the "sum" of the Law of Moses? (one sentence)

47. When Christ Jesus spoke of his fulfilling the Law, what did he mean? (two sentences)

48. a) What must we have in order to please the Lord God Almighty? (one sentence)
    b) Who is its author, finisher, and perfecter? (one sentence)

49. Are Christians supposed to live their lives according to Levitical Law? Please explain. (two to three sentences)

50. What is the danger of using Levitical Law in assessing or judging others? (two to three sentences)

51. Did Christ Jesus ever break Levitical Law? Explain with examples. (three to four sentences)

52. In what ways was Molech worshiped? (one to two sentences)

53. What important link exists between 1 Kings 14:24 and Leviticus 18:24? (two to three sentences)

54. Considering the link that exists between 1 Kings 14:24 and Leviticus 18:24, as well as the lead-in of Leviticus 18:21, what is the context of Leviticus 18:22 and 18:23? (three to four sentences)

55. a) According to *The Expositor's Bible*, what is the context for the prohibition against male-male sex in Leviticus? (two to three sentences)
    b) How does Leviticus 18:1-5 support this view? (two to three sentences)

56. After reading Chapters 18, 19, and 20 of Leviticus, explain why there is a double reference to male-male sex in Leviticus 18:21 and Leviticus 20:13. (three to four sentences)

57. Why did the Lord God Almighty take such a seemingly hard-line stance against transvestitism? Is transvestitism *per se* morally wrong? (three sentences)

58. Does the Lord God Almighty really care about hair length or clothing type? Why or why not? (three to four sentences)

59. In what way was castration used to honor fertility goddesses? (three to four sentences)

60. Are males who accidentally lose both testes (testicles) really prevented from entering into the congregation of the Lord? Please explain. (three to four sentences)

61. In what ways are the contexts different for Deuteronomy 23:1 and Leviticus 21:20 relative to individuals missing one testis (testicle) or both testes (testicles)? (three to four sentences)

62. Define *prototype* and *anomaly* and discuss how eunuchs might be considered ancient prototypes for modern-day homosexual people. Be sure to include references to Leviticus 21:20, Deuteronomy 23:1, Isaiah 56:3-5, and Acts 8:26-40 in your discussion. (approximately 250 words)

63. In what ways are homosexual people *physiologic eunuchs*? (three to four sentences)

64. Referring to Isaiah 56, why might Christian homosexual people have "a better name" in heaven? (In other words, why might oppressed people who are faithful to Christ Jesus receive a greater reward in heaven?) (three to four sentences)

65. What might be the significance of the churches of Smyrna (Revelation 2:8-11) and Philadelphia (Revelation 3:7-13) in relationship to Christian GLBT people? (three to four sentences)

66. What might be the significance of John 16:1-4 to Christian GLBT people? (three to four sentences)

67. Was Christ Jesus himself cursed by the letter of the Law of Moses? Use scriptural references in your answer. (three to four sentences)

68. How does 1 Corinthians 1:27-29 relate to the issue of homosexuality? How can these verses help to solve the issue of condemnation of homosexual people and transgender people once and for all? (three to four sentences)

69. Who can tell the Lord God Almighty to whom He should extend His mercy and grace? (one sentence)

70. How does Acts 10:15 relate to Christian homosexual people? (two to three sentences)

71. How could you use Romans 5:1 and 8:33, 1 Corinthians 6:11, Galatians 2:16-17, and Titus 3:7 to help someone who wants to justify his or her homosexuality to family members or friends? (four to five sentences)

Questions for Chapter Six

72. What does Scripture tell us to do when someone has sinned or trespassed against us? Why is this especially important to Christian homosexual people? (four to five sentences)

73. According to 1 John 4:18, why should homosexual people not be afraid of their sexual orientation? (one to two sentences)

74. According to the Holy Bible, what is *sexual immorality*? (one sentence)

75. What is *serial monogamy*? (one sentence)

76. What are the spiritual and sexual responsibilities of heterosexual people and homosexual people? (two to three sentences)

77. How can you honor God with your body? (two sentences)

78. Why should homosexual people be encouraged to have holy unions and be married? (three to four sentences)

79. Discuss what homosexual people have in common with Christ Jesus? (answer length will vary)

80. What are spiritual healing and restoration and how do they relate to Christian heterosexual people and Christian homosexual people? (three to four sentences)

81. a) Map out a strategy you might use to share the gospel with non-Christian homosexual people. (answer format and length will vary)

b) How would you respond to those individuals who express that homosexual Christians are "self-loathing freaks seeking acceptance from people who hate them." (approximately 250 words)

82. Create an outline of topics with scriptural references that you can use to help minister to hurting homosexual people who, though they have accepted Christ Jesus, believe that he does not accept them because of their sexual orientation. (2 page outline)

83. Do you have any additional questions that have been left unanswered by this book? Please Email your questions to Dr. Pearson and he will be pleased to respond: DrJPearson@aol.com or drjosephadampearson@gmail.com

God Bless you as you continue to seek our Lord's Will for your life!

P.S. The chapter questions in Appendix B can be useful in small or large group discussions after participants have read the chapter(s) to be discussed.

APPENDIX C

Fast Facts for Distribution Purposes

For the purpose of mass distribution, the following three documents — entitled *Fast Facts* — can be photocopied. When photocopying, no alterations may be made with the exception of removing the book page numbers from the footers on each page.

Fast Facts
About Christianity and Homosexuality

by Rev. Joseph Adam Pearson, Ph.D.
International President, Christ Evangelical Bible Institute

Question

How do you reconcile your Christian beliefs with the passages from the Bible that relate to homosexual practices?

Answer

First, I make a distinction between "same-sex behaviors" and "homosexual practices." Practices between people of a homosexual orientation are different from same-sex activities that may occur between people of an unresolved sexual orientation. I write "unresolved" not to describe internal conflict or how the people view themselves but, rather, to describe that it is indeterminate within the Holy Bible whether the behaviors often used to condemn homosexual people are really between homosexual people as opposed to obligate heterosexual people and/or people involved in ambisexual activity (*ambisexual* here referring to a complete indifference to the gender identity and/or sexual orientation of a sexual partner).

With that said, I also turn to historical and literary contexts, Hebrew and Greek etymologies (i.e., word origins), and hermeneutics to properly divide the word of truth.

The often-quoted story of Sodom in Chapter Nineteen of Genesis is a story of intended brutal group rape and not a story of homosexual people who are each involved in a committed, covenant-based, and lifelong monogamous relationship.

The reference in Chapter Eighteen of Leviticus is properly understood only within its historical and literary contexts. Verse 3 of that Chapter clearly states that the children of Israel were to avoid the practices of the Egyptians and the Canaanites, for which practices the Lord God Almighty was "going to cast out the nations before them" (verse 24) — which practices are more specifically referred to in 1 Kings 14:24 as the practices of the *Qadeshim* (the male temple cult prostitutes who served as religious functionaries in the worship of both male and female fertility pagan gods and goddesses). The Hebrew word *Qadeshim* was translated as "sodomites" in the 1611 edition of the King James Version of the Holy Bible and, hence, has been assumed erroneously to refer to modern-day homosexual people.

The Apostle Paul uses the Greek words *malakoi* and *arsenokoitai* in 1 Corinthians 6:9. *Malakoi* in this verse has a pejorative slang meaning that St. Jerome translated into the Latin cognate as *molles*. *Molles* is a Latin word that is a synonym to *effeminati*, which word St. Jerome used to translate the Hebrew word *Qadeshim* into Latin. Both *effeminati* and *molles* are referring to the transvestite male temple cult prostitutes who served in the sexual "worship" of various Canaanite fertility gods and goddesses, including Baal, Molech, and Ashtoreth (later known as Ishtar and Astarte) as well as the Greek and Roman fertility goddesses Cybele, Magna Mater, Anaitis, Hecate, Artemis, and Aphrodite. *Arsenokoitai* is a coined Greek word that St. Jerome translated into Latin as "concubitores masculorum," which literally means "the bought [i.e., *paid for*] male sex slaves of men." So, St. Paul was not referring to homosexual people joined in holy union but people who were involved in idolatrous and/or prostitutional sexual activity.

Chapter One of Romans is referring to same-sex activity in cult temples and other common areas that involved idolatrous pagan worshipers rather than homosexual people *per se*. The use of the Greek word "phusiken" that is often translated as "natural" also means "instinctual," which brings forth a whole other discussion about biology, hormones, embryonic and fetal development, brain morphology and physiology, and cognitive and developmental psychology as they relate to, and influence, genital identity, gender identity, and sexual orientation.

Ironically, the "strange flesh" reference in Jude 7 (KJV) is translated from the Greek words "heteros sarkos." I write "ironically," because if one wanted to strain out gnats and swallow camels, one could write a scholarly treatise on how the phrase is referring to heterosexual people (it's really not). Though many would like to make the reference in Jude a same-sex issue, it is clearly referring to the different kind of "flesh" of the angels that the people of Sodom wanted to rape.

Distributed with permission from the author.

Fast Facts
The Bible and Transgender People

by Rev. Joseph Adam Pearson, Ph.D.
International President, Christ Evangelical Bible Institute

The most often quoted Biblical citations used against exceptions to gender norms include:

So God created humanity in His image, in the image of God humanity was created male and female.

Genesis 1:27 KJV Paraphrase

God blessed them, and God said to them, "Be fruitful, and multiply, and replenish the earth, and subdue it…"

Genesis 1:28a KJV Paraphrase

To be sure, the above passages express the general rule but are not universal or absolute. Exceptions to this general rule are found both in nature and in Scripture itself:

From a biological standpoint, the presence or absence of genitals is a state of nature; and gender is a state of mind that is ultimately responsible for an individual's instincts. If you think that transgender people are perversions of nature, then you have made "male and female" an absolute or universal law, which law is contradictory to the full spectrum of what occurs in nature. Indeed, such an absolute fails to take into consideration the myriad departures in nature that deviate from the norm (*norm* defined here as "that which occurs most frequently").

Such an absolute also fails to take into consideration spiritual law that states in Christ "there is neither male nor female" (Galatians 3:28). Spiritually speaking, God does not discriminate using gender or sexual distinctions. Certainly, in heaven such distinctions do not exist. As Christ Jesus explained:

> "In the resurrection, people neither marry nor are given in marriage, but are as the angels of God in heaven." Matthew 22:30 KJV Paraphrase

True science does not contradict pure religion nor does pure religion contradict true science. True science shows that there are exceptions to the so-called absolute scriptural rule of "male and female" (Genesis 1:27) in the form of intersexuals (i.e., individuals whose physical nature is somewhat ambiguous or uncertain with regard to sexual identity or genital identity); and pure religion shows that there are exceptions to that rule in the form of eunuchs — of whom, Christ Jesus said, "some are born that way" (Matthew 19:12). In other words, intersexuals serve as biological prototypes for transgender people, and eunuchs serve as scriptural prototypes for them. Thus, God accounts for exceptions to the general rule of "male and female" both naturally and scripturally.

Scripture not only acknowledges that there are exceptions to the rule of anatomic males and females but also acknowledges that there are exceptions to the directive for them to reproduce (i.e., "be fruitful and multiply"). If anatomic males and females were a universal law, and reproduction was an absolute, God would not have consoled eunuchs as He does in Isaiah 56:3b-5:

{3b} The eunuch must not say, "Behold, I am a dry tree" {*dry tree* connoting the inability to reproduce}. {4} For thus says the Lord to the eunuchs who keep My sabbaths, and choose what pleases Me, and abide by My covenant. {5} I will give to them in My house and within My walls a place and a name better than of sons and of daughters {*sons and daughters* here referring to those who do reproduce}: I will give them an everlasting name that will not be cut off {the expression *cut off* is *double entendre* because it also alludes to the eunuch who has had something *cut off*}. Isaiah 56:3b-5 KJV Paraphrase {brackets mine}

So, why the seemingly hard-line stance by God when He states:

A woman shall not wear that which pertains to a man, neither shall a man put on a woman's garment: for all that do so are abomination unto the Lord your God. Deuteronomy 22:5 KJV Paraphrase

He that is wounded in the stones {i.e., testicles} or has his privy member {i.e., penis} cut off, shall not enter into the congregation of the Lord. Deuteronomy 23:1 KJV {brackets mine}

These previous verses were written partly because idolatrous temple practices involved in the cult worship of fertility goddesses included castrated young male prostitutes dressed up as women: 1) to emulate the feminine form of their "idol" as well as 2) to attract and better satisfy the heterosexual procurers of their ritualistic sexual *sacrifices*. So, transvestitism (i.e., "cross-dressing") in itself is not bad; it was the context in Biblical antiquity that was evil; it was the intent that was bad.

Finally, whenever we are tempted to judge another on the basis of his or her apparel, we need to remind ourselves that "as many of us as have been baptized into Christ have put on Christ" (Galatians 3:27 KJV Paraphrase). In other words, in the reality of God, when we accept the Lord Jesus Christ as our personal Savior, we are "dressed" in him. We also need to remember that in heaven we will be clothed in God's glory! Truly, God cares not one whit about how we are dressed other than that we are dressed appropriately for inclement weather or that we are dressed modestly. (Our Creator-God is like that, you know.)

Distributed with permission from the author.

Fast Facts
About Marriage for Homosexual People

by Rev. Joseph Adam Pearson, Ph.D.
President, Christ Evangelical Bible Institute

Hindering marriage, or holy unions, between homosexual people contributes to immorality and not vice versa.

When slavery was legal in the United States, people of African descent were prevented from legally marrying in the slave states. However, many of them participated in a ceremony of "jumping the broom" to signify that they were mates to one another. Even some of the more benevolent slavemasters attended these ceremonies. Unfortunately, the "marriage" ceremony generally consisted of the intended partners merely jumping over a broom. Was this ideal? No, of course not. Why? There were no vows exchanged.

To be sure, when laws prevent marriage, we do what we can do in order to present ourselves to each other and to signal that we are committed to one another. However, it is not sufficient either to just jump a broom or simply move in together. Scripture teaches that:

Marriage is honorable for all, and one's bed should remain undefiled because God will judge fornicators and adulterers.

Hebrews 13:4 KJV Paraphrase

Marriage specifically involves an exchange of vows between two intended spousal partners who desire to live in a committed, lifelong, and monogamous relationship with one another in the sight of God. For those who might say that marriage between two people of the same sex should not be performed where such marriages are not legal, I would respond that the laws of God are higher than governmental laws. In other words, it is God who desires that we should marry in order to escape sexual immorality. (Please read Chapter Seven of 1 Corinthians.) Consequently, marriages between homosexual people should not be hindered. Christ Jesus said, "What God has joined together, let no one pull apart" (Matthew 19:6b KJV Paraphrase).

Scripture teaches that sexual intimacy between two people seals the vows that they have made between them "so they are no longer two but one flesh" (Matthew 19:6a KJV Paraphrase). If sexual intimacy takes place without the exchange of vows, then the potential for all sorts of problems is set up:

Do you not know that one who unites with a prostitute is one body with {him or} her? For "The two {who join themselves sexually}," {God} says, "will become one flesh."

1 Corinthians 6:16 Modern Language Version {brackets mine}

Joining oneself to non-spousal bedpartners produces all sorts of unhealthy natural consequences such as shared sexual addictions, shared emotional instabilities, and shared sexually-transmitted diseases. Furthermore, Scripture is clear that God is against fornication (i.e., sex outside of marriage).

Because marriage, or holy union, is God's ideal, homosexual people who profess love for one another should exchange vows. With the exchange of vows comes rights, responsibilities, expectations, and trust that honor the love that two people share. That is why marriage should be honored by all, homosexual people and heterosexual people alike.

The author was Senior Pastor of Healing Waters Ministries in Tempe, Arizona from 1998 to 2007. During that period of time, if two people came to me to perform a holy union, I counseled them over a period of time and helped them determine their answers to the following:

1. Have both partners accepted the Lord Jesus Christ as their personal Savior?

2. Is the couple seeking to make the relationship permanent through lifelong commitment?

3. Is the couple willing to stay together, and remain faithful to one another during extended periods of sickness or unemployment until death separates them?

4. Do the partners have a long term history of mutual respect?

5. Have the partners disclosed to each other their respective incomes, assets, liabilities, and obligations?

6. Is each partner willing to completely share his or her income and assets with the other; and is each partner willing to jointly assume the debts, liabilities, and obligations of the other?

7. Is the couple willing to demonstrate their commitment legally through joint ownership of property, shared banking and checking accounts, medical powers of attorney, and naming each other as beneficiaries in wills and on insurance policies?

8. Is the couple willing to state their commitments to one another in the form of written and/or spoken vows and promises?

9. Is the couple willing to state what would make their commitment to one another null and void?

If the answer to any one of the previous questions was "no," then I would not perform the ceremony until such time as each answer was genuinely "yes." Otherwise, the couple would be unequally yoked together, or their relationship based on false assumptions, and their partnership would be headed in the wrong direction.

May our Lord Jesus bless you as you jointly seek His Will for your lives!

Distributed with permission from the author.

Bibliography

Angier, Natalie. "Intersexual Healing: An Anomaly Finds a Group." *The New York Times*, February 4, 1996, E14.

"Answers About Homosexuality," prepared by the Oregon Psychological Association and distributed by the Arizona Psychological Association, 202 East McDowell Road, Suite 170, Phoenix, Arizona, 85004.

"Answers to Your Questions about Sexual Orientation and Homosexuality," American Psychological Association, 750 First Street NE, Washington, DC 20002-4242.

Barton, Bruce B., David R. Veerman and Neil Wilson. *Life Application Bible Commentary: Romans*. Tyndale House Publishers, Inc., Wheaton, 1992.

Bauckman, Richard. *Word Biblical Commentary: Jude-2 Peter* (Volume 50), Word Books, Waco, 1983.

Boswell, John. *Christianity, Social Tolerance, and Homosexuality*. The University of Chicago Press, Chicago, 1980.

Brenton, Sir Lancelot C.L. *The Septuagint Version: Greek and English*. Regency Reference Library, Grand Rapids, 1990 (originally published by Samuel Bagster and Sons, London, 1851).

Burr, Chandler. *A Separate Creation: The Search for the Biological Origins of Sexual Orientation*. Hyperion, New York, 1996.

Constable, Thomas L. "1 Thessalonians." *The Bible Knowledge Commentary by* John F. Walvoord and Roy B. Zuck (eds.), Victor Books, 1983.

Crow, James F. *Genetics Notes: An Introduction to Genetics* (8th edition). Prentice Hall, New Jersey, 1987.

Duberman, Martin Baumi, Martha Vicinus, and George Chauncey, Jr. *Hidden From History: Reclaiming the Gay and Lesbian Past.* New American Library, New York, 1989.

Dunn, James D.G. *Word Biblical Commentary.* Volume 38: Romans 1-8. Word Books, Dallas, 1988.

Grant, Michael. *A Social History of Greece and Rome.* Charles Scribner's Sons, New York, 1992.

Greenberg, David F. *The Construction of Homosexuality.* University of Chicago Press, Chicago, 1988.

Hartley, John E. *Word Biblical Commentary.* Volume 2: Leviticus. Word Books, Dallas, 1992.

Haqq, Christopher, Chih-Yen King, Etsuji Ukiyama, Sassan Falsafi, Tania N. Haqq, Patricia K. Donahoe, and Michael A. Weiss. "Molecular Basis of Mammalian Sexual Determination: Activation of Müllerian Inhibiting Substance Gene Expression by SRY." *Science,* Volume 266, December 2, 1994, pages 1494-1500.

Hu, Stella, Angela Pattatucci, Chavis Patterson, Lin Li, David W. Fulker, Stacey S. Cherny, Leonoid Kruglyak and Dean H. Hamer. "Linkage between Sexual Orientation and Chromosome Xq28 in Males but not in Females." *Nature Genetics* 11, November 1995, pages 248-256.

Kimura, Doreen. "Sex Differences in the Brain." *Scientific American,* September 1992, page 119-125.

LaVay, Simon. "Brain Structure Difference Between Heterosexual and Homosexual Men." *New England Journal of Medicine,* Vol. 162, Issue 9, 1995, pages 145-167.

Luther, Martin. *Die Bibel oder die ganze Heilige Schrift des Alten and Neuen Testaments.* National Verlag Kompanie, Deutschland, 1967.

Meyer-Bahlburg, Heino, Anke A. Ehrhardt, Laura R. Rosen, Rhoda S. Gruen, Norma P. Veridiano, Felix H. Vann and Herbert F. Neuwalder. "Prenatal Estrogens and the Development of Homosexual Orientation." *Developmental Psychology*, 31, 1995, pages 12-21.

Milgrom, Jacob. "Does the Bible Prohibit Homosexuality?" In *Bible Review*, December 1993, page 11.

Miller, Madeleine S. and J. Lane. *The New Harper's Bible Dictionary*. Harper and Row, New York, 1973.

Miller, William Lee. *Arguing About Slavery: The Great Battle in the United States Congress*. Alfred A. Knopf, New York, 1996.

Nicoll, Reverend W. Robertson (Editor). *The Expositor's Bible*. Volume 2 (Leviticus), Volume 3 (Deuteronomy and Joshua), and Volume 6 (Kings). Funk and Wagnalls, New York, 1900.

Partridge, Burgo. *A History of Orgies*. Bonanza Books, New York, 1960.

Patterson, Charlotte. "Sexual Orientation and Human Development: An Overview" in *Developmental Psychology*, 31, 1995, page 3-11.

Pearson, Joseph Adam. "Do Homosexuals Need to be Healed of their Homosexuality?" United State Copyright Office: TXu000643369, 1994.

Rahlfs, Alfred (Editor). *Septuaginta*. Deutsche Bibelgesellschaft Stuttgart, 1979.

Ratzinger, Joseph Cardinal. "Letter to the Bishops of the Catholic Church on the Pastoral Care of Homosexual Persons," given in Rome at the Sacred Congregation for the Doctrine of the Faith, October 1, 1986.

Scroggs, Robin. *The New Testament and Homosexuality*. Augsburg Fortress Publications, 1994.

Senior, Donald and John J. Collins (Editors). *The Catholic Study Bible*. Second Edition. New York. Oxford University Press, 2006.

Seper, Franjo Cardinal. "Declaration on Certain Questions Concerning Sexual Ethics," given in Rome at the Sacred Congregation for the Doctrine of the Faith, December 29, 1975.

Singer, Isidore. (Editor) *The Jewish Encyclopedia: Volumes 1-12.* Funk and Wagnalls Company, New York, 1944.

Stern, David H. *Jewish New Testament.* Jewish New Testament Publications, Jerusalem, 1989.

Strong, James. "Dictionary of the Hebrew Bible" and "Dictionary of the Greek Testament" in *Strong's Exhaustive Concordance of the Bible.* Crusade Bible Publishers, Inc., Nashville, 1890.

Sullivan, Andrew. "The Catholic Church and the Homosexual" in *The New Republic*, November 28, 1994, pages 47-55.

The Comparative Study Bible: A Parallel Bible: New International Version, New American Standard Bible, Amplified Bible, King James Version. Zondervan Bible Publishing House, Grand Rapids, 1984.

The Layman's Parallel Bible: King James Version, Modern Language Bible, Living Bible, Revised Standard Version. Zondervan Bible Publishers, Grand Rapids, 1973.

The Holy Bible, New International Version®, NIV® Copyright © 1973, 1978, 1984, 2011 by Biblica, Inc.®

Tilsen, Rabbi John-Jay.
    URL in 2000: http://www.uscj.org/ctvalley/beki/crossdress.html
    URL in 2014: http://www.beki.org/crossdress.html

Tortora, Gerard J. and Sandra Reynolds Grabowski. *Principles of Anatomy and Physiology* (7th edition). HarperCollins, New York, 1996.

Vine, W.E., M.F. Unger, and W. White, Jr. *Vine's Complete Expository Dictionary of Old and New Testament Words.* Thomas Nelson Publishers, Nashville, 1985.

Webster's II New Riverside Dictionary, Riverside Publishing Company, 1984.

Whitam, Frederick L, Milton Diamond, and James Martin. "Homosexual Orientation in Twins: A Report on 61 Pairs and Three Triplet Sets." *Archives of Sexual Behavior*, Vol. 22, No. 3, November 3, 1993, pages 187-206.

Wilson, Jean D., M.D. "Sex Testing in International Athletics." *Journal of the American Medical Association*, Vol. 267, No. 6, 1992, page 853.

Wilson, Marvin R. *Our Father Abraham: Jewish Roots of the Christian Faith*. William B. Eerdmans Publishing Company, Grand Rapids, 1989.

Wyngaarden, James B. and Lloyd H. Smith, Jr. *Cecil Textbook of Medicine* (17th edition). W. B. Saunders Company, Philadelphia, 1982.

Zondervan Parallel New Testament in Greek and English. Zondervan Bible Publishers, Grand Rapids, 1975.

A Message from Christ Jesus

Although members of my Church have rejected you, I have not rejected you! Though you have been persecuted by members of my Church, I ask that you forgive them for their trespass against you.

Since you have accepted me as your Savior, Lord, and Sovereign King, then reflect me in all of your daily social and sexual attitudes and behaviors!

Hold tightly to the faith and righteousness you have in me, for I am returning soon. At that time, all things wrong will be set aright.

WATCH AND PRAY!

Books by the Author

As I See It: The Nature of Reality by God by Rev. Joseph Adam Pearson, Ph.D., Christ Evangelical Bible Institute, Copyright 2012. ISBN 978-0615590615. *Print-on-demand* copies of this book can be ordered at https://www.createspace.com/3768013 or at www.amazon.com. (The e-book Kindle format is also available at www.amazon.com.)

God, Our Universal Self: A Primer for Future Christian Metaphysics by Rev. Joseph Adam Pearson, Ph.D., Christ Evangelical Bible Institute, Copyright 2013. ISBN 978-0985772857. *Print-on-demand* copies of this book can be ordered at https://www.createspace.com/4327421 or at www.amazon.com. (The e-book Kindle format is also available at www.amazon.com.)

Divine Metaphysics of Human Anatomy by Rev. Joseph Adam Pearson, Ph.D., Christ Evangelical Bible Institute, Copyright 2012. ISBN 978-0985772819. *Print-on-demand* copies of this book can be ordered at https://www.createspace.com/3920989 or at www.amazon.com. (The e-book Kindle format is also available at www.amazon.com.)

The Koran (al-Qur'an): Testimony of Antichrist by Rev. Joseph Adam Pearson, Ph.D., Christ Evangelical Bible Institute, Copyright 2012. ISBN 978-0985772833. *Print-on-demand* copies of this book can be ordered at https://www.createspace.com/4050171 or at www.amazon.com. (The e-book Kindle format is also available at www.amazon.com.)

Christianity and Homosexuality Reconciled: New Thinking for a New Millennium! by Rev. Joseph Adam Pearson, Ph.D., Christ Evangelical Bible Institute, Copyright 2014. ISBN 978-0985772888. *Print-on-demand* copies of this book can be ordered at https://www.createspace.com/4775617 or at www.amazon.com. (The e-book Kindle format is also available at www.amazon.com.)

Hello from 3050 AD! by Rev. Joseph Adam Pearson, Ph.D., Christ Evangelical Bible Institute, Copyright 2015. ISBN 978-0996222402. *Print-on-demand* copies of this book can be ordered at https://www. createspace.com/5385974 or at www.amazon.com. (The e-book Kindle format is also available at www.amazon.com.)

Intelligent Evolution by Rev. Joseph Adam Pearson, Ph.D., Christ Evangelical Bible Institute, Copyright 2017. ISBN 978-0996222426. *Print-on-demand* copies of this book can be ordered at https://www. createspace.com/6301821 or at www.amazon.com. (The e-book Kindle format is also available at www.amazon.com.)

The author may be contacted
at
drjpearson@aol.com
and
drjosephadampearson@gmail.com

Visit the author's legacy websites
at
www.dr-joseph-adam-pearson.com
and
www.christevangelicalbibleinstitute.com

About the Author

Dr. Joseph Adam Pearson is a college and university educator with more than forty years of classroom and administrative experience. Dr. Pearson has been the International President and Chief Executive Officer of Christ Evangelical Bible Institute (CEBI) for over twenty years. At the time of the latest publication of this book (2017), he still oversees thriving branch campuses of CEBI in India, the Philippines, and Tanzania.

Currently, Dr. Pearson spends the majority of his time developing, designing, and deploying curriculum for Christian education nationally and internationally. And he preaches, teaches, and leads international crusades as well as provides group pastoral training in global mission settings.

During his professional life, Dr. Pearson has also served in the role of Senior Pastor of Healing Waters Ministries in Tempe, Arizona and as Dean of Instruction for Mesa Community College in Mesa, Arizona — where he was founding instructional dean for its Red Mountain Campus as well as Director of its Extended Campus.

Dr. Pearson holds a Bachelor of Science degree in Biology from Loyola University (Chicago), a Master of Science degree in Biology from Loyola University (Chicago), and a Ph.D. in Curriculum and Instruction with specializations in language, literacy, linguistics, and statistical analysis from Arizona State University. He has also taken additional doctoral level coursework in advanced anatomy, biochemistry, cell biology, chemistry, advanced histology, and advanced physiology.

Dr. Pearson believes that after we are saved, and at the same time we are being sanctified, our individual lives and deeds are part of an "application" for the jobs that we will each hold during Christ Jesus' Millennial reign on earth. Dr. Pearson's greatest goal is to be one of the many committed Christian educators who will be teaching during that period of time.

Made in the USA
San Bernardino, CA
01 December 2019